DRIVEN

By Tred Barta and Donna De Weil

Driven

By Tred Barta and Donna De Weil

COPYRIGHT © 2016 BARTAWAY LLC

ALL RIGHTS RESERVED. NO PART OF THIS BOOK MAY BE REPRINTED OR REPRODUCED OR UTILIZED IN ANY FORM OR BY ANY ELECTRONIC, MECHANICAL, OR OTHER MEANS, NOW KNOWN OR HEREAFTER INVENTED, INCLUDING PHOTOCOPYING AND RECORDING, OR IN ANY INFORMATION STORAGE OR RETRIEVAL SYSTEM, WITHOUT PERMISSION IN WRITING FROM BARTAWAY LLC.

PRODUCT OR CORPORATE NAMES MAY BE TRADEMARKS OR REGISTERED TRADEMARKS, AND ARE USED ONLY FOR IDENTIFICATION AND EXPLANATION WITHOUT INTENT TO INFRINGE.

FOR FURTHER INFORMATION ON THE BOOK OR TRED BARTA, GO TO:

WWW.BARTAWAY.COM

CHAPTER HEADING ILLUSTRATIONS BY: SAM GIBBONS

ISBN: 978-0-9981830-1-5

*For Grant and Mary Lou,
thank you for your
friendship and support
SAM C. GIBBONS
BFA RISD*

NOTE TO OUR READERS

Thank you for purchasing this book. The charts and photos contained in this book are available on a special page on Tred Barta's website. To view this content visit: http://www.bartaway.com/book-extras . As a buyer of this book, you have access to this information as well as updates and additional photos. To access, please enter the password which is: FRIGATE.

We invite you to join and enjoy Tred's digital scrapbook. In honor of Tred's many achievements, we are assembling a digital scrapbook of his life and achievements. If you have a photo of or with Tred and would like to be a part of this exciting project, please scan the photo and send to admin@bartaway.com . Please be sure to identify the individuals in the photo, location and dates (to the extent possible). All photos will be posted at http://www.bartaway.com/scrapbook .

Contents

Foreword: Cave Fregata Nomine Tred 1

Foreword: Tred's North Star 5

Preface by Donna De Weil 9

1. Just Ask Tred 13
2. My Childhood 17
3. Major Events Towards Manhood 27
4. My Dreams with John Wayne 35
5. One Mission One Goal 39
6. My Beginnings in The Canyon 45
7. A Touch Short Handed 53
8. Surface Swordfishing 67
9. Primeval Real Estate 75
10. Science Is My Friend 79
11. Respect Earned 81
12. Welker and Lydonia Canyons 85
13. Out of Ice 113
14. Hydrographer 117
15. Nantucket Bound 129
16. Canoe Paddles Required 133
17. When the Earth Stood Still 143
18. My Father's Death 153
19. To Set a World Record 157
20. Walker's Cay and The Barta Blue Marlin Classic 167
21. The Barta Boys and Girls Club Billfish and Inshore Tournament 183

22.	A New Reality	189
23.	The Next Chapter – Returning to the Longbow	199
24.	My Old Friend Badger	203
25.	Piñas Bay, Panama – Tropic Star Lodge	209
26.	A Slippery Slope	219
27.	Weightless	225
28.	I Can Do It!	233
29.	Bamboo Barta	243
30.	Rebirth of Makaira	247
31.	Four Twelve	259
32.	A Truly Great Woman	271
33.	My Bucket List	277
Reprint of the "Barta Bigeye Bible"		287
Reprint of "Barta's Bluefin Bible"		301

Index of Charts and Diagrams

Chart 1 - Tred's beginnings in the Canyons	50
Diagram of "Barta Porcupine Rig"	64-65
Chart 2 - Tred's shorthanded journey through a Nor'easter to bring home five bigeye tuna	66
Chart 3 - Tred's surface swordfishing journey out of Montauk	74
Diagram of "Barta Throttle Dance"	107
Chart 4 - Tred's epic three-day journey to Welker and Lydonia Canyons (includes flight path and fishing conditions)	108
Chart 5 - Tred's epic three-day journey to Welker and Lydonia Canyons	109
Chart 6 - Tred's epic three-day journey to Welker and Lydonia Canyons (includes Marine National Monument designation)	110
Chart 7 - Tred's swordfishing journey with his father	141
Chart 8 - Walker's Cay	178

Foreword
CAVE FREGATA NOMINE TRED
Latin: "Beware the Frigate Named Tred"

SCIENCE IS ONLY recently catching up to the wisdom that our world's best fishermen have known for centuries. Frigate birds (fregata), live, survive, and thrive on our highest seas in ways that are unimaginable to most of us.

Mother Nature motivates frigate birds starting with huge limits. Their feathers lack waterproof plumage, unlike most other birds that depend upon salt water. With no help from others except the winds, they courageously set sail across every ocean on our planet knowing full well that there's no safe place to land. Recent sensors placed on these birds from scientists now confirm that they can stay a flight for months, traveling thousands of miles over water, while flying at altitudes below freezing levels. To pioneers like Tred Barta, frigate birds represent the past souls of our best sailors and explorers.

It seems hard to understand how a young frigate bird would learn to leave the nest of its parents to pursue its true calling as the world's most efficient adventurer. However, I personally would imagine it to be much like the extraordinary upbringing of Tred Barta by his parents Joseph and Judy Barta.

Frigates must be forced quickly to trust their own instincts where they belong – in the sky, over water they cannot swim, and amidst storm clouds that will feed their bills. Such is the beautiful irony of so many events within the life of Tred Barta that are detailed here in this book. What may seem to be a series of life setbacks become magnificent set ups to inspire others to live out their dreams.

Everything that a frigate bird needs to dance with the Earth's winds is already found within their hollow bones. Every cell within a fregata's body seems designed to excel for conditions thought unfit to most other species. Thanks to its unique aerodynamic design, its wing load enables it to travel great distances with fantastic stamina. Without a B29 squadron leader for a father, it is equally doubtful that Tred Barta could have touched so many apex predators in his lifetime of flying, floating, and stalking.

As an instrument-rated private pilot, it seems very unusual how a frigate bird would knowingly choose to fly into a cumulus storm cloud without some internal consciousness weighed against this certain risk. Tracking ornithologists have now proven that frigates deliberately fly into building storm clouds to leverage their turbulent updraft lifts over angry seas. These same clouds are precisely what can bend the metal spars of airplanes like that Tred has flown, sold, and used on so many expeditions. Imagine how these birds close their eyes into a complete cloud fog that must feel a bit like a heavy shoe inside the fastest spin cycle of a wash machine. What seems to risk death to many is precisely what empowers life to others.

Harnessing the cloud's altitude climbing energy is not the only advantage given to the fregata with this native act. It turns out that the cloud's very existence over the ocean's deep waves helps settle the surface to encourage plankton and baitfish to appear in greater frequency. By trusting its instincts, and living its bold purpose, the frigate bird is driven towards its best chance for survival. Thus, the frigate needs the storm cloud much like the suckerfish needs the shark.

This quest to always ride upwind of your game is native to the legendary events surrounding Tred Barta. Reading this book will take you on some fantastic journeys of Tred's life. However, it will also help us understand the magic of our planet's remaining wilderness areas: our greatest underwater canyons of the North Atlantic, the resilence of a tiny chapel slapped with back-to-back hurricanes in the Bahamas, and the biodiversity of the Panamanian jungle. Jigging across a few chapters of this book can remind us of the amazing torpedo power of a big eye tuna, the unspoken grace shared with our horse, and the native power of the right string release from a hand-built limb of wood.

Earth's apex predators are our best barometers that all is in proper balance. Without future generations to troll the seas for 892 pound mako sharks from Block Canyon like Tred, each of us stand to lose something more. The hunter's existence at the northeast edge of a warm core eddy days off Nantucket Island remains an important check that the jugular vein of life from our Gulfstream is alive and well. An old school captain still rigging his bait dockside for tomorrow in Islamorada helps keep alive the marine wisdom from those passed before us. The return of a Panamanian bow hunter spotting a fresh Jaguar print in the mud is our best sign that the fast will outlast the weak in our jungles.

For many years, it may have been the peripheral sight of a frigate bird flying low that helped turned Tred's lonely week around towards success. Where frigates signaled baitfish and whales, Tred knew that marlins and swordfish may soon follow on his lines. Just like a dorado dolphin side-speared, but not deterred by a marlin, Captain Tred Barta will live on making and sharing his purpose.

With this book, his flights become ours. With each chapter, his reading of deep waters is shared with us. By absorbing his dreams and adrenaline, our own visions can become more attainable. Just like the frigate bird leads us to life under challenging waters, Tred's book is intended to inspire others to keep going that distance. *Cave Fregata Nomine Tred*. Beware the frigate soul named Tred Barta. His presence may stir your spirit to find the razor's edge in your life.

What are you waiting for? Hook up one of his amazing stories right now!

Travis H. Brown

Foreword
TRED'S NORTH STAR
A Must Read

I DON'T KNOW why I was born so different from other people. I don't know why the very fabric of how I relate to the world brings me to a different path in life. I don't know why at every institution, every prep school, every college, every training camp and in absolutely every situation in life I don't follow the manual, the agenda, the book, or often advice given. I only know one thing. There is only one constant that transcends my life and the way I judge everything and that is the consistency and inconsistency of nature. The North Star to me always points north and this is my moral compass.

I also am a believer in the Lord and I believe He created the earth.

I relate to everything in the world on the basis of how nature lives and moves in its most natural form every day. For example, when tracking a grizzly bear in British Colombia I don't just follow his track; I become the apex predator myself. What is the great bear thinking? As I follow his tracks I wonder what his movement means? Is he passing up areas of fresh blueberries on a mountain and looking for a kill of fresh meat.

If the grizzly's tracks meander past a cool glacier fed stream and he doesn't drink, this means to me he simply is not looking for water. The animals of which a grizzly savagely feeds on all have a great sense of smell. If a grizzly is working into the wind and you think he may be trying to ambush his unsuspecting prey, I guarantee you he will work into the wind where his scent is undetectable. What I am describing to you is much different than just following the track. The sight of a frigate bird pinned against a brilliant blue sky 80 miles offshore, is an immediate signal to me that he is not on vacation. He is there for one reason and that is to feed.

For the frigate to be successful he must swoop down at the precise moment. A dorado, wahoo, or marlin is chasing bait whether it be ballyhoo or flying fish. The frigate from his aerial perch can see the entire scenario unfold of life and death, as the prey jumps out of the water trying to escape being eaten. As I watch that frigate, he will tell me the precise time and place I need to be trolling my baits.

I see everything in life like this. Over the span of my life many people have suggested that my ADD/ ADHD or severe dyslexia has driven me onto my own path. I could not perform or conform in almost every situation like other people.

For my entire life, I could not read an entire book because I see it in choppy fleeting passages upside down and backwards. However, if read to me orally, my retention is excellent. In learning complex turbine engines, I spent time physically working on the engine with mechanics and could ask questions to get a better understanding. Normally a person reads the manual. By the time we are both finished I always seem to have a greater practical understanding of the engine.

I was brought into this world with an extremely strict military father, a cut throat world class athletic mother and for some reason formed a relentless curiosity towards apex predators – the great giant tuna of the northeast, the patrolling swordfish, a blue or black marlin on the hunt, and the lion or leopard. I believe since I was driven away from socialization in my youth and found little love from my parents that I tried to order the world from the only constant that would not talk back to me, not make fun of me, would not judge me, and that is nature.

When I was a child growing up I did not conform and since I did not I was left behind and often labeled "retarded." I could not play team sports but I would be a true champion in individual sports such as running and skiing. On group picnics I was uncomfortable. I would leave the group and I would walk in the woods to see a great spotted owl. I found a wonderful warmth and confidence alone in the woods or alone at sea. Why is it? How is it?

In nature the rulers are the apex predators. A 900-pound mako shark fears nothing. A mature killer whale does not even have a handful of enemies. With the inadequacies that I was born with, I would let nature be the judge of how great I was and how great I was becoming.

As most people proceed in daily life, they buy their food at a grocery store, they have the oil changed in their vehicle at a garage, in their spare time they have movies, theater, games on their phones, and before you know it what direction the wind is blowing from is no longer significant. If you are in a city you may not see the sunrise or sunset, a garden, or fish. The life and death that is played out every day at the oceans edge is not even recognized. Technology tries to solve every situation sometimes making the natural world insignificant.

Prior to the tragedy of my life confining me to a wheelchair I could survive almost anywhere with just a knife. I am a hunter. I am a gatherer. I am an apex predator.

As you read this book I beg you for your forgiveness. In the beginning the editors came very short of saying, "you can't publish this. The book is choppy. It doesn't have a beginning and an ending. People come and they go and are not developed characters throughout the book. The book does not flow like a normal novel."

The reason for this is that I think in "events" and the events of which I write are those that have been significant in my life, a turning point. When I tell a story of fishing for bigeye tuna in the northeast canyons where no sport fishing boat may have ever gone had I not ventured there, my ADD/ ADHD, and dyslexia are in hyper focus of that adventure. I am not capable of blending a description of that trip as it relates to the next chapter or the following chapters. That's Tred.

When I took the SATs for the first time, the test showed me as a complete failure. I was devastated. When new legislature in the educational system was approved for those with ADD/ ADHD and dyslexic, I was allowed to take my SATs orally. I scored in the 98.6 percentile just short of the label genius. Today that means nothing but I think it explains just how different I am.

I hope the book *Driven* gives you a greater understanding of the world we live in and what happens to people when they start to explore and have a commanding understanding of nature itself. I hope this book makes you look at the North star in a different way. I hope that *Driven* excites a spark in your life allowing you to step out of your comfort zone of everyday life. *Driven* will hopefully make you think outside of the box. It will show you what the human spirit is all about.

I will tell you what it feels like when a doctor tells you "you have one week to live." One thing is for sure, if I followed all of the rules I would not be the man I am today and if I followed all the rules I would not have accomplished all that I have done. It is a plain and simple fact. So perhaps you can step out of your own box. I believe in life and you do not surf on the wave, you make the waves.

I have found and lived my life under the Panamanian stars, underneath a frigate bird leading me to success, following the finback whales to the bigeye tuna, and by facing a charging African buffalo at ten yards. Man is the greatest apex predator in the world. Perhaps my reason for living today is to open your eyes to something we can't control but can only live with and that is the vagrancies, the power, and the unpredictability of what happens every day right in front of us.

The true confidence that a man or woman possesses is tested in how they can survive in nature. If you are dropped off on an Alaskan mountaintop 200 miles from the nearest road and two months later you walk out carrying a spear, bow, fishing rod, wearing a bearskin robe, moose hide slippers and a belly full of fresh meat, then you can do anything. Where will you be when the lights go out?

As you read this book I beg you not to judge for its continuity but judge it as hard as you want by its content. Never give up! Never say never!

Tred Barta

September, 2016

PREFACE

TRED BARTA IS a strong, rugged man. People who watched his TV show saw him kill a grizzly bear with a longbow and a handmade arrow from mere feet away. They witnessed him catching International Game Fish Association (IGFA) world-record fish.

One of his close friends once said, "People either love him or hate him. There is no in-between." Over the years, I've come to agree with this friend, but the people who don't love him should know how much more there is to him than what they see or hear.

The first time I went out to a restaurant for breakfast with Tred, five men in their early 20s sat at a nearby table. He bantered with them throughout their meal. Nobody ever accused Tred Barta of being shy. Tred whispered to our waitress that he wanted to buy their entire table breakfast. When the waitress let him know the cost, Tred not only paid for all of their meals but gave our waitress a $50 tip for our $10 meal. The shocked young men came over to Tred, thanking him profusely. They explained how they attended college and didn't have much money. They really appreciated his generosity. Tred replied, "Pay it forward. Do something nice for someone today." They all promised they definitely would. I said, "That is nice what you did for your friends." Tred informed me that he never met those young men before. He just wanted to do something nice for them. In another restaurant, Tred asked a couple what they were eating because it looked so good. Before long these strangers ended up sitting at our table and we had a lovely evening. He asked if they liked to fish. Look out if someone tells Tred they like to fish but don't have the time! He'll have none of it, and before long, those people look at their busy lives and say, "You're right! I'm going fishing next weekend!"

Tred looks at life kind of like a five-year-old child, meaning there are no "Adult Rules." If there is a rule he thinks it does not apply to him. It is this way of thinking that has made him phenomenal and break all of those world records, because he never listened to the people who deemed it impossible. The child in him also makes life fun. He can make the most boring thing exciting – like going to the grocery store for celery and eggs… you never know what will happen but you know it will be an exciting adventure.

We both like to travel, and one day we were discussing where we would like to travel. Tred said he would like to travel to Antarctica. I said, "We can't go there!" because I was worried that he would freeze in that climate and moving about in the wheelchair would be difficult. His response was, "I can go. Why can't you?" Simply put, Tred lives his life on an extremely accelerated course.

When Tred first moved to Islamorada, he met a young man trying to start a charter-fishing business. Tred saw the young man working tirelessly on his boat and wanted to help. He bought this young man a bait pen and then generously filled up his fuel tank. Tred never asked for recognition or boasted about helping this young man. He just wanted to help out of the goodness of his heart.

Tred's passion for the fishing world spans five decades and he always helps others whenever he can. If he developed something that worked well, he quickly shared his fishing knowledge. I once rigged lures with Tred and he showed me a swivel. He nonchalantly said, "I developed that." I asked if he had a patent on it and he responded, "No. I gave it to friends to use and eventually someone manufactured it." Dozens of times, I have been in World Wide Sportsman in Islamorada, Florida where Tred planned to buy just one pack of Mustad hooks. It always sounded good in theory, but while in the hook aisle, he'd see someone looking at tackle with a puzzled expression. Tred would ask them what they want to fish for and where. Armed with those bits of information, Tred would help them pick out the best tackle to buy. If someone needed more intense help, Tred often wheeled around the store with the person, picking out what was needed. As if that wasn't enough, he'd then proceeded to give the person a crash course on how to rig it or to do whatever they were trying to do. If others saw them, they'd listen in and before long, an actual crowd — with hundreds of dollars-worth of items pulled off the shelves so everyone could duplicate what Tred was teaching — would march up to the cashier! Instead of just being in the store ten minutes to pick up Mustad hooks, we'd end up there for hours.

Tred reminds me of a bumper car – bumping, banging and careening his way through life. But if he sees someone who needs help, he quickly gets out of that bumper car and does whatever he can for that person to make their life better. That's the inner Tred Barta I wish everybody knew!

Over the years I have known Tred, he has told me many stories of his childhood, hunting, fishing, and what he did to return to his passions after being confined to a wheelchair. It is these exciting stories and adventures that I felt Tred should share. In this book, Tred has opened up his heart and poured the facts of his early upbringing, fishing adventures, and his passions. It is a fact that during the writing of this book some chapters became very painful, often draining us emotionally. I personally found many of the stories of his upbringing significant. When you understand Tred's childhood, you really start to understand his behavior in adult life. Although Tred was privileged in many ways he saw it as a curse. He constantly searched for recognition and love from his parents and then the world.

Tred may be confined to a wheelchair for the rest of his life but he will never limit himself to sitting in front of a TV every day. He will continue to be adventurous throughout his life and will continue to help others with his "If I can do it, you can do it" attitude.

As co-author of the book, *Driven*, I feel this represents a true insight in what many call the last living legend of an era. I hope you enjoy it because I enjoyed writing it.

Donna De Weil

September, 2016

Chapter One
JUST ASK TRED

THROUGHOUT MY LIFETIME, many people have recommended that I see a psychologist or psychiatrist, apparently for the sole purpose of quelling some anger I supposedly have with my upbringing. Though when I examine those examining me, I often see something that disturbs me.

Many men and women today no longer know how to change a tire on their mode of transportation which replaced the horse. They don't know how to start a fire in a rain storm, or to survive in the wild. Forget about these people taking care of themselves, but what about saving their families from starvation. These skills I learned growing up and feel are critical to life. Of course, I don't live in a multi-million-dollar high-rise penthouse on Central Park or work on Wall Street in an office all day.

I am going to tell you what I see is wrong with the world from my perspective. All you really have to do to be successful in life and for your children to be successful is to rip out this page from the book and stick it on the refrigerator door for your entire lifetime. It is a fact, since the beginning of time, men hunted for food. Although women rarely went on the dangerous hunt, they played a critical role in civilization by growing and gathering food and raising the children. From the beginning of time, men and women had different skill sets and bodies built differently. But both shared equally in responsibility and were equally important to survival. If a man could not hunt, or had some type of "inner caveman experience" making him "not one of the men," he would either be stoned to death or die of starvation. Men who did not hunt didn't exist nor did women who didn't do their share. As time progressed mankind started to change its thinking on how to effectively and efficiently do things. Only then did the concept of free time arise. Free time allowed one group of a society to be hunters, another set to be builders, and other sets, (jumping way ahead in the evolution of mankind,) to be poets, musicians, artists, and philosophers. History of mankind has proven that when everything fell apart, the only ones that survived were those with the skill sets to hunt, fish, and gather. Without these basic skills one could not survive against the lion, buffalo, or an intense weather change. The simple philosophy that I am building and trying to reinforce is what I call a baseline. The baseline DNA that runs through all of us is called survival. Without survival skills, we die.

Now rocketing forward to modern society where men and women no longer need to hunt and fish to survive. They have no need to perform any single skill faced with the consequence of being ostracized from the group or worse. We live in a society where baseball, football, and golf rule family life. We live in a place where terrorists prey on innocents and yet we tolerate specific areas at LaGuardia Airport where people can pray to Allah. We live in a society where anything goes and nothing is forbidden. Our society can buy fish, fowl, and meat with a credit card and yet the very next day protest hunting and fishing, when in fact you recently killed everything you ate with that credit card. We live in a society where all services and goods may be purchased, including everything as minute as tuning your cello or killing a water buffalo for a rare or special dried meat.

What is wrong with our society today? Just ask Tred. Today men's and women's skills have blended, no longer clearly defining the roles that have served society since the Stone Age. People do not have the basic skills to survive in Nature any longer. Today's critical survival skills involve hostile takeovers, sub-prime mortgages, and minimum wages.

People constantly ask me why I hunt and fish when it's no longer necessary. I can buy meat and fish in a supermarket. Each one of us probably has a different answer. But I would like to think we are all saying the same thing. I hunt and fish to prove my manhood as well as to claim my particular place in the world. Being part of the ancient circle of life wherein I harvest God's creation, preparing, preserving, and eating the wildlife which I have harvested gives me a real refreshment of what life once was. I am aware, of course, that many do not share my philosophies. Life activities today are well camouflaged in many different ways. People constantly insulate themselves from Nature. Even just driving down a highway on a beautiful, clear, cool day, more cars than not have their windows closed with the occupants bathing in the artificial environment of air conditioning!

I recently went fishing in Islamorada, Florida. Onboard my boat, *Makaira*, were my friends Doctor Jeffery Bennett, Donna De Weil, and our mate, Evan. We found a coral reef with an abundance of sea life. Within a few hours, we filled our cooler with numerous different species – mangrove snapper, hogfish, grunts, and porgies. We took care of our catch by icing it down. Back at the dock, we cleaned all of our fish. We fed heads and guts to the tarpon, sharks, jacks, pelicans, and egrets while tourists took pictures with their cameras and phones. Donna and I cleaned and packaged the catch so it could be shared and eaten among friends. For a brief moment after the entire process had been finished, I felt peace come over me — that all was still okay. To add to the peace I felt that day was the extra pleasure of knowing every single aspect of my boat, a 26-foot Andros, both electrical and mechanical, and that I could take my Evinrude outboard apart piece by piece. Although I haven't asked Donna how she feels when she prepares our catch, she always has a gleam in her eye, a celebration of satisfaction when she serves a meal we caught ourselves to family and friends.

Most Americans today probably consider what I've written as chauvinistic or profoundly shallow, but that's just the way I see it. At what point should any man be able to go through life without overhauling an engine, without changing a tire, without being able to hunt or fish and prepare his bounty for the table? Am I a cave man, am I ignorant or stupid, or do I just not get it? Or have I hit the nail on the head? I can go on and on offering examples, but the truth is that celebrating and putting into action the very basic rules of survival is what still motivates men and women in almost all activities they pursue. I want you to think for one second like me.

Why do thrill-seekers bungee jump off a bridge or sky dive? My opinion? Since civilization can no longer participate in a spear hunt for wooly mammoths, they prove their manhood or womanhood by jumping off a bridge.

Many people disagree with me but here is what I believe: all men and women should know how to hunt, fish, gather, clean, and cook fowl, fish, meat or grain so as to give sustenance to their family; all men and women should know how to change a tire, know how an internal combustion engine works, and have the basic skills to survive; and, all men and women should be able to nurture and hold the family together, know how to care for children, and maintain and defend the family home without depending on the rest of the community. If you think I'm a dinosaur, so be it.

I hold the responsibilities of men and women to be one hundred percent equal and I truly mean it. One cannot help but notice today how much time and effort the media spends posturing about the end of the world. There are countless movies and books centered around this concept. When the power grid goes down, no electricity or computers, no planes or cars… then what are the true survival skills men and women will need? To me the answer comes extremely quick. You'll need to care and provide for your family by knowing how to hunt, fish, build a shelter, make a fire, and defend the family unit. Wow! Isn't that interesting? It kind of sounds like the way I started this chapter. Shouldn't every man and woman have these basic skills and shouldn't they teach their children these skills?

Just ask Tred.

Chapter Two
MY CHILDHOOD

TO UNDERSTAND ME and why, throughout most of my life, I have sacrificed everything toward a single goal, one must take a brief moment to understand how my childhood molded me to be the perfect offshore fisherman. Looking back, the chances that I took and even subjected my crew to, were — in many ways – unspeakable. But we all knew the risks and we were all driven to succeed in spite of them.

I came into this world with a silver spoon in my mouth, the product of an incredibly successful father, a competitive bulldog of a mother, and access to wealth that most people cannot fathom. I don't remember the silver spoon, but I do remember Father's belt across my rear end until it welted bright red. I clearly recall a couple of incidents that — now in the autumn of my years — I look back on as particularly significant.

The facts are that I suffer from ADD/ ADHD and dyslexia. With the dyslexia I have a difficult time organizing and sequencing thoughts, translating printed words and I mix up my speech. My father gave me 4 words per day and I had to learn how to spell them, what they meant and how to use them in a sentence. I have a difficult time distinguishing left from right. I read books upside down and backwards. I scored in the top ¼ percentile on my SATs (which I was allowed to take verbally). I was always in trouble but never from alcohol or drugs; mostly for killing things and eating them or for just breaking the rules. I wasn't an angry child. My family simply drilled into me that the rules were not for me and if I didn't dig my own ditch then I wasn't meant to be on this earth.

At Hinckley Preparatory School in Waterville, Maine, just outside of Skowhegan, I was a stud of 147 pounds of unequivocal blue twisted steel, with less than 2 percent body fat, captain of the ski team, captain of the soccer team, captain of the tennis team, and the U.S. Olympic Biathalon team coaches had their eyes on me. As is common in wealthy families, my parents sent me away from home for both summers and school years starting when I was just eight years old.

I had just come back from Red Lodge Montana, where I trained all summer skiing giant slalom. Back at school, I was about to run in the New England Prep School Championship Cross-Country race. As I recall there were just under 100 runners competing against me. Father flew in from New York on the family Lear jet. Like a personalized license plate, the plane's tail number 50JB which stood for Joseph Barta.

Father rarely came to my events. But as it turned out, this one was exceptionally important as from within the first 15 places of this particular 6.5-mile race would come four future United States Olympic runners! I thought to myself, "in this race I will win his love."

The race course wound through Maine's autumnal wooded areas — flooded with brilliant red and golden colors of oak and maple. The gun went off and I held my own in four through eight places until I got my second wind on a monstrous hill that dove down sharply through a stream that could be easily jumped. I slipped, fell and lay on the ground just long enough to watch the frontrunners disappear. Instant horror came over me and a shot of pure adrenaline kicked in like nitrous in a race car. Within minutes I was challenging the first three runners. I had trained my whole young life to look for the weakness in others and I sensed it. I made my move on the front-runner. I saw him gasping for breath and I knew I had him. I stayed beside him for what seemed an eternity, though certainly it was only a couple of seconds. I kept shouting at him, "You can't beat me!" I tormented him without mercy. I made my move to first place with all cylinders firing. When

I entered a large open field which took us by all of the spectators, I saw my father waiting at the finish line way in the distance. He was always urbane and the best dressed with his World War II aviator sunglasses, carefully combed-back gray hair and a long, tan camelhair coat.

I knew I would be challenged over that last half mile and everything in me said, "just hold the lead and then give it everything you've got at the end." But I didn't. I gave it my all right then and widened the gap. I was leading but my lungs were burning, my legs felt like rubber and within 1/8 mile of the finish line the third place runner blew by me and I simply could not catch him. As God is my witness, I had no more in me. I could have dug no deeper. I finished in second place and the first person who greeted me was the representative of the U.S. Olympic Biathlon team and right alongside of him was a scout for the University of Colorado. I approached my father and he looked sternly at me. When I asked, "Dad what's wrong?" He replied, "You will learn that in life, there is no second place." My father walked off the field, went to the airport and flew home in his Lear jet. He did not come to my commencement events for graduation.

I was heartbroken. But in my world, simply doing your best was unacceptable to the family. You had to do your best *and* win. Six months later I won the U.S. Junior Olympic Biathlon Championships in Lake Placid, New York. I collapsed at the finish line and threw up uncontrollably for what seemed like a long time. I didn't know it, but Dad had flown in to watch without my knowledge. At the finish line, as I approached him literally being carried by a coach under each arm, he said to me, "How does it feel to really win?" I broke out in tears! I thought for sure that it was his way of saying, "Good job Tred! I love you!"

As I thought about it subsequently, I always wondered about the definition of giving it your all. Is it when you think you can't give anything more or is it when you actually collapse? An interesting question.

Looking back, I often wonder what I remember of my childhood and if what I remember is really the way it happened? I suppose it makes no difference. I do remember being baptized at the Dutch Reform Protestant Church in Bronxville, NY. We lived at 28 Locust Lane, a part of upper Westchester jam-packed with McMansions. Father came from the poorest of the poor families in Pennsylvania. Dad's father was a coal miner with a shovel and his grandfather an immigrant from Czechoslovakia. Father was a man of steel. He climbed out of the poor, immigrant class quickly via his B29 flying squadron of 100 bombers which he led into battle during WWII. During his service to the U.S. military Dad lost a total of three crews of nine each. They were shot up and mutilated in battle. On 12 different occasions, my father carried the torsos of his fallen crew out by himself. He would never allow an ambulance crew or anyone else to lay the men under his command to rest. Father spoke little of the war and when he did his eyes welled up with tears, though I never saw my father actually cry… ever. He went on to command the B29 pilot school and was an unmitigated war hero. I have never seen any man possess more "grace under pressure." Dad was strict, stern and unfair, but in a consistently fair way. I don't know if that makes sense but I think I nailed it.

My mother came from a German Luftwaffe-type of stock. Her family social status was 20 times higher than my father's and I believe my father hated that fact. Mother, a competitive tennis player, headed the Women's United States Lawn Tennis Association. It is so unfortunate, that my recollections of Mother inspired me to create the term "man-woman." Certainly she possessed qualities of femininity, maintaining the home and cooking, but her persona seemed always one of show and social climbing rather than sincere motherhood. Of course I loved my mother like most any child would and of course I still love her today. But as memories unravel, my observations will become clear. Mother loved wiping men off of the tennis court 6-0, 6-0, and 6-0. My father feared nothing but being banal and poor. Mother stressed over the thought of missing the benefits of not being rich. Between these two titanium personalities formed the perfect storm, ultimately creating the boiler room for one Captain Tred Barta.

Father reveled in being a full partner in William C. Wold Associates, later to become Joseph T. Barta Associates and later still Barta-Iso Aviation, a company specializing in the purchase and sale of corporate aircraft. He tapped into the right place at the right time. He invested shrewdly in vehicles such as Black and Decker Machine stock, IBM, Texas Gulf Sulfur, TransCanada Pipeline, and TWA stock and within three years my father's net worth grew 250%. Welcome to my world. I was four years old, had two parents cooking in grease. My mother started Ball Boy Corporation making the first tennis ball throwing machine and rebound net for teaching. She also founded the Leighton-Barta tennis school for teachers. We had fresh capital and lots of it, churning it out on both sides. On my mother's side we owned a "mini-estate" on Rangeley Lake in Maine near Hunter's Cove.

Father traveled close to seven months a year, much of it internationally – Korea, China, Japan, Near East, Far East and everywhere in between. He bought from TWA and sold to Korean Airways and then bought the aircraft back from Korean Airways and resold them to companies like Rhodesian Airways and New Caledonian with gigantic markups.

When I was six years old, everyone in school was concerned that I was different… very, very different. I seemed to have a learning disability, and yet, if I learned something verbally or could see it (which demanded direct eye contact from the person teaching it) I was nothing short of brilliant. I was diagnosed with ADD, then ADHD, then dyslexia, not exactly what my father and mother envisioned for me. Of course back in those days they had no real idea what any of this stuff was or how to treat it. I was called stupid, ignorant, a dummy, and the repeated use of these words from not only peers but teachers as well started making scars. However, being called lazy hurt me to my very core because I always tried my best.

Somewhere around age six I stole a candy bar from a local store in downtown Bronxville. Father found the wrapper and tricked me into admitting I had no money and I had taken it. Father called the local police chief (whom he gave a large donation to each year). Two squad cars came to the house, "arrested me," and took me to down to the jail. They booked and finger printed me. Father actually beat me to the jailhouse. I was terrified and cried like a baby. Father surreptitiously slept in the jail cell next to me (and the jailers never mentioned it). I never knew he was there. I cried most of the night and — to their credit — policemen constantly visited me trying to calm me down. I believe this to be the most horrifying experience of my early life. I thought my father and mother had abandoned me and that I could never trust them again. But it also set my moral compass on true north for life. I would never steal again. In the morning my father came to me in the jail cell and told me that he made a special deal to get me out.

For example, at age 16, while in Vermont, I bought several items in a hardware store. I drove some 30 miles before realizing that I inadvertently had not paid for an extension cord. I stopped at a dairy farm in Rutland and called the local and state police. I told them what I had done and that I wanted it to be on record that I was driving back to pay for the extension cord.

From age 7 to age 16 I never returned home for a summer, never lived at home during school. I attended pre-boarding schools, boarding schools, special dyslexic training schools (one of which was in Lyndonville, Massachusetts), then to Hinckley Preparatory School, then high school in Hinckley. Summers found me at Outward Bound, climbing school, music camp, survival school, pilot school, piston, turbo prop and jet schools, American Airline's weather courses, glacier-skiing training courses, martial arts training, and pre-school tutoring in every damn class I would be taking for every semester in every school. I knew my mother and father loved me but it sure didn't feel like it.

I was starting to develop an insulating barrier of concrete between how I acted and how I really felt. With every situation, every new place, I felt abandoned. I hated sympathy. I hated losing. I hated being mediocre so I started to equate success with love. I started to realize that being number one engendered attention, position, self-worth and therefore I did not allow myself to feel lonely. Keep in mind that added to the table scraps of love from my parents were non-human perquisites like offshore fishing boats, a family Lear jet, a Schweitzer 232 glider in Sugarbush, Vermont, a Rolls Royce, Lamborgini, Jaguar XJ6, and a Cadillac Seville (replaced by an Oldsmobile Toronado, quite the wizbang in its day).

I learned to succeed at an early age. Unfortunately, in so many situations, success took not only skill and drive, but also knowing how to look for, expose and ultimately capitalize on competitors' weaknesses. And I learned it well! At the tender age of 14 in survival school orienteering championships, I discovered that my counselor and four of the competitive runners were scared witless of lightning. They chose to wait and start the race in the morning. I took a short nap, woke up and ran and hiked all night in the most horrendous lightning and rain storm that I had ever been in. By the time the little girls – okay, I mean boys and men — woke up the next morning, I had already won the race.

Father and Mother kept drilling into me at an early age what I was good at, how I was different from other people and what makes some people great and others mediocre. I think saying that I was turning into an animal would be unfair at this age but I was certainly developing into the worst guy to compete against.

I would have traded anything in life to have a normal childhood, but looking back I never knew what normal was. By age 42, I had amassed 7,500 hours of total flying time, 22 ocean crossings as pilot in command, 16 pilot training courses on turbo props and jets with 50 hours flying left seat in a Hercules C130 four-engine transport aircraft. I attended schools and actively trained flying bush planes including Otters, Beavers on floats, Grumman Goose and Grumman float planes, and I even had about 200 hours in Bell Jet Ranger helicopter time. Even with all that, I was a lonely kid, overly loquacious, and verbose. But I knew what I was talking about and I performed. My god what a childhood! I wouldn't wish it on anybody.

People with dyslexia have a hard time multi-tasking but can concentrate on one task and do it well. Due to this concentration some of the greatest people in history have dyslexia including Albert Einstein, Thomas Edison, Steve Jobs, Leonardo da Vinci and Ludwig von Beethoven. Looking back, maybe I was specifically-designed for the major event millstones that lie ahead.

My Childhood

Thumper (St. Bernard on left), Heathcliff (Sheepdog on right), and Judy Barta (Tred's mother)

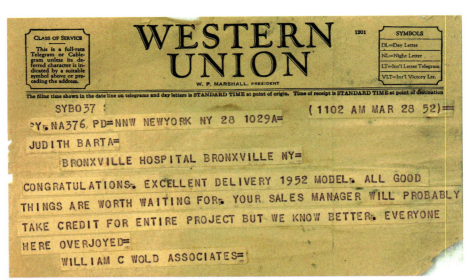

Congratulatory telegram on Tred's birth

Tred Barta and his mother

Tred Barta and his mother

Tred's martial arts training

Tred Barta (#35) as a member of Hinckley Preparatory School Ski Team

Tred at 16 years old with marlin he caught in Cabo San Lucas, Mexico.

Chapter Three
MAJOR EVENTS TOWARDS MANHOOD
"OR"
PASSING BY CHILDHOOD

I COUNT THREE specific events in my development that I consider milestones. Most people might judge them harshly, but that's okay.

My mother's family owned a beautiful camp on Rangeley Lake in central Maine. From there come my earliest memories of where fishing, hunting and shooting became ingrained in my life. They constitute my fondest memories of Father and yet some of the most painful ones.

I fished off of the dock for hours at a time. One evening I caught the largest trout in the entire world. It must have been a whopping six inches! Mom and Dad ran down from the cabin, placed the trout in an aluminum bucket and released it into a big old-fashioned porcelain bathtub. I was probably six years old and I guess everything seemed huge to me. The bathtub was filled with lake water that we drew directly for the camp with an old gas-powered pump. The two-cylinder engine had a leather fan belt and made a sound like a steam train engine. I loved when Father first arrived at camp and we fired the old girl up. I never grew tired of the sound. It's amazing what you remember looking back. The porcelain tub, whitish with chips of differing shades of black around the sides, made the fish look smaller. Nonetheless I knew I had caught a monster and the fish seemed very happy.

At about 3 AM, I knelt by the bathtub, crying. I woke Mom and Dad and insisted that we release the fish down at the lakeside. Mother seemed overwhelmed at my sensitivity at such a young age. Dad seemed irritated. The fish swam away under the full moon, and I was hooked on the sport. My sister, Susan, seven years older, was very supportive of my decision and I loved her very much, as I do today.

When I was seven years old, (an extremely socially unacceptable seven), I already felt comfortable out in the woods and wilderness. I could trap, had my own .22 rifle, and could navigate as well as many adults. For my birthday, I was given the best gift of my life: a 17-foot Rangeley Lake Classic Guide boat, dark green with open ribs of varnished cedar, seats woven with cane and a mighty Mercury motor with a green bonnet. The denizens of Rangeley Lake were amazed by my boat-handling skills, but more so that a father would allow a seven-year-old to travel the 14 square mile lake by himself. I always pushed the limits.

Soon after receiving this great gift, I told Dad that I was often scared when the sea got rough. That very night, it blew some 30 knots out of the northeast. In rough weather we usually moored the guide boat on a buoy (a large concrete block which the family had delivered by barge) and secured it. As the gale winds picked up, Father came into the living room with an old metal lunchbox. I remember it had a silver patina kind of like a tarnished candle holder and the hinges were loose. I always considered it beautiful. Dad also carried a frayed and dirty LL Bean canvas tote bag containing my rain gear, a pair of boots and a life preserver. Dad and I went out to the boat and transferred it from the dock to the buoy. My goodness the waves seemed huge; cresting, with the tops blowing off in almost a mystical spray. It took 10 minutes for me to attach the pelican clip on the bow to the buoy. The boat kept lifting and falling in the swells and as I remember I was just a little short of petrified. Once attached, the boat rose and fell on the huge waves. Father looked at me and said, "You will no longer be afraid of rough seas and you will never get sick again. I will see you in the morning."

Father jumped overboard and swam to shore. I have never felt so scared and alone in my life. Even with the howling wind I heard my mother try to characterize this action as cruel and as undeservedly harsh punishment. I don't remember exactly their conversation, but it was not pretty. So, now, I'm a little kid, riding out a gale. It was so rough that I had to lay down in the bottom of the boat. I had to bale with a rusted coffee can about every 20 minutes. I hated my father more than ever that night! I cried and sniffled and yelled for help but none of it worked. So with life preserver and rain gear on, I lay down in the sloshing water to ride the night out.

What an interminably long night and for a seven-year-old virtually unbearable. The wind didn't let up, but at one point, about 3 o'clock in the morning, I snapped! I sat on the cross seat and welcomed everything that Mother Nature could throw at me. I was no longer scared and the boat's violent movements seemed more like an amusement ride than the terrible bucking bronco ride like when I first arrived. All I could think about was how I would act when my father arrived on the dock. And then it dawned on me how I could really show him that I was not afraid.

I started the mighty engine on the first pull. I don't remember how I got unhooked from the mooring but I did. And off I went to Smith's Cove, some two miles away straight into the jaws of the gale. With every wave, white water showered over the bow onto me. I knew this was dangerous and that I had to be extremely careful. Finally, in the calm-water of Smith's Cove, I took a deep breath and knew then and there that my future would be spent on the water. I also suspected Mother and Father would be going berserk. It was payback time!

I went way up into Smith's Cove (which turns into a river) where I often went to fish for perch, and nestled into the alders where no one could find me. It seemed like I stayed there for hours. With the concept of time being what it is to a small child, it could have been 15 minutes.

Cruising down-sea back to our camp, I realized how dangerous my decision had been. It took a sensitive and deft touch on the tiller and throttle in those rough seas, but I learned that I really could handle the boat that day.

Back at camp, Mom, Dad, the local police, and two gentlemen dressed in dark-green, Department of Forestry uniforms stood on the dock. I remember their yellow, sewn-on badges seemed to glow in the sun.

Surprisingly, I felt neither afraid nor intimidated. When I tied the boat off to the dock, Father started to unload on me about how what I did was stupidly unsafe. I had already heard this diatribe in my mind on the run back from the cove. I turned to the officers, and stated in an extremely sarcastic voice, "Ask my dad to tell you about how he left me in the boat alone all night during the storm!" Things got very quiet and I heroically walked up to the cabin.

The second seminal event came at age 17 in my senior year at Hinckley Preparatory School. As an "A" student, I was allowed to do an independent study project. I chose to write a paper entitled "Who Am I?" I recall being extremely influenced by Christian existentialists during that period of my life as well as by Walden's Pond. I planned to stay at the camp in Rangeley and have no contact with anyone for three weeks while I researched and wrote. My father was outraged by this project. I can just see him stomping around in his office saying "Whoopie! My son is writing a philosophy paper."

The first week I was visited by Hinckley's own best philosophers as they checked in on me amidst tremendous suspicion that all I would do was hunt and fish. And it turned out that's exactly what I did.

During the second week Father showed up at camp in a red and green Bell 206B Jet Ranger helicopter. He invited me in and we flew north. Shortly after liftoff there were no houses and no roads; nothing but wilderness from there to the Canadian border and beyond. We landed in a muskeg field with several rivers feeding the marsh. Father presented me with a Marlin .22-long rifle and a rucksack containing copper wire, a change of clothes, rain gear, a small tent, compass, two Zippo lighters, matches, fishing kit, K-bar knife and a topographical map.

Dad suggested that I should travel north, not a difficult heading by the way, until I crossed into Canada. A major logging road traveled east to west and basically couldn't be missed. This sudden departure from my school plan took place so fast that I really couldn't even comprehend what was happening. As the helicopter fell out of sight I quickly realized the gravity of my situation.

No amount of understanding could temper my anger, my disappointment, and my lack of trust. Fifteen minutes later I came upon a cow moose. I had the wind right and placed a .22, 30-grain hollow point right between her eyes. She dropped like a lead sled. I took a right rear quarter, boned it out, and headed for a deeply forested bench where I set up camp and ate like a king. To this day I cannot reconcile whether I dropped that moose on a basis of survival or the moose represented the rejection that I felt from my father.

During the next ten days I followed a course of true north, unadjusted for any variation. I was cold and wet. I had moments of frustration when I balled like a baby, but towards the end I was able to catch fish with my fishing kit, kill and eat beaver, porcupine and my dried moose meat. I developed severe diarrhea and was very dehydrated. Interestingly though, I never really suffered from fear. What I realized about myself, and later wrote in my philosophy paper, was that I didn't like being alone. I still don't. I realized that the human condition — unless shared with others – is in many ways meaningless. The adage "No man is an island" is very true. I had been alone enough in my life.

I crossed the Canadian border three or four days overdue. Everyone had been looking for me. A logging trucker stopped me — having my picture on his dashboard. I announced I was Tred Barta and he announced that my father had offered a $5,000 reward for any information as to my whereabouts. I hoped that I could get the reward higher so the trucker could get more, but the two of us couldn't figure that one out.

The helicopter arrived at the logging camp. The pilots brought me back to our camp at Rangeley Lake. Most of my professors never knew what happened and I think Father paid off those who did.

After the school's overly pedantic philosophers graded my paper, I ended up with a D! They claimed it was too simple and that I simply quoted other people. I argued that in many ways life is simple and that everyone's truth is different. In any event, the pilots flew me home after graduation.

Father had a huge wine-colored mahogany desk which in those days' cost about $20,000. I called it "the Power Desk." Father was definitely always the man in charge. When I arrived home, he was having a sales meeting with six other men. I walked into his office and had planned on presenting him with my K-bar knife. But before I could get it out, Father asked, "Are you a pussy anymore?" With that I drove the knife four inches deep into the blotter on his desk and said, "Your son's home. I wrote the philosophy paper and I am still a man" and walked out.

My third formative event happened a year later. I had already attended rock climbing camp, music camp, survival camp, orienteering camp, been to several certification courses on Beechcraft King Airs, Lear jets, was flying left seat (pilot in command) in Mitsubishi turbo props, all while training constantly in Alpine and Nordic skiing during the summer and of course competing in the winter. It was just before a serious push took place to get ready for the Junior Olympic Biathlon tryouts. And to be quite honest I was just tired of the B.S.

Yes, I could hunt, fish, survive, cook, scuba dive and fly. I know it sounds like a great life, but looking back I realize they never allowed me to be a kid. In fact, while attending the University of Colorado I completely missed the happy days. All I did was train my butt off.

I finally had two weeks off at home before finishing up my senior year at boarding school. Father announced I would be going to the last camp in my life for two weeks in Louisiana. This was an adult survival program; eat on the run, military style evasion camp and people actually hunting you down. Can you imagine?

They give you a knife and a compass. When you get to a predetermined flag you follow an approximate course line for a week while the counselors attempt to capture and torture you until you break and give them a five-digit code which you are not supposed to reveal. Really? I am pissed! I don't want to play in my father's sandboxes any more.

I became arrogant, rude, obtuse, and made no bones about not being willing to take this crap any more. I will skip the additional details of this camp because today it seems so boring. The object was to eat, run and survive. The Cajuns gave us a five-hour head start. All of the other participants apparently had their fathers training them for this camp. They all left at early light and ran across a big open field with cattle.

I chose to sleep in and somehow I went unnoticed. At approximately 10 AM a counselor came into my tent yelling and screaming. By the way, I had been trained in martial arts and had been beaten up and defeated many times. This guy did not even raise my blood pressure. As a matter of fact, I thought I could take him and seriously considered it. Right then five other counselors came in and started yelling and screaming, too. When one of them pushed me, I tackled him by the waist and we fell over two beds and the others pulled me off.

I got dressed, put my pack on, and sheathed my K-bar and walked to the yellow flag that marked the start of my survival route. They all started screaming, "You better run! You have less than five hours!" I purposely walked slowly across the cow pasture. Approximately 200 yards into the farmer's field stood a black and white Holstein heifer. I cut her throat and watched her fall to the ground and bleed out.

I pitched my tent right there, started a fire from dried cow patties, fed it with a couple of dried old fence posts and planned to eat steak for a week. Oh my God! Talk about a cluster! Here comes the farmer, the counselors, and I am sure my father was there on the phone. All the counselors stood outside the pasture, yelling and screaming at once, threatening that I am about to be captured. I just stood my ground slinging profanities right back at them while holding my K-bar.

As they got closer, I kept yelling, "Someone is going to get hurt!" I really had had enough. I consider this experience one of my scariest. I honestly didn't give a damn and was prepared to take them all on! And I would have. They all knew it.

Father flew in on the family jet. I remember he paid $1,100 for the cow. If he paid $5,000 it wouldn't have mattered to me. In the aircraft, the two pilots — who had saved me from being thrown out of countless places — gave me a high-five, which further enraged my father.

Dad was wearing a Brooks Brothers plaid jacket, khaki pleated pants, an alligator belt, and tan buck shoes with a yellowish ascot. We took off without saying anything. We started to talk when I grabbed him by both lapels, thrust him back in his seat, and said, "I am not going to take this anymore. It is over." My father did not push back at all. I have never been so angry.

We landed at Westchester Airport and as I walked to the terminal, I heard my father say behind me, "We have a man on our hands now." How monumentally disappointing; my father finally announcing my manhood.

That day, and for the rest of my life I feared no man and I truly did not fear any situation. One day I mourned deep down inside as I watched a high school kid pull out of a parking lot in a red Mustang, with his blonde girlfriend, hair blowing in the wind, radio blaring; how much of my youth I had lost.

Many who read this will probably view my youth as cruel, uncaring and irresponsible. But as I came back from the University of Colorado and started my fishing career in the northeast canyons you will soon understand from my eyes, my heart, and my upbringing, the mindset which I took to the canyons. Was it further proving myself? Was it trying to win my father's love? Was it pure passion for the ocean? Or perhaps all three? Welcome aboard!

Judy Barta, Tred's mother, and Tred at Rangeley Lake, Maine

Tred's sister, Susan, and Tred riding horses in Rangeley, Maine

Chapter Four
MY DREAMS WITH JOHN WAYNE

MY FATHER WAS a tall, handsome man, one who carried himself in stately stature and always stood out in a crowd. If he wore his uniform it was tailored, starched to perfection, and stood out amongst others. He had an incredible command of the English language and knew innately what sophisticated words to use, when, and to whom. He would never talk over a workman's head, but he definitely changed his words when talking with someone like Stavros Niarchos, a very wealthy Greek business tycoon with whom my father did business.

By the time I reached my early teens, ADD/ADHD and dyslexia specialists had basically given up on me. Fifty years ago, when I was a boy, the world didn't know what we know today about these illnesses. My family's solution was to send me to special schools during the year and send me to special summer camps after that.

Due to always being away from home, I fantasized about John Wayne and in my nightly dreams he became my dream father. I actually met him twice in California. It amazed me when John Wayne stood next to my father, how they both carried that identical indestructible, one-in-a-million-type look.

Embarrassed to even take the subject up with either parent, every night for four years I found myself beside John in almost every movie he ever did. With guns blazing, horses galloping, fist fights, roping, drinking at the bar, or even swooning with the ladies, the greatest acknowledgement I ever got happened when John Wayne would turn, look me directly in the eye, and give me an approving wink.

My obsession with John Wayne started to bother some of my school counselors and summer camp doctors, to the point that they recommended me for psychiatric counseling. That idea didn't gain much traction as my father loved John Wayne more than any man alive. He said, "What's the matter with these people? What a great dream to have!" I usually stayed in the psychiatrist's office for about ten minutes of an hour session. Not being a "normal" kid, I felt it was ridiculous. I accepted no bulls**t from anybody. I had already been around the world twice. I had lived through three or four solid years without seeing my parents for more than two weeks at a time. Those two weeks inevitably consisted of a battery of tests to see what I had learned.

One night, after fighting a fierce battle alongside John Wayne and riding off into the sunset, I dreamt of Shady Creek, of a place populated with large cottonwood trees and the ground covered by soft moss and grass. It smelled like spring coming out of a bottle. The clean stream water made a gurgling sound, rolling over rocks that caused huge ripples in the water. John would always lay on the ground with his head on the saddle blanket on top of his saddle, turn over on his side with his right hand almost touching his pistol, and he would then pull his cowboy hat right to his eyebrow so he could still see. I did the same thing some ten feet away. The camp fire smoldered beneath the blue porcelain coffee pot suspended over the flames. The horses grazed quietly behind us. Just before John Wayne would fall off to sleep, we would make eye contact, meaning to me that all was okay, I had done a good job, I was a trusted friend, I covered his six, and tomorrow would be a new adventure.

Sometimes in my dreams, we never talked much in the morning when I would wake up out on the trail with John, but our gestures spoke volumes. He would send me down river to look for Indians and do a general recon. I knew that he trusted me with his life and embraced the fact that he never felt the need to question whether or not I could do it, tell me how to do it, when to do it, what to look for, and consequences of my behavior. All John said was, "check down river."

I saddled and mounted my horse, my colt on my hip, Winchester in my scabbard, sun at my back, shoulders high, and rode off to do the job. This is really all that I wanted from life or perhaps going deeper, the only thing I wanted from my father.

I obviously consider this a very embarrassing chapter in my life. I have never discussed these dreams with anyone. Certainly, a shrink would say that John Wayne represented my father, providing me with the love I never received or never earned from him. Or perhaps I did receive it but I just missed seeing the wink or the eye contact. Despite this, I still believe to this day my father was the greatest man who ever walked the face of earth.

One of his bombardiers told me later in life, while leading a squadron of B-29s the flack was so bad that you couldn't even hear yourself talk. Over twenty B-29s on that raid crashed to the earth. Dad took the other B-29s to the target and bombed the living crap out of the enemy. And at the absolute worst of it he yelled down the aircraft, "what does it take to get a cup of coffee up here?" That was my Dad, fearless, intelligent, cool, honorable, and a man's-man.

Joseph Barta's certification

Tred Barta with statue of John Wayne

Chapter Five
ONE MISSION ONE GOAL

BY THE TENDER age of 18, I decided (or should I say my father decided) that after winning the Junior Olympic Biathlon; spending a week at Dartmouth College where I couldn't do the work; and then being drafted by Bill Marolt at the University of Colorado who coached both the CU ski team and the U.S. Olympic ski team, that I would be simply the best skier in the world. I was okay with that and gave it my best. The problem? I just wasn't good enough. In fact, at one of the best cross country races I ever skied, I came in 35th. You might say I saw the writing on the wall when two Czechs, a Russian, and a Norwegian — all with legs the size of oak trees and all women beat my times. Half the Finnish, Swedish, and Norwegian teams regularly skied 50 miles in the morning to go to high school and 50 miles back home again.

Biathlon is a sport of shooting and cross-country skiing. I was an incredible shot but the skiing technique just never came. I didn't really give a damn about school as by this time I had been around the world three or four times flying corporate aircraft. I also knew that I probably would never work for anyone else other than my father or myself. School just wasn't in my DNA. I was brought into this world not to surf on waves but to make them; not to follow, but to lead.

In my sophomore year at the University, I had a Business 101 instructor named Professor Bowen. He wore a black eye patch, was a real prick, and he did not like me. I held him in contempt from the first moment he opened his mouth in the amphitheater where he taught. He is what I call a little, big man.

Being around wealth, success, and hard-working people my entire life, I considered this pint size man dressed in his little corporate gray suits a "wannabe." For goodness sake, he didn't even know how to tie a double Windsor knot! He pontificated endlessly about the marginal propensities to consume and save and worse, how smart he was in business. He droned on and on about desire and passion.

The first week of class, I stood up and yelled for all to hear, "If you're so smart, why is it you make $35,000 a year, drive a VW bus, and rent an apartment. Why is that?" The man hated me ever after and several times suggested I leave the class as there was no way I was going to pass it. It enraged me that the Peter principle would allow such a jerk to have earned quadruple PhD's in Business. It enforced in me that school was a joke.

So I rebelled again. With my monthly allowance from Dad I purchased a light-blue Lotus Europa, a hot little European fiberglass sports car. But I noticed every other kid on campus bought or borrowed someone else's Volkswagen. One evening I hatched a business plan; I sold the Europa, convinced my father that people like us didn't belong in a dorm, and got my allowance tripled to live off campus.

At the end of each school year, graduating seniors would sell their Volkswagens at bargain prices and move on with their lives. The new freshmen class would gobble these up, their daddies and mommies writing these checks with scarcely a second thought. In fishing vernacular, I considered it nothing short of a Volkswagen feeding frenzy. Very similar to hundreds of sea birds swooping up the scraps from a tuna bite.

With $5,000 in seed money, I went around knocking on seniors' doors. I chatted up all over campus and immediately put down $50 to $300 deposits on each VW. Actually, they were more like options to buy their VWs by a certain date rather than deposits. Before I knew it, I had fifty VW bugs and buses tied up and stood to literally triple my money on each and every one. What an absolute riot! I had a calendar filled with option and delivery dates. I moved more VWs than any two Boulder, Colorado VW dealers combined. Daddy would come into town with his little freshmen baby, drive the vehicle around the block, and bingo… I would make $800 to $1,500 a pop!

I experienced only a few, minor problems: I paid no income taxes; I neither collected nor paid any state sales tax; and, I was not a certified car dealer. Surprisingly, all are required by law. I guess I had missed a couple of details in Professor Bowen's class after all.

With my proceeds, I ended up buying a 1952 Rolls-Royce Silver Wraith —the model with the monstrous headlights and sweeping lines like a Cagney mobster movie. You expected the door to open up at any moment revealing a guy with a machine gun blasting away. Instead out I climbed with my long hair. Oh, and I usually towed a waterski boat behind the Rolls-Royce. That year I generated income just under $60,000. Hey everybody, this was around 1972 so that would be equivalent to approximately $200,000 today.

Then one day they showed up on my doorstep en masse. Officials of all stripes served me with lawsuits, subpoenas, notifications, salutations, invitations, all of which begged for a pre-trial hearing. Father (who was gloating in my success), hired the best of the best attorneys in Denver. Resolving the problem proved to be much simpler than expected. The State of Colorado, the local car dealers, and the University of Colorado wanted Tred Barta to disappear without any media coverage. I proved to Father that I turned out to be exactly what he had hoped for: a confident, successful prick. I had been taught from an early age not to take crap from anybody. Dad decided I was ready to move into the family aircraft business.

At the hearing, I was told that I would leave the university and State of Colorado, I was never to buy or sell cars in the state again, and in exchange, I asked that the car dealers buy my remaining inventory of 67 vehicles options at a 50% profit. My father blanched but held his tongue. On my closing transaction alone I made another $ 36,000.

I exited the University of Colorado with $ 87,000. Just before all of my papers were signed (and believe me the State of Colorado was never so happy to get rid of somebody) I added one more caveat. I insisted I be allowed to attend one more class with Professor Bowen.

I remember my reparations for that class visit cost me $193. Why the heck I remember that number I have no clue. But that's what it cost me to print out all of my sales agreements, my initial option plan agreement, a list of my purchase option contracts, pictures of my ski boat and Rolls-Royce, and a 500-word essay on what a jerk I considered Professor Bowen. The amphitheater filled up and Captain Pint-Size came in after all 100 students were seated. I had already placed on each seat a nine-page collated and stapled report on my activities proceeded by my essay. Mr. Bowen took the podium. He used to carry a little white orchestra-type baton for effect, which I am sure was 400 times the length of his genitalia. When he saw his copy and skimmed the essay, Professor Bowen threw the report to the floor and screamed, "Where is he?" Well "he" was me, and I was already climbing out of flight level 18,000 headed for flight level 41,000 in route to New York in the family Lear. Had I failed in school, had I failed in business, had I failed on the ski team, or was it all just a preamble for one of the greatest accomplishments of my life? This was the true beginning of my blue water career.

My Grown-Up Job

Now living with my family for the first time in over a decade, I quickly realized that in many ways our corporate pilots, which were many over the years, were always more accepting of me than my immediate family. Lou Enborg was one of my favorite pilots. After all they had rescued me and retrieved me whenever I was expelled from school, kicked out of camps or just bringing me to and from my father's boot camps all over the world.

My family owned 200 acres in Pleasantville, New York, just outside Armonk and the IBM headquarters. The family business, Joseph T. Barta Associates, bought, sold, and leased executive airplanes globally. The company was big, well-honed, and successful. I became an immediate success, a gifted salesman, and was obviously razor-sharp at self-promotion. I did all of my own delivery trips, ending up with 22 ocean crossings. I literally flew around the world at least three times in some of the world's most incredible aviation equipment such as Lears, Hawkers, Beechcraft King Airs, and G1s, G2s, and G3s. I spent a week with Stavros Niarchos in San Moritz, Switzerland as my father had sold him the Ling Tempco Voight Bac-111 executive jet. Stavros liked me and here I was experiencing opulence on a level which I had never seen before.

I soon purchased a condominium in the Excelsior building on 57th Street and 2nd Avenue in New York City. Father sold the Lear 24B and our company purchased a twin engine Cessna 310 which would be perfect for commuting from Westchester Airport (HPN) to Suffolk County Airport (FOK) on eastern Long Island.

After a year of exhausting the vices of New York City, I chose to live in Southampton, New York and commute to the office for the next 30 years of my life. I had three sports that required an incredible amount of money to support: big-game hunting with a longbow, water fowling, and offshore fishing. By this time in my life, I had fished with Father and his clients throughout the Bahamas, Mexico, Venezuela, and all over the Caribbean. I had fished Cabos San Lucas extensively, and was fairly seasoned. I had been to Tropic Star Lodge eight times in Piñas Bay, Panama. I had a tremendous interest in light-tackle angling and throughout the years set numerous IGFA world records on light and conventional tackle.

Stephen Sloan, my mentor in light tackle at that time, co-authored a book entitled "Ocean Bankruptcy" with another gentleman, Larry Furman. Both world-class anglers taught me a lot. About that same time, I purchased my first fishing boat, a 19-foot Mako. My friend, Oak Gentry, at White Water Marine reconditioned the vessel, adding extra fuel, new wiring and steering, a fighting chair in the bow, outriggers, and rocket launcher rod holders aft. I planned to break several world records in this boat. Of course it was way too small and in many ways turned out to be a disaster. It certainly became the laughing stock at Indian Cove Marina in Hampton Bays, New York.

Aboard this little "skiff," I attempted on many occasions to set a bluefin IGFA world record on 30-pound test, but I suffered one heart break after another and never did land one. The mystique of the canyons — the edge of the North American continental shelf where America drops off into the deep ocean that runs from North Carolina all the way up past Georges Banks — consumed my life for the next 20 years. There, my life on the 100-fathom line started.

Chapter Six
MY BEGINNINGS IN THE CANYON

FROM THE VANTAGE point of my wheelchair, I look back now at that time in my life when the only value of money to me was to finance an all-out campaign to understand the mysteries of the Continental Shelf and the unexplored wilderness of what seafarers call "The Canyons."

In 1972, leaving from Shinnecock or Moriches Inlets, I would fuel the Mako, then insanely add a 50-gallon drum of gas as well as a secondary fuel bladder! I was 20 years old and my boat qualified as a 19-foot-long fuel barge! With only my transom tied to the dock and my Chrysler outboard running in gear, I added to the weight of fuel by loading eight rods, numerous swordfish rigs, coolers filled with ice, a wet suit, a gallon of milk, ten cans of Spam and Vienna sausages, a loaf of TipTop white bread, and a carton of Twinkies. I revved the outboard up to about 1,500 RPM and the dock hands would simultaneously cut the transom lines with serrated knives. I immediately poured the coals to the rig and on an almost flat sea would head between 145 to 170 degrees traveling at 24 knots for 4 to 4-1/2 hours. I had no radar and Long-Range Navigation (LORAN) was in its infancy. I had a compass, watch, and a hand-held VHF, which from my height above the water offered a range of about two miles. Upon arriving on the 100 fathom line (some 80 to 100 miles offshore) I never really knew exactly if I was there, but knew I was somewhere between 90 and 300 fathoms.

On my first such adventure, I met the Russian fleet. The Chinese and Japanese had not shown up off our canyons yet. Three Russian longliners (whom I got to know extremely well) — the Kreefe, the Kokomo, and the Bladsteeg, were 90 to 200-footers.

I used to carry a three-by-six-foot piece of 5/8-inch plywood with me, and seeing the Russian fleet meant it was time for me to refuel. The bladder tank I carried in the bow gravity fed into the floor tank under the center console. Then I'd roll the 50-gallon drum up and over the 5/8-inch plywood, all while maintaining 10 knots so the boat wouldn't sink. Then the full fuel drum, the plywood, four hi-flyer buoys, my anchor, anchor rope, and two large containers containing bait and fresh water were jettisoned. I was now 100 miles offshore by myself with my "health food stash" and a full tank of fuel — ready to fish.

The story I am about to tell is only known to a very few people. I don't know why I have kept it a secret but perhaps in the day I was afraid to tell it. The first time I saw a Russian trawler bearing a huge red hammer and sickle insignia, I honestly thought I had sailed off the end of the earth. Russian-American relations festered in the midst of the Cold War. Under such circumstances, I couldn't help but wonder why in the world the Russian fishing fleet worked a mere 90 to 120 miles off eastern Long Island?

Although I developed a friendly relationship with three of the captains of these factory fishing ships, I later saw smaller vessels of some 80 to 100 feet unloading catch boxes containing what I assumed were swordfish, tuna, and assorted ground fish. I loved watching this fascinating transfer process. Rigid inflatable boats (RIBs) powered by twin outboards launched out of the transom of the factory vessel in "James Bond" movie fashion. They transported fish between the trawlers and the factory ship.

It amazed me to watch the processing operation continue around the clock. On one occasion, a huge "mothership" showed up. I thought it very strange as it had no Russian markings and sailed under a Rhodesian flag. I don't know how large the ship was, it seemed four times the size of the biggest processing ship. A conveyor belt stretched from the highest point of the processing vessel to the lowest point of the mother ship. Six long conveyor chutes transported boxes of frozen fish up into the hull of the mother ship.

Then, one strange morning, I woke up to a flat-calm sea and the entire fleet had completely disappeared. It was mid-August as I remember, and for two weeks Coast Guard Falcon jets, Hercules C130 transports and U.S. Navy fighter jets patrolled along the 100-fathom line, flying less than 200 feet overhead. It scared the living crap out of me. I have always wondered where the Russian ships came from. From what port did they leave? Where did the fish go to that they caught? And why was the United States of America allowing it?

One weekend back onshore, four nondescript gray and black government vehicles arrived in front of my house in Hampton Bays. Seven men approached the house, showed very official-looking badges of some sort and handed me several pictures of my Mako tied up to or being towed by one of the Russian trawlers. They asked questions about my relationship with the vessels. They already knew everything about me and it quickly became quite apparent to all that I was nothing more than a kid trying to catch tuna. After explaining in great detail the potential consequences of my actions and how I could be prosecuted every which-way to

Sunday, they disappeared as quietly as they came with these parting words: "This meeting never happened and make sure we see no more pictures like these!" That's the last I saw of them until several years later.

I always brought five bottles of Johnny Walker Black scotch out fishing with me as the crews and officers of the Russian fleet absolutely loved it. I spent many a night tied off to a Russian trawler. They let me shower, fed me, and quite a few spoke English. Of course this probably violated every international rule in the book. I heard that there were other sport fishing boats in the canyons at this time, but over a period of two years between the Hudson Canyon and the Fish Tails, I never saw a single one! Not once!

On approximately my 15th overnight canyon trip by myself on my little 19-footer, I came back into Shinnecock or Moriches Inlet with grandiose stories of fish lost. On every single trip I got buggered by between four and eight bigeye tuna on at one time, big enough to simply strip all the line off my reels, break my rods, or get loose when on the wire. For sure I just couldn't catch one.

The Russian fleet liked me, watched me and looked out for me – the crazy kid 100 miles offshore in a tiny boat! Sure, they thought I was crazy but I earned their respect and I enjoyed their camaraderie. I remember on two separate occasions I had lost all of my fuel, food and bait with the current. I usually fished within a five-mile grid of my floating fuel source. I remember the Russian fleet always helped me get back to it.

Sometimes at night, seas got so rough that I lay in the bottom of my boat in my wetsuit truly believing that I wouldn't see the sunrise. My childhood adventures brought me to a point where I wasn't afraid to die, and fishing out there affirmed my life's purpose. Nonetheless, I finally sold my 19-foot Mako and purchased a 32-foot Forest Johnson Prowler powered by a pair of Chrysler 440-hp gas inboard engines. I named it *Makaira*, the Latin taxonomy for Marlin.

I also upgraded my tackle and greatly improved my wiring and gaffing skills. Folks back on the docks judged me as arrogant, stupid, and reckless. The new *Makaira* had an oscilloscope Loran-A. By matching a run line with a bell shaped green arch isolator one could actually come very close to locating your position.

I remember one particular day really well: the flat-calm seas and high stratus clouds cut out about 80 percent of the sunshine, making the ocean battleship gray. In fact, from earth to sky presented a study in 50 shades of gray. I decided to troll just one rod; a real renegade technique. I actually trolled three other rods that had lures without any hooks (appropriately called teasers). Suddenly, here comes the wolfpack! Every teaser line got ripped off of the boat. The teasers, huge expensive jetheads, were combinations of yellow and green, silver and blue, and green and black. What looked to be a black Volkswagen inhaled my 50-pound rig with a 12-inch bait with a three-ounce chin weight and a single, 16/0, closed-gap, welded-eye Mustad 7754 hook rigged on number 19 silver piano wire.

Line screamed off the black Penn Senator spooled with white Cortland Dacron braid. The reel got so hot that I could hardly touch the side plates with my hand. The clicker completely burned out.

As I applied maximum pressure to the white Cortland line, it actually twanged like a violin string. I fought this fish for almost two hours. I finally got the leader and used a meat hook rather than a gaff to boat it. Unbelievable.

Popular fishing out of eastern Long Island during this period included surface fishing for swordfish, as well as trolling for white marlin, small- to medium-size yellowfin tuna and of course giant bluefin tuna – all in depths of 40 fathoms or less. I caught my tuna in 558 fathoms, just 42 miles east of the Fish Tail. My Russian neighbors all praised me as I headed for Shinnecock Inlet with one massive dead tuna on the deck.

In retrospect, I think it's strange that I remember one significant fact from so many years ago: I remember asking myself why I couldn't wait to tell the Russian fleet or our company pilots of my success rather than my father or my mother? I don't know what it means nor do I seek to understand it. I just remember thinking it.

When I got back to Shinnecock, Long Island I was met by several of my detractors, all experts of course, all more experienced than myself and many of them true captains at grilling hot dogs back at the dock. About 90 percent of the time they did not go fishing because it was too hot, too cold, wrong tide, too much wind, not enough wind, rising barometer, or falling barometer. Personally I think they were just sissies and wimps. If you are so afraid of failing, you cannot win!

The tuna weighed in at 298 pounds! All of the dock-bound experts (including the real experts) failed to identify the species. Woods Hole Department. of Fisheries were immediately notified and flew into Westhampton Beach to meet me and Eddie Laureson, marina manager of Indian Cove Marina. After one solid hour of extracting backbone and liver samples, they determined that all my stories of broken tackle, heartbreaks, broken leaders, and straightened hooks just may have been true! The first bigeye tuna (*Thunnus obesus*) had hit the dock in Shinnecock. Here begins what I consider my true life story.

While my fishing success had barely scratched the surface, and though still very young, people – even the best-of-the-best fishermen in the world – started taking me much more seriously.

I now contributed to every issue of *Sport Fishing* magazine and appeared frequently in *Marlin* magazine, *The Big Game Fishing Journal*, granted over 50 radio interviews per year and had a four-page feature article about me in *Sports Illustrated*. Newspapers like the New York Times, New York Post and other syndicated mediums followed me very closely. **The "Barta Bigeye Bible" and "Barta's Bluefin Bible" are included at the end of this book, courtesy of Big Game Fishing Journal.**

It is at this time that I started to weave the very fabric of my knowledge. Even the best offshore captains knew my knowledge of the Continental Shelf was well earned. Everyone knew I had passion, guts, stamina and the resources. Now was my time to become a great fishermen.

Out Of The Stone Age

The introduction of Loran (Long-range Radio Navigation) basically divided my northeast canyons into numeric grids running north/south and east/west. It was like God himself designed a visual mosaic for a man inflicted with ADD and ADHD. I grew to know every inch of those canyons. Every intersection had a value and over the next three years, I spent another couple hundred thousand dollars validating, researching, and confirming the value of warm core eddies (swirls of water peeling off the Gulf Stream), how to fish them, and why I'd consistently find game fish at certain locations and certain times. My research and findings made *"Team Makaira"* almost unbeatable from the early 1970s through the mid '80s.

Follow Tred's journey aboard his 19 foot Mako as he encounters Japanese and Russian fleets and brings the first bigeye tuna back to Shinnecock, by viewing the following chart.

12300
UNITED STATES - EAST COAST
APPROACHES TO NEW YORK
NANTUCKET SHOALS TO FIVE FATHOM BANK
Starting Area
Shinnecock Inlet
First
Bigeye Tuna
Weighed in at
Indian Cove Marina
Map of Ocean Currents.
Where warm Gulf Stream
meets cool northern currents
at atlantic continental shelf.
Red Circle Surrounds where journey took
place
Block Canyon
Atlantic Canyon
Veatch Canyon
Hudson Canyon
Floated Fuel
Jettison Fuel
Hendrickson Canyon
Toms Canyon
Middle Toms Canyon
South Toms Canyon
Berkeley Canyon
Carter Canyon
Early Russian
and
Japanese Fleets
NORTH ATLANTIC OCEAN
Tred's Handwritten comments
supplemented for legibility
12300
12300

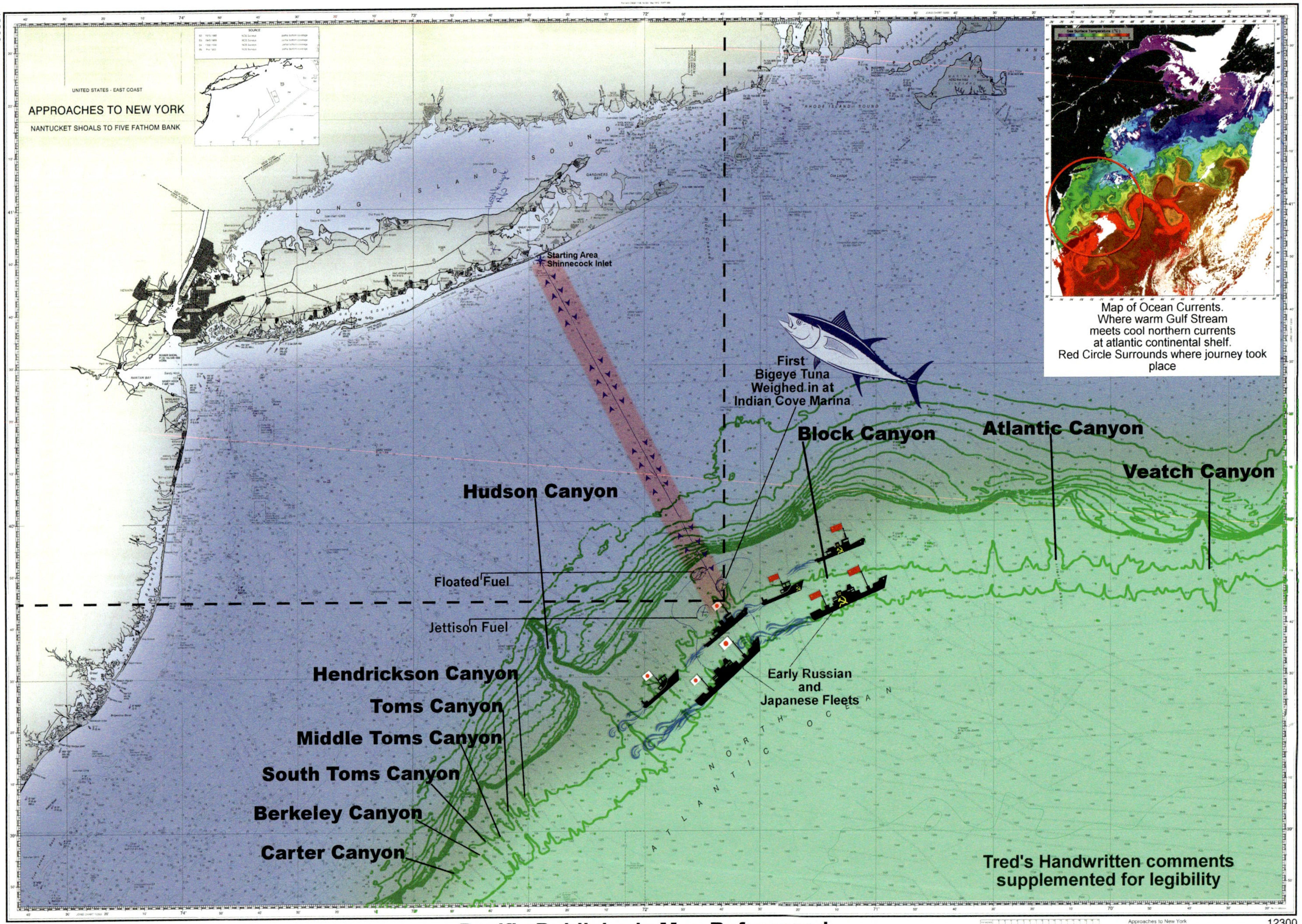

Pacific Publisher's Map Referenced

CHART 1

Tred Barta on his 19 foot Makaira, the vessel Tred would spend 3 days on, 100 miles offshore and then brought the first bigeye tuna into Shinnecock, Long Island

Chapter Seven
A Touch Shorthanded

I FINISHED A real head-banger of a day selling corporate aircraft at Joseph T. Barta Associates. A Japanese company from whom I had purchased an aircraft apparently preferred to conduct business face-to-face and so asked for a meeting to discuss a contract they'd already agreed upon. Pardon my language, but what an unmitigated cluster. At the last moment, my partner, John Iso, was selected to represent us. He showed up in the office with a mocha java Peruvian of caramel designer coffee and six books on Japanese customs. As the day ended he was trying to get me to practice bowing. It was not going to happen. Anyway I would get to revisit this charade on Monday.

I had worked from 6 am until 9 pm for five days. That is a long time sitting on your butt screaming and yelling at people in six different languages who don't understand you to start with. When I finally escaped, my twin-engine Cessna 310 started up like a little tiger. The Cessna knew its way to the Suffolk County airport in Westhampton Beach, New York like the back of her hand. Something in me pushed the weekend button. "Tower, 27 Tango Bravo ready to taxi at Hangar D." "Roger 27 Tango Bravo. Runway 24, barometer 2987 millibars, winds light and variable. Have a good weekend."

About 23 minutes later I was on a short final approach to Francis S. Gabreski Airport in Westhampton. The ocean in the distance looked like a sheet of glass. It beckoned and shimmered in the early evening sun. I hated the thought that some boats had already left on their way out to fish the canyons. As I secured the aircraft, three line boys approached me. I said to myself, "they are *not* going to make me move this damn airplane to another location." All three of them had the largest baggies made in their hands. They asked, "Tred, what's the chance of getting some yellowfin tuna this trip?" We all laughed, but I took the baggies.

I jumped in my camouflage Bronco — I mean fully camouflage — with not a space on the vehicle that was not covered. The Bronco growled upon start up. After all, for some reason I found it necessary to have a glass-pack muffler. Curiously, those who know me said it was to draw attention to myself. Can you imagine? At this time in my life, my personal closet had 21 khaki shirts starched to military perfection with Captain Tred Barta monogramed on them and matching khaki pants. Outfits numbered 1-32. Add two sets of penny loafers with Brooks Brothers white and blue monogramed button down dress shirts.

As I drove to Indian Cove Marina in Hampton Bays, New York, Mike Forman sat on the dock rigging a 15-inch squid for night swordfishing. Mike had a lot of talents, but rigging baits was not one of them. I planned to leave that evening, but didn't see my mate, Willy Dickson. I yelled to Mike, "Hey, where's Willy?" Silence. I beat Mike to his next sentence. "Mike, where is he?" He explained that it was Willy's birthday and his entire family plus guests were having a big shebang this evening to be followed by more festivities the next day.

Mike went on to say that I was to be surprised by a second mate coming, who I often used and tried to hire twice. This mate however apparently got drunk in Montauk the night before and literally ran into a parked car with his bicycle dislocating his shoulder and breaking his nose.

By now, it was getting late and we decided that Mike and I would force ourselves to go to the Lobster Inn, visiting one of my closest friends, Skip Tollefsen, the owner of the restaurant. As we drove to the restaurant over the Shinnecock Canal Bridge not a breath of wind stirred. At dinner, I gave Mike six phone numbers for six different mates. As he returned to the table he said, "Tred, every single one of them are going to Willy's birthday party." So we enjoyed our dinner and I headed back to my Hampton Bays house.

I planned to meet Mike at the boat at 10 am. Surely by then we would have a third crew member and leave at noon. It's an unmitigated fact that I loved my crew. In essence they were my family. Willy Dickson — a part of the rich fabric of Hampton Bays fishing families in terms of his offshore career — was still just a kid. Gary and Jeff Dickson as well as George and Glades Dickson, their parents, played a huge part in my life. I am sure everyone thought it callous and rude to not attend the birthday bash, and it probably was. But in those days I only had one objective: hunting bigeye tuna.

The night came and went to find Mike and me on the boat, *Makaira*, still with no mate. Inside I was absolutely furious. My fishing operation supported no fewer than 15 families and I sure in h**l expected at a minimum to have my crew ready to go. So it was that at the crack of 1:52 am, Mike and I departed for the canyon by ourselves on my 47-foot Ridgeway.

As always, we had prepared the boat to perfection. Ice, food, Kosher salt, rods and reels – all in in perfect order and carrying full fuel for the trip ahead. Mike and I always hated Hudson Canyon. For some reason, every rude "New Yawk" fisherman showed up there using heavily accented profanity. It turned into an ugly place where most anglers ignored the tradition and heritage of the sport. There had been a recent bigeye tuna bite along the eastern wall of the Hudson from the boot to the first corner. We planned to fish the night bite, lay overnight on the canyon wall trying to catch a swordfish and then catch the morning bite.

Makaira cruised at only 19 knots, a polite way of saying we really only made 17. The trip to Hudson proved uneventful and for a second day not a ripple could we see on the water. Mike and I laughed three quarters of the way out telling old fishing stories and just discussing life in general. I always enjoyed Mike's great sense of humor. My old Cummins diesels left an ugly, brownish exhaust trail over the beautiful ocean.

Somewhere near the 40-fathom line, a school of porpoise some hundred strong joined us. Damn they were beautiful. It seemed like they were leading us to Hudson Canyon and stayed with us for miles. With them traveled black-back gulls and terns. It felt surreal. I remember sensing an interesting dichotomy on the magnificent seascape: a well-tuned bigeye killing machine headed to Hudson Canyon and yet it blended in to the ebb and flow of life just as naturally as the porpoise did. I compare it to how magnificent a lion is, how cuddly and beautiful his mane looks — right up to the point that his jaws crush the neck of an impala as it struggles towards its death. As the lion sinks its massive teeth in, literally disemboweling its prey, blood dripping from his muzzle, does a secondary appreciation of the reality of life and Nature sink in. *Makaira* was the lion prior to the hunt.

The weather forecast called for it to be absolutely gorgeous until late Sunday morning when Mother Nature planned to puff out of the east at 25 knots. This perfect forecast for Mike and me would let us fish and be on the way home before the blow. I knew this forecast would dissuade many of the offshore boats from coming to the Hudson Canyon and I felt very comfortable with our weather game plan.

As we arrived at the eastern wall of the Hudson Canyon it struck us how few boats we saw. We trolled our normal nine rods using the Barta Porcupine Rig, even though we were short crew. As we trolled the eastern side bumping from 500 to 1,000 feet just on and off the canyon shelf, we both noticed how little current as well as how little life there was. We found mahi-mahi under all of the lobster pots. Mother Carey's chickens sat by the hundreds on the water, half asleep. The terns and big gulls seemed very apathetic and lazy. The thought occurred to us that everything that lived in the canyon may have gone to Willy's birthday party as well. We couldn't beg a bite. We switched to ballyhoo, tried rigged flying fish which I had imported from Hawaii, and as darkness started to surround *Makaira*, we hadn't a single bite nor seen any encouraging signs.

Mike and I decided to tie off to a lobster pot, normally Willy's job. Willy would tie us off as Mike held onto the high flyer (pole, flag and radar reflector) of the lobster pot. This actually was a very dangerous task as often when you let go of the high flyer the metal radar reflector on top would whip back into the ocean with enough force to easily rip your throat out. In rough conditions, tying off qualified as one of the most dangerous tasks at hand. Tonight, in a placid sea, Mike couldn't find Willy's tie off rope anywhere. This special rope had a pelican clip with a quick-release mechanism so that we could get off the ball in an instant. For some stupid reason Mike tied off with 200-pound test mono. We both laughed. The ocean was so calm that leader material was actually light enough to hold us! What the heck — it worked so we left it alone.

Both being pretty tired, we arranged to split the night watches. Mike took the first on the bridge while I enjoyed the comforts of my state room. I knew one thing for sure: If we ever caught anything, it would stay cold! We had 1,800 pounds of ice on board. I had installed a Northstar LORAN in my cabin with an alarm that alerted me if the boat left a quarter-mile circle. I remember dozing off as *Makaira* lay still and sleep came quickly. I always trusted Mike on night watch. Although sometimes it felt impossible not to doze off, Mike fought it by always keeping busy tending the fishing lines and checking the baits. These days preceded the practice of massive chumming. We often got three or four swordfish bites per night and we considered catching a sword standard rather than a novelty. At midnight, Mike woke me to take over the night watch. I am convinced that my sleep habits made me perfect for canyon fishing. I could go on for days if I could sleep between 9 pm and 1 am. My time clock ideally suited this pastime.

Mike settled into the forward V-berth while I checked the reel drags in the cockpit. I started to clean up the cockpit, but quickly noticed that Mike had it in perfect condition. My set of blue welding gloves were on the fighting chair and in a precise row sat two sets of white cotton gloves, a knife, rigging needle and twine, Cyalume glow nightsticks and a bag of rubber bands. Two straight gaffs hung hooked to the tower ladder with their lines neatly coiled and attached to the cleats, ready for action; one on the starboard side and one on the port. The generator hummed a reassuring sound saying, "A-OK."

Early on, while outfitting *Makaira*, I had invested in four quartz night lights. They lit up the ocean behind the boat and proved a real asset in attracting big fish and for fighting fish at night. We also felt it was a great asset for night safety as you could see us a mile away. One of the tower lights faced forward lighting up *Makaira's* bow in white glare and making us more visible to oncoming vessels. As I started to climb up the ladder to the bridge a very soft and gentle breeze hit me in the face. This was the first essence of a breeze the entire trip. When on watch one does not sleep, but occasionally, on three- and four-day trips, your eyes inevitably close at some point. It seems like you are constantly waking up — realizing it is your responsibility not to sleep. I must have had my eyes closed as I flew off the bridge bench and slammed onto the floor. At first I thought I had fallen asleep and Mike was proving a point but there was no Mike nearby. I awoke to a wall of wind that was blowing no less than 35 knots. From 0 to 35 knots in five minutes.

In all of my years, not only as a pilot but as a boat captain, I had never seen this happen. *Makaira* laid hove-to in the troughs and the riggers had just over 30 knots of wind humming a lonely and always very unnerving tune. As I went down the bridge ladder I met Mike in the doorway to the salon. His words were clear and direct, "What the heck?" I tried to get an updated single sideband weather report as well as to speak with other boats in the canyon. I could reach nobody. While not the first time by a long shot that I ever laid to in 35-knot winds, it was the first time that a storm crept up on me so quickly. Both Mike and I suited up in our Grundens and Helly-Hanson rain gear and the canyon white boots three sizes too big so if we over went overboard the boots would come off quickly. By the way, there were no gloves or rigging material on the fighting chair any longer. They had been blown over board. Mike and I were truly shocked. We were in the southeast corner of the Hudson Canyon, ridiculously low on crew, and now drifting in six to eight foot short, ugly seas which were building by the second. The temperature plummeted almost 15 degrees.

After reeling in the deep swordfish rigs, checking bilge pumps and the engine room, Mike and I lay side by side on the salon floor in our rain gear awaiting the morning light. It was a long damn night! Waves crashed into the cockpit filling her sometimes with six inches of water. A flying fish was washed aboard and kept trying to take off to gain its freedom and would slam into the cockpit. Mike and I laughed that we finally caught something. This flying fish was hilarious. It finally caught a puff of wind and off it went.

Offshore sailors engage in a nervous banter when things get edgy. It's like you are talking to each other but are really saying nothing. The gravity of the situation was sinking in every second. Mike and I tied down the riggers as swaying side-to-side was placing too much pressure on the supporting arms. We discussed tying off to another lobster pot but decided it was too dangerous without our third crew member. If Mike went into the drink he would be dead.

I have often said in life that friendship and camaraderie is not built in the best of times but in the worst of times. In the worst, most trying of times, true friendship is forged. Unfortunately, or fortunately, this was one of those times.

As we headed into the gray light of morning, the wind blew a solid 30 knots and gusted to 40. You couldn't wear a baseball hat in the cockpit and stowing the bridge canvas was not even an option. I don't know if any of you have seen isinglass ripped like a piece of paper. I have and it results in edges as sharp as a knife. In high winds this can kill you.

The top of the ocean was one big froth of white and sea birds seemed not to be hunting for their morning breakfast as much as engaging in survival mode. Seas ran an honest eight to 12 feet. It was time to get the heck out of dodge, but both Mike and I knew we couldn't. I can remember him glancing at me the way Doc Holliday glanced at Wyatt Earp in the movie *The OK Corral*; wordlessly saying to the other, "it is a great day to die."

Mike and I put out eight rods with the biggest lures aboard: huge kona heads with 14/0 and 16/0 hooks and 500-pound mono leaders attached to 300-pound wind-ons. I tried to troll up sea but mountains of white water rose above the bow and swept across the bridge, drenching me from head-to-toe with no isinglass to block it. The cockpit bucked wildly enough that Mike playfully and nervously could jump at the right time and gain almost a foot of the deck as the bow came crashing down into the bottom of the next oncoming wave.

Truthfully, we could only troll down- or quartering down sea. Too bad this carried us farther offshore by the minute. As an approaching front from the East grew, silver-metallic, winter-like high stratus clouds formed a razor-edge line across the sky. The sun, obscured by clouds, created an artificial metal look to the waves. I remember it as an omen of something bad about to come. It felt wrong and Mike and I should not have been there. Add to all of this the bilge alarm lights — all six of them, along with the audible alarms kept sounding off. We weren't sinking, but I discovered some seepage from the deck to hull joint. Minor bilge water sloshed by the huge seas set off the high-water alarms. Mike joined me on the bridge. He'd automatically taken out two survival suits and two throwing rings attached to lines just in case one of us went overboard.

Deep down inside, we each hoped that we wouldn't get a bite. In these seas, Mike and I couldn't possibly land a fish, but nor could we return home without trying. Mike left the bridge to bring me a microwaved turkey Hungry-man TV dinner. Although *Makaira* had a cockpit steering and control station, looking around the corner of the cabin and being met with 40 knots of sea spray made for poor navigation. Mike and I had the inevitable big talk. We would have to turn towards Shinnecock soon and the ride home would be absolute h**l itself. No way we could run more than 8 knots and broaching would be a constant threat. *Makaira* was a wooden boat, and although she had a fiberglass bottom, she was old and fragile. Just as the big conversation started, our worst nightmare hit. Charging through a wave, a black torpedo engulfed the right flat lure. Mike bellowed, "hooked up, right flat, bigeye!" As Mike hit the cockpit floor from the bridge the left long rigger came crashing down. I saw neither bite. Line peeled off both reels as I did the only thing I could… idle slowly down-sea. Normally I'd employ my signature Barta Throttle Dance where I take power on and off the engines while turning violently to the left and to the right, begging the ocean to relinquish the rest of the wolfpack behind our transom. I yelled to Mike to reel in the other lines quickly.

I had sincere doubts that we could catch either of the two bigeyes. As Mike reeled in violently getting the left flat out of the water, the swivel nearing the rod tip, the water exploded pushing water back into the cockpit drenching Mike. I'll never forget the look he gave me: "Hooked up! Three ON," he screamed. Simultaneously the right long and center riggers fired. I have never heard Mike's voice crack like that. "Five on! Five on!" I came off the bridge, taking over the cockpit controls heading down sea. At least I needn't worry about running into anyone or anything. We qualified as the only humans within a hundred miles! We had one rod which had not hooked up yet. I reached up and cut the line with a knife. Although the lure no longer connected to the rod, the wind fouled the cut line with the 9920 rubber band pinning it to the left rigger. So the lure still dragged in the water. Like a 30-ought-six going off on a cold morning in deer season, the lure ripped from the wing rigger, exploding the clip and breaking the halyard. Unfolding in front of me was one of the most challenging battles of my life. Obviously we had to fight these fish while heading down-sea as holding the bow into the wind was just not an option. I have seen much bigger seas, but these were steep and close together. As we got ready to do battle, sea foam started to fill the cockpit like five kids blowing bubbles all at one time. An amazing sight.

One of the keys to catching multiple bigeye tuna is to put the hammer down with maximum drag on the last fish to hook up as it's inevitably the closest. I buckled Mike into the fighting chair. The Altenkirch rod moaned in agony as the guides actually started cracking and the wrappings started to split under the guide seats. All of my reels during those days were modified by Mr. Cal Sheets in California. The 80 and 130 Penns could deliver 65 pounds of drag, absolutely amazing for the timeframe. We knew full well that we had to catch the first two fish quickly or intentionally break them off.

Mike never did well without first eating breakfast. Added to the lack of sleep, the pressure of our current situation, and the gut-wrenching reel drag put Mike in an almost convulsive situation, giving him the dry heaves. As Mike fought the tuna, I reeled in the flat line inch-by-inch. With my welding-gloved left hand on the line towards the reel and turning the handle with my right hand, I could start to recapture a foot or two of line at a time.

I had so much drag that the rod tip submerged in the seas every few minutes. Even in the intense wind, you could hear the wrapping starting to pop. Mike's dry heaves finally turned into a world class barf — the wind catching the puke — the wind blowing it all over my neck and across my back. With all that was going on around us, I still chuckled at what obviously had been two Hungry-man dinners both with broccoli last night. The remains of these little green critters were now all over me. Luckily, to wash off, all I had to do was lean my torso two inches outboard of the cabin and Nature's wall of water took care of the rest.

With little warning, the massive 130-pound swivel appeared at the surface, the 500-pound leader attached to a brass ring, wired on to what we called a "coat hanger rig." Yes, we really made them from wire coat hangers placed through the kona head lure, then onto a Mustad 7754 closed Martu tuna hook. A triple X of course, with the eye welded closed. Finally, I had one wrap on the leader, then a second. Mike knew from that point on, I'd never let go under any circumstance. As Mike left the fighting chair, leaving the reel with just enough drag to avoid a backlash if the fish ran, he grabbed the starboard straight gaff. I had now wired the fish all the way up the 17-foot leader and knew if the tuna got a moment's relief combined with the massive seas, it was gone. I yelled for Mike at the top of my lungs and half way through my scream Mike reached over my right shoulder and stuck the bigeye right in the gill plates.

I will never forget the color of the blood on that first fish: A crimson red, and the wind disbursed it behind the boat in a way I had never seen. We couldn't open the tuna door as the seas would rip it off its hinges! Our footing became dangerous as the transom bucked like a bronco in now solid 12-foot waves. I grabbed a meat hook and slammed it into the fish's head. As the next big wave rolled green water over the boat's transom, Mike yelled, "Now!" and as we pulled, the 300-pound bigeye literally floated into the cockpit. One fish and Mike and I were both already exhausted, sitting in six inches of swirling water. Mike looked better until the reality that we still had four on hit us like a brick wall. Mike secured the first fish on the starboard cleat. I handed Mike the left flat that I had previously wound on. He went to work in the fighting chair only this time on an 80-pound rig.

Makaira's designer located the cockpit controls on the starboard side against the bulkhead. Keeping us heading down-sea without broaching proved difficult. With the waves pushing the boat forward combined with maximum drag on the reels, it was a wonder the rods and the line held. Fifteen minutes later the second fish broke the surface about sixty yards behind the boat. The sickle on its dorsal and the yellow finlets along the tail lit up like a neon sign in the cold, steel-colored sea. It was dark, ugly scary, but somehow this flash of iridescent yellow added color to the situation which we greatly needed. Mike poured on the drag and I missed the leader, lost my footing and ended up on my back. In fact, I missed the leader three more times. I just couldn't reach it. Each time I tried, the great fish made another run. We had no right to catch this fish, but we did. Another slob hit the deck in the high 280s and we secured it to the port-side cleat. We worked on two more rods moving them to the port and starboard flat-line rod holders. We planted the remaining rod in the fighting chair so the line would be above our heads. It came last as it was the farthest out.

What a surreal battle! Empty coolers floated around the cockpit, all four bilge pump lights blazed constantly and pretty soon, we would be swept up on the western wall of Hudson Canyon where the relatively shallower water would push the seas ever higher, making large waves into massive ones! We had to land these fish and we had to land them now!

Both of us hammered the drag somewhere into the low 50s. Mike yelled, "I can't get any line" and said, "Can you try backing up?" I yelled, "Are you crazy?" The slightest touch of reverse could bury *Makaira's* transom in a wave and easily sink her. After what seemed an eternity, Mike's tuna finally came straight up and down. The leader — this one on double 19 wire to a coat hanger rig — broke the surface. The lure we used was a yellow Sevenstrand with a pinkish-red and dark-blue skirt (that I currently have on the wall in my home as I recall this adventure). As I finally got the bigeye's head up, Mike's gaff again came out of nowhere (as it usually did), right on time, in the right place, kind of like Big Ben in London's Palace of Westminister chiming high noon. Always reliable. Our count now stood at three bigeye tuna in the boat and and worse conditions at the canyon's west wall imminent.

Mike has a very dry sense of humor. If the boat were sinking, just as it was about to go under, you could expect Mike to say, "Well, it looks like my toes are getting wet." As Mike glanced at the white foam flying off waves to the west, he said, "It's going to get a little bit interesting…" and that it would. Both of us operated on adrenaline-times-four. I assumed Mike looked worse than I did. Despite him being exhausted, I put him back in the fighting chair. After all, I had to run the boat and keep her afloat. I caught Mike slacking, meaning that he was not pumping the rod and was just hanging on for dear life. Just as I started to lay into him, I realized just how absurd my thoughts were.

Within minutes, Mike recovered enough to get back to work and quickly gained back more than half the line. These last two tunas had been swimming free and by now had pulled massive amounts of line into the ocean. I alternated from the controls to gaining line on a flat-line rod and back to the controls. We worked both fish almost hopelessly. Then we hit the west wall of the canyon almost like an explosion.

Mountains of water rose out of the sea. Honest 15-foot waves. The wind blew their tops off almost creating a white-out. I honestly thought we might lose *Makaira*. I was so driven in those days that I was prepared to lose our lives, but was more worried about the boat; the typical attitude that permeated Team *Makaira*. While I focused on the sea and the best way to meet the waves, I ignored Mike. When I next looked, the fish was close. The riggers continued their moaning sound. From what I hear, it's just like the sound a tornado makes when it gets close. Damn eerie! Usually you only hear the riggers sing like that when the wind tops 40 knots.

Mike's tuna broke the surface to swivel out of the water and moved left to right. I got the leader but it dragged me up the port gunwale. I lost my footing and was well on my way overboard when I felt Mike's hand on my Helly Hanson's. Back on both feet, I got three really good wraps. Mike reached out with the straight gaff but missed. I don't think I had ever seen him miss. We were now both leaning over the gunwale into the wind and spray, both of our torsos no longer sheltered by the cabin. It felt like a fire hose unleashed on us. Mike yelled, "I can't see." Finally, the gaff struck home and there was only one bigeye tuna left to fight: the one farthest from the transom!

Fighting the fish out of the starboard rod holder, Mike summoned the strength from somewhere. It was almost scary. It seemed like someone just lit him up. Halfway through this battle, however, I spelled him and Mike took over the controls. Suddenly, *Makaira* got violently knocked off course. It wasn't Mike's fault; this particular wave came so big and fast that we both got thrown to the cockpit floor. *Makaira* now sat beam to the seas, perhaps the worst possible attitude, as a big wave can roll a small boat like ours in an instant! I held on to the fighting chair pedestal and of all things Mike was hanging onto the tail of one of the tunas as the boat rolled all the way onto its beam end. Strangely enough, we looked at each other and started to laugh. When I asked what was so funny, Mike pointed to the rod in back — still hooked up. That was a close one! The last fish had no chance. Mike and I took turns and in short order it was wired and dispatched to the transom floor.

Mike and I laid on the deck, so tired that we had difficulty getting up. I tried to crack a joke, mustered all of my strength and yelled to Mike, "Let's get them out and catch five more". Without moving a muscle, Mike said something that I had never heard one of my crew say ever in my fishing career. I heard the word quietly but emphatically said: "No."

We secured the five tunas as best we could though we were both so tired that we couldn't get the tuna from the cockpit floor and into the coffin. Usually this was child's play. I rigged a block and tackle from the bridge and we hoisted the fish one by one into the chill box. Then, believe it or not, came the worst part of it all: Our homeport of Shinnecock Inlet lay some 90 nautical miles north. Our heading took us straight into the jaws of this Nor'easter which apparently came from out of nowhere, surprising everyone, including National Oceanic and Atmospheric Administration (NOAA) weathermen. I could run all of 10 knots and even at that speed the bow kept stuffing itself under a few feet of green water. The front hatches leaked, allowing water into the forward V-bunks, but that was the least of our worries.

I figured Mike had fallen dead asleep below, and heaven knows he needed and deserved it. But next thing I knew a miracle occurred! Mike showed up on the bridge with a triple-egg *Makaira* sandwich, steaming hot with bacon and melted cheese on a magnificent crusty hard roll and wrapped in aluminum foil. Nothing ever tasted that good! In fact, I can close my eyes as I sit here and still taste that sandwich, because it meant much more than Mike doing something extra nice. It meant to me that everything had returned to normal and we were going to make it back home safely.

That night it blew a gale at Shinnecock, yet getting through the inlet proved a piece of cake. Most everybody came from Willy Dickson's birthday party and met us at Shinnecock Inlet. Two fishermen returning from 15-foot seas and — against all odds — going five-for-five on bigeye tuna, all heavier than 280 pounds cleaned! In other words, despite being severely shorthanded, every fish we caught weighed in the low 300s before removing the guts and the head.

I have no explanation why, after the celebration at the dock closed down, Mike and I ended up sleeping on the salon floor. I don't even remember lying down and grabbing a pillow. But I do remember that at 10 am the next morning Willy Dickson opened up the salon doors with coffee and a deli egg sandwich for each of us. What an epic fishing trip! As luck would have it, due to the high seas along the US Atlantic coast around then, the Japanese buyers paid the highest price of the year for our tuna.

As I reflect, I think about the wonder which unfolded. A wolfpack of bigeye tuna hunting in the middle of a Nor'easter and despite the massive waves they cruised just below the wave surface for food. How was it possible that those fish found us? Just the thought of how life and death can unfold in an angry ocean makes me feel so humble yet so very privileged.

See the following diagram of the "Barta Porcupine Rig".

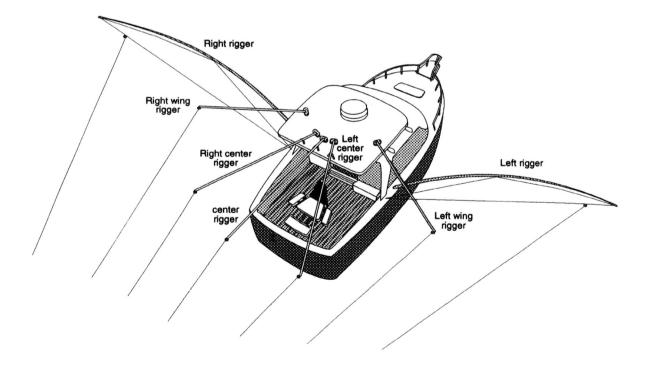

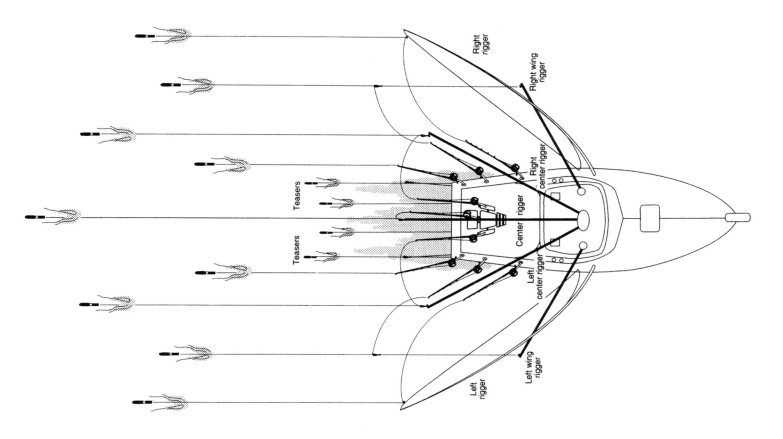

Nine single-hook lures and four teaser – this is the setup that took Capt. Tred and crew six years to develop and prove. There is not a team around who will not testify that the Barta Porcupine is the killer rig on bigeye tuna. Notice all lines on equal riggers are equidistant from boar – 180° turns will not result in a single tangle. Big Lures can be trolled at 7.8 knots with good action, #084 rubber bands and bronze clips with or without tag lines on every rigger and flat line. When Barta does the bigeye throttle dance by adding and ripping off power – acceleration and deceleration with hard turns to port and starboard spilling the wakes, the lures look like a school of bait fish running for their lives. Watch out, here comes the wolfpack with multiple hookups from Mr. Bigeye Tuna. Capt. Barta has been accused of destroying custom boats with this ugly and ridiculous rigger system. Maybe so – just don't fish against him.

Follow Tred's "shorthanded" journey as he trolls through the night encountering gale force winds and 12-14 foot seas and brings home 5 bigeye tuna, by viewing the following chart.

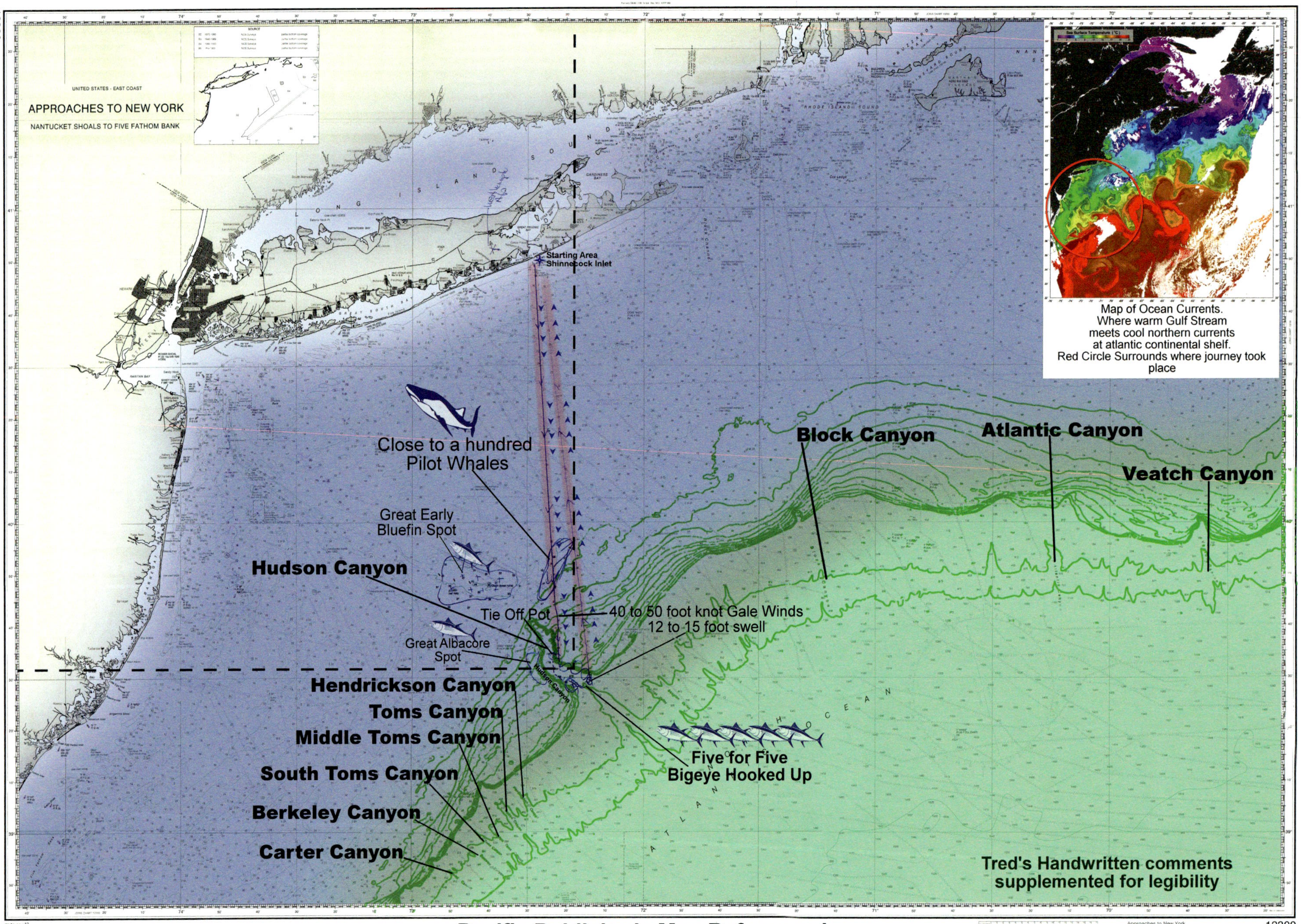

Pacific Publisher's Map Referenced

CHART 2

APPROACHES TO NEW YORK
NANTUCKET SHOALS TO FIVE FATHOM BANK
UNITED STATES — EAST COAST

Starting Area
Shinnecock Inlet

Close to a hundred Pilot Whales

Great Early Bluefin Spot

Great Albacore Spot

Tie Off Point

40 to 50 foot knot Gale Winds
12 to 15 foot swell

Five for Five Bigeye Hooked Up

Hudson Canyon
Hendrickson Canyon
Toms Canyon
Middle Toms Canyon
South Toms Canyon
Berkeley Canyon
Carter Canyon

Block Canyon
Atlantic Canyon
Veatch Canyon

Tred's Handwritten comments supplemented for legibility

Map of Ocean Currents. Where warm Gulf Stream meets cool northern currents at atlantic continental shelf. Red Circle Surrounds where journey took place

Chapter Eight
SURFACE SWORDFISHING

I KEPT MAKAIRA berthed in Shinnecock, Long Island in the early 1970s. We often stopped at Montauk for fuel and provisions. Montauk sat approximately 35 miles closer to the eastern canyons of Hydrographer, Welker, Lydonia and Oceanographer, so it made more sense to leave Shinnecock and stop in Montauk for fuel, ice, bait and groceries.

A lot of people think that eastern Long Island from Montauk to New York City runs east to west. It actually runs northeast to southwest. If one examines the Continental Shelf between Hudson Canyon and Oceanographer its baseline also runs northeast to southwest.

Carl Darenberg Jr. (I called him " Senior") purchased Montauk Marine Basin from George Miller in 1955. The best way to describe Carl Darenberg would be a John Wayne twin. Darenberg — larger than life — represented a stern, but kinder father figure than the one I had. He could see through imposters with a blink of an eye. Carl knew the real players and could spot a wannabe a mile away. He was a burly man with a frame over six feet and huge hands. When I shook his hand and looked him straight in his eyes, I saw compassion and a softness of heart that you wouldn't expect based on his appearance. Carl and his family were kind people.

During that time, Montauk Marine Basin became the epicenter of big-game fishing on the northeast coast. Although canyon fishing was in its infancy, inshore fishing at Montauk qualified as indescribably fantastic. Fluke, tautog (black fish), whiting, butterfish, ling cod, striped bass, bluefish, cod, and haddock were abundant. Many knowledgeable Northeast anglers considered it the most fertile fishing grounds bar none. The legendary fall run of stripers made the art of jigging wire line, using a buck tail with pork rind for them an art form. On the offshore side, we had giant bluefin tuna, which in those days could be found a mere seven miles off Montauk Point. Some of the best surface swordfishing took place in that area, too. Then we had the late-summer migration of white marlin that flooded the 30 fathom line. Everybody came to Montauk to partake in that legendary fishery.

Meanwhile, every ounce of energy and money I could muster was spent on the exploration of the canyons. Montauk's fleet of charter boats held some of the saltiest, most experienced captains of the world. They fully understood the tides, rips, and the bottom contour in the area around Montauk Point — a game that took me half a lifetime to learn.

On any crisp, fall day, Montauk blurred with activity and the finest fleet in the world passed Shagwong Point for Montauk Point. They lined up across the rips on the change of both tides; an incredible sight to see. There was no space available for recreational boats that didn't know what they were doing. Montauk also became a great oasis, for after a day of fishing, the game turned to drinking. Back in those days, fishermen could really hold their liquor. *Salivars*, a local watering hole, filled with the roughest souls that Montauk could dish out, and the women came even rougher. I considered Montauk the Jackson Hole of the east; the Wild, Wild East rather than the Wild, Wild West.

In the middle of all of this activity, Carl Darenberg ran a marina with a full-blown shipyard. Carl kept much of the fleet in business. If you had a problem, like a blown engine with the next 50 days booked for charter, Carl and his crew of mechanics would work all day and night. He literally saved many a fisherman from losing their livelihood, house, and for that matter even their pickup truck!

Through all the hustle and bustle at Montauk, I would come in from two and three-day canyon trips, unload double-digits of bigeye tuna, and sell our catch across the Montauk Marine Basin dock.

I loved Carl Darenberg, and in his own burly way he loved me. I spent many hours with him learning how to master surface swordfishing. With Carl, I shared my adventures of the northeast canyons where very few of the fleet ventured. Carl recognized the fire in my belly. He saw my passion and totally understood the sacrifice it took to accomplish my goals. I believe Carl to be one of the greatest surface swordfisherman the world has ever known. During the 1960s, you could regularly see five to fifteen swordfish on the surface every day. Carl owned a 41-foot Hatteras that he painted the ugliest shade of brown one could imagine. Why that color I have no idea. The Hatteras had no outriggers, but sported a huge tower by today's standard. I'd call it pretty typical of sport fishing boats of that era. It cruised at a whopping 16 knots.

It's ironic that over the five decades I knew Carl, we only got to fish together a dozen times. He was always busy saving someone's livelihood. He had a mind-boggling knowledge of diesel engines! One mid-summer's day, Carl called me at home. I remember his words even now. "Tred? Swordfishing tomorrow. Flat calm. You in?" "Yes," I replied without hesitation. He ended the conversation with, "Rig five baits." Hearing many people talking in the background I simply replied, "Yes sir." I rigged five huge squid, two with double hooks and three with single hooks on #19 wire. I sewed the rigs with a needle and waxed floss thread. I placed the finished baits in a small Igloo cooler with newspaper separating the squid from the ice.

Early the next morning, I loaded the baits aboard the Hatteras and in total darkness, I waited for Carl. Before I knew it, the lights came on and Carl brewed us a thermos of coffee as I made sandwiches for the day ahead. After a very few grumpy niceties we shoved off. We cleared Montauk Inlet and soon passed Shagwong Point. We made our way inside Serberus Shoal around Montauk Point. Then we worked our way to the 20-fathom line. A mammoth fire ball rising from the east made for a magnificent sunrise. Several boats had stopped at the point for bass and bluefish. Another fleet dispersed on the way to the shark grounds. The great white shark hunter, Capt. Frank Mundus, ran the greatest fishing-circus side show ever to be seen around this time. Frank was a professional captain and a showman of Hollywood caliber. He was also Benchley's inspiration for the book and movie, "Jaws."

As we ventured out to the southeast, we saw our first swordfish on top, displaying its fins like a peacock. One curved butt 80 with white Dacron line rested in the fighting chair rod holder. Carl drove from the tower taking the fishing line and bait up with him. As Carl maneuvered the boat, holding the line in his hand, he threw the bait in a gentle arch, a long way away from the fish. I stood in the cockpit with the reel in freespool as I watched Carl gently come across the fish's path in a half-moon arch. Often during this procedure Carl pulled the squid in by hand while I took up the slack down in the cockpit, or he'd ask for more line which I gently pulled off the reel as he let the line slip through his fingers.

As a fellow fishing captain, I stood in absolute awe as Carl carefully put the double hooked bait right in front of the swordfish. This entire maneuver accomplished with neither the wake nor the noise or pressure wave of the boat disturbing the swordie's reality. By baiting the fish from the tower and getting way in front it, our quarry never had a clue of our presence. What a magnificent fish, too! Solidly above 400 pounds. This particular fish made an unusual lunge at the bait during the first pass. As it appeared to swallow the bait, Carl let go of the line creating a very gentle but sizable drop back. When the line came tight to the rod tip I locked the reel up and reeled as fast as I could. Carl moved the boat forward with a billow of black smoke from the engines. The rod buckled over and came tight. Hooked up! I climbed into the fighting chair, buckled myself in and the fight began! The first hour of fighting time went quickly, but it seemed to serve no purpose whatsoever… the fish didn't appear to be affected one bit. Although in shallow water, we made very little progress. The next fifteen minutes we saw the fish surface three times. I remember this particular fish had a purple and black color. Extremely short-handed for the task at hand, at one hour and forty minutes into the battle, Carl came off the bridge, took one wrap on the #19 wire and the great fish stood on its side in all of its glory — the eye about the size of a softball. A National Geographic cover times five! As I started to get out of the chair to grab the gaff, the hooks pulled and Carl, stumbling from the release of pressure on the leader, and fell backwards flat on his back.

For some reason which I will never understand, I jumped on top of Carl as if I was in a football game and we both wrestled on the deck laughing so hard tears streamed down Carl's face. For some reason my mentor and I found the situation incredibly funny. We ended up legs stretched out with our backs leaning against the gunwale both happy for the experience. Technically, we had released the swordfish under IGFA rules as Carl had touched the leader. We had both accomplished one of the great feats in the sport fishing world. We had baited a swordfish successfully on top using Carl's techniques. I particularly remember the warmth of the sun and the feeling of camaraderie with such a fantastic man. Somehow I knew that as long as I lived I'd remember this experience… and I have.

With the day still young, we decided to go out farther — touching the 30 fathom line, running east to an area called the "dump" to find another fish we could bait. During the next two hours we baited three more fish and as expected Carl presented the bait perfectly. We ended up with one kinked leader and two fish that sounded before we could get to them.

America wrestled with an era of intense political tension with China, Asia, and Russia during this time. As we approached the 30 fathom edge, three large ships stood out on the horizon. One of the ships made a huge billow of black smoke from a dry exhaust — a telltale sign to those who spend a lifetime on the ocean — that some type of trawler was in the process of retrieving its nets.

As Carl and I witnessed this from the bridge, we knew where we had to be. As we approached the vessels, it came as a complete shock to see a black insignia with a red hammer and sickle on the transom and bridge, the Communist symbol of Russia. Oh, my! A Russian fleet fishing in our waters right off of Long Island! How could this possibly be? Off on the horizon, a huge vessel turned out to be the mothership for the several Russian trawlers in the area. I can't explain to you what an unsettling feeling we had approaching three Russian trawlers during that political climate. One of the three boats was hauling its nets, and to this day I don't remember what species were caught and placed in blue plastic bins. They appeared to be sorting by size and species. Two men used wide, shiny shovels to remove the bycatch or cull off the deck. Each shovelful held squid, small ling, and cod which all floated dead on the surface down the net line as the main net came aboard. Most bycatch seemed to be juveniles.

The crew of the Russian trawlers, obviously at sea for months at a time, seemed jovial and waved frantically to us. I think they were happy to see another boat. The contrast of knowing that Russia was the mortal enemy of the United States at that time while the men on board seemed so friendly that it made me realize that all of us in the world are pretty much the same. The hard working people of Russia weren't our enemies. I guess our respective governments held those positions. Nonetheless, we felt pure amazement that this fleet could be fishing so close to the United States.

At that very moment, we both saw a huge bluefin rolling in the wake of the Russian trawler. Closer inspection revealed at least 50 bluefin following the trawler in a bycatch feeding frenzy! Carl and I climbed the tower and could see one after another 500- to 800-pound tuna rise on the side of the ascending nets and inhale the bycatch floating on the surface. Hundreds of birds circled the trawlers and at times, the bird noise became unnerving. A life and death mosaic presented itself before us. What a spectacular sight! The Russian trawlers harvested the bounty below, the bluefin tuna fed and sustained themselves on much of what had been killed above. The fish from the nets, over time, would obviously feed many hungry Russians thousands of miles away. Yet Carl and I just hunted for whatever opportunity the bounty of the sea afforded *us* that day.

If you could take a snapshot of what lay before us, that image has been branded upon my brain and soul for the rest of my life. I am physically and mentally there with absolute clarity as I write this. I even remember details like the rust on the trawler hull. Most of the crew wore oversize pants with suspenders and old seafarers' caps, common at the time among European fishermen. What to do, what to do? Both of us were speechless. Should we call the U.S. Coast Guard? Or start fishing for the giant bluefin that kept crashing the bycatch being shoveled overboard? One crewman controlled a large fire hose and assisted the shovelers by spraying an abundant amount of water over the deck, cleaning most of the bycatch out the oblong scuppers. At this very moment, we sat in the cornucopia of life. It felt like we had walked into a story of Greek mythology with great ships and sea monsters.

Carl and I looked at each other — obviously thinking the same thing. Look at what we'd found that nobody else knew about. How long had the Russians been fishing here? How long had the giant tuna been following the Russians? Both of us came off the tower to the bridge. I will never forget Carl's words, "Shall we try one of these on for size?" "Yes," I agreed, "It won't take very long." Carl maneuvered his ugly brown Hatteras to less than 10 feet off the trawler's hauling boom, the name *Orlan* glaring at us from its transom. I don't know if it said that in Russian, but it looked like that in English.

Carl retrieved his giant tuna rig from the salon: A Fin-Nor 130 stump puller with a mammoth Fin-Nor 14/0 reel, which in addition to a complicated drag system also had a leather brake — a large leather strap that you could push with a thumb and forefinger to add extra drag on the spool. Obviously, one of Carl's wealthier clients (of which he had many) once owned this rig.

We approached the trawler on our starboard and I tossed the large single hook squid on #19 wire towards the trawler. As soon as the bait struck the water Carl went to neutral on the controls. I pulled line over my back sending the squid back into the wake of the boat as if it were floating with the bycatch. When I had the right amount of line out compared to our drift I stood behind the reel and put the drag up to strike. About two seconds later, a giant black torpedo came out of the water and inhaled the squid. I watched the entire bait disappear down the great fish's gullet. I'd say we had hooked up!

By this time in my life I regularly caught hundreds of tuna offshore and totally understood the tackle of the day. I had spent my younger years dedicated to learning how to catch tuna. As much as I'd like to claim we fought a heroic battle, that wouldn't be quite honest. I laid into the fish with every bit of drag the Fin-Nor reel could muster and on top of maximum drag, pressed down hard on the leather strap, adding extra drag to the spool. The stump-puller rod I used — an old-style, long tuna rod — was so massive and stiff that it could double as a telephone pole! I had a solid 60 pounds of pressure on this fish. The depth was only 180 feet so the fish could only go that far down. I fought this fish out of the rod holder. Carl — one of the greatest captains I ever fished with —kept maneuvering the boat in such a way that no matter where the fish ran he would stay on top, and then pull away. He maneuvered the boat with such skill that I constantly muttered to myself, "it just can't be done any better." After 15 minutes into the fight, we had slowed this fish down and coerced it into the death circle. We had the fish on its side in well under one hour. I took double wraps on the #19 wire. Carl came off the bridge and put a harpoon right through the tuna's gill plate. We had the fish! It was ours! We hoisted the fish on the starboard side using a block and tackle. The giant bluefin gently lay on its side.

On the way back to the Montauk Marina Basin we saw *Cookie*, the Murray Brother's family boat, and two other custom rigs that had come up from Palm Beach for the summer, heading right towards the Russian fleet. We assumed that several of the giant tuna insiders knew about the Russians.

We arrived at the dock where the fish tipped the scales at 705 pounds, about an average size giant for that timeframe.

That summer the entire fleet found the Russian trawlers, waited for them to haul back their nets and then caught fish the identical way Carl and I did. One day several Coast Guard cutters and Coast Guard helicopters patrolled the general area we had fished with the Russians. The Russians had been reported by other boats. Suddenly the Russian fleet disappeared and nobody ever saw them again. One must assume that a lot went on between the U.S. Coast Guard and the Russian fleet. We'll never know the truth of why they fished here or to where they disappeared. But I guarantee you somebody knew. Once in my fishing career I fished alongside Russian ships. I met a Russian seaman some twenty feet away. Life at sea offers some marvelous experiences!

I knew Carl Darenberg Jr. and his son, Carl Darenberg III for most of my adult life. The great Carl Darenberg Jr. died in 2010. Carl Jr. was legendary in the fishing industry of Montauk and was instrumental in making Montauk world known. I truly loved the gentle giant. He taught me so much and always provided a welcoming face as I turned into Montauk Marine Basin from a three-day canyon trip. Carl used to wrap his arm around me and put me in a friendly headlock. Then he would say, "Sonny, have you learned anything about the tuna yet?"

Follow Tred's surface swordfishing journey out of Montauk with Carl Darenberg, by viewing the following chart.

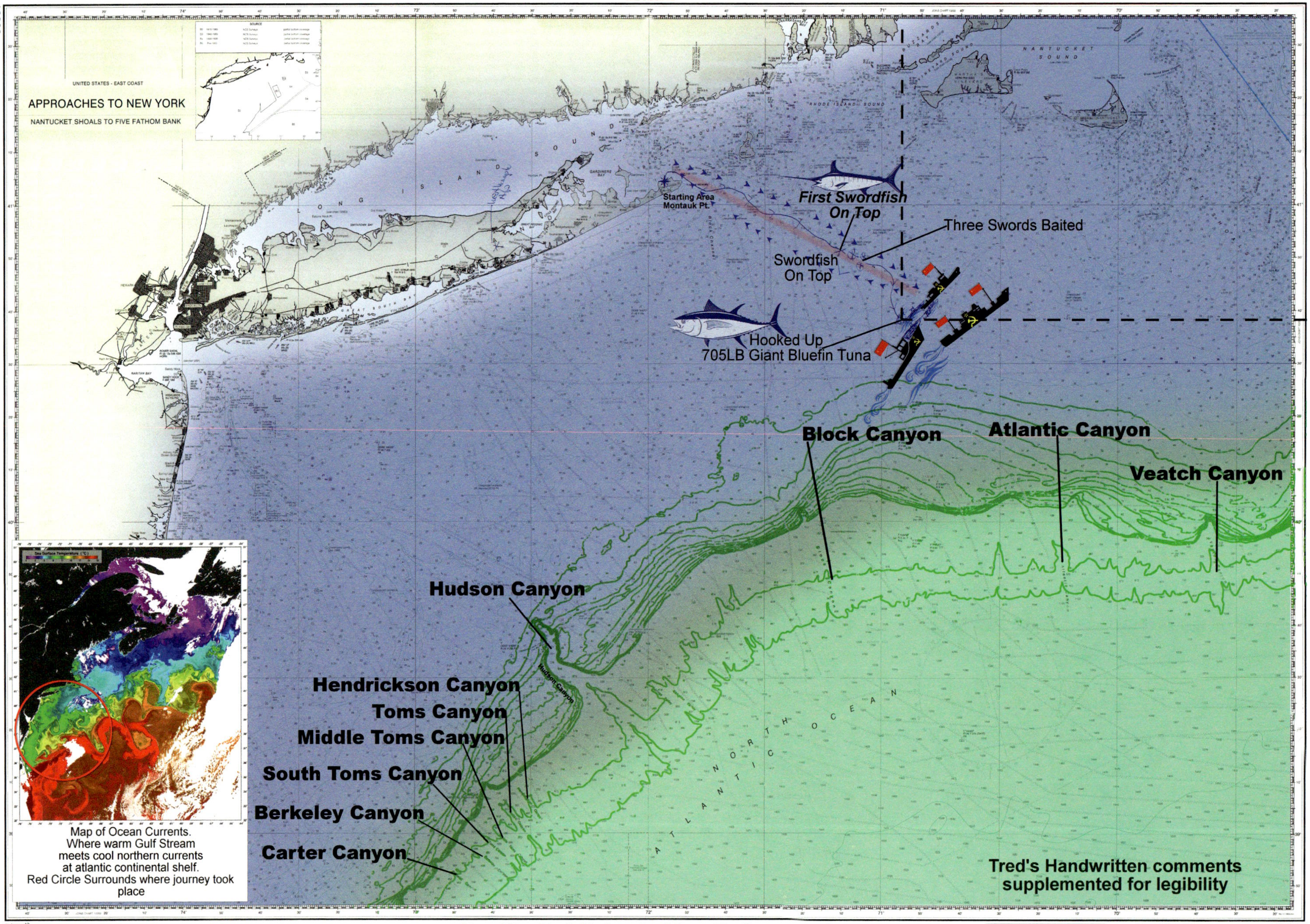

12300
UNITED STATES - EAST COAST
APPROACHES TO NEW YORK
NANTUCKET SHOALS TO FIVE FATHOM BANK
Starting Area
Montauk Pt.
First Swordfish
On Top
Three Swords Baited
Swordfish
On Top
Hooked Up
705LB Giant Bluefin Tuna
Block Canyon
Atlantic Canyon
Veatch Canyon
Hudson Canyon
Hendrickson Canyon
Toms Canyon
Middle Toms Canyon
South Toms Canyon
Berkeley Canyon
Carter Canyon
ATLANTIC
NORTH
OCEAN
Map of Ocean Currents.
Where warm Gulf Stream
meets cool northern currents
at atlantic continental shelf.
Red Circle Surrounds where journey took
place
Tred's Handwritten comments
supplemented for legibility
12300
12300

Pacific Publisher's Map Referenced

CHART 3

Chapter Nine
PRIMEVAL REAL ESTATE

AT 20, IN yet another effort to slip the chains of my father's iron rule, I ventured to Africa by myself in search of life's truths. I knew I could find them if unencumbered by my father's manipulation. I knew *some* things for certain already. For example, no matter how hard I worked at it, I would never be a biathlon world champion. I had been to Johannesburg with Dad on several occasions, delivering and purchasing aircraft: insignificant trips.

A lot of people have said that the Dark Continent draws you to her nipple to feed on the savagery which unfolds every single day. Africa — unyielding and uncooperative — will have its way with you. The stakes do not favor man and many things can kill you. Even when you're cautious and plan carefully, Africa can still kill you. It is a prehistoric place. The sights, sounds, sunrises, morning breakfast in the bush before a hard day's hike, the fresh lion tracks right through camp ten feet from your tent, serve as reminders of your constant vulnerability.

Upon landing in Johannesburg, I proceeded north to Limpopo Valley near the Botswana border. Today this area is cut up into one dude ranch after another, but back then not a fence could be found. On my first day of hunting, my professional hunter announced there was a civil war going on in Botswana with everyone there armed to the teeth. I felt relatively safe carrying a pair of 45 caliber pistols.

At mid-morning I arrowed a nice impala doe which ran down to the river. I looked across the river to Botswana. As we followed the impala's blood trail, a gunship came upstream and discovered six young men wielding machetes on the Botswana shore. All of us face planted on the moist forest floor, not moving a muscle. The gunship opened fire and cut the men down. In a seeming microsecond, everyone was dead, collapsing in the undergrowth. I was amazed, but neither shocked nor in awe.

This wasn't the first time I had seen death come like this. Human beings had expired in my arms. Ten yards in front of us lay my impala on the river bank. As I closed in to retrieve the animal for camp fare, a 1,000-pound crocodile exploded out of nowhere and dragged the impala into the river. One more step – one less second — and it could have been me being pulled into the river. The savagery that the crocodile exhibited reminded me of the bigeye tuna "wolfpack" exploding on its prey at the exact opportune moment in the Northeast canyons. The canyons to me was "Africa" but just a different location. I wonder if the crocodile was watching me approach the impala and at the exact moment he thought I was stealing his prey. He took it from me. As we sat on the bank my professional hunter slapped me on the back and said, "Welcome to Africa!" Over the next several years I set numerous world records with a longbow, including beating the venerable Fred Bear's warthog record set in 1952, the same year I was born.

Why do I use Africa as a lead-in to explain the Northeast canyons? After traveling all over the world, I've determined there are no other places like wild Africa and the wild Northeast canyons. I know most of you have watched National Geographic's *Blue Planet: Seas of Life*. What an incredible series! The Northeast Canyons from Maine to North Carolina following the Continental Shelf is *Blue Planet* on steroids squared twice. I once represented a Louisiana attorney wanting to buy a big boat, hire crew, buy tackle, and he asked for my help. Most of these guys don't want to learn, but pretend they do. Both of us had the weekend off. He picked me up in his Lockheed Jet star and at my request we flew to the Grand Canyon. I asked him to have two folding chairs on board and to have a Suburban waiting for us at the airport. Most wealthy people hate surprises and I refused to give up the plan. As we sat on the East Rim together I said to him, "Look…" and he got it. The Continental Shelf is very similar to the Grand Canyon. How do the winds, tides, currents, salinity, rotational warm core eddies, and orographic lift set off an explosion of life like a burning furnace? Some scientists believe these facets of the oceans may be the engine of all life. We looked across the canyon walls at one angle and then hiked up the trail one mile and looked at the exact same spot from another angle. My client said, "it does not even look the same." I replied, "not only does it not look the same but how would you fish it in different conditions?"

For the sake of clarity, let me say that addictions to golf, badminton, tennis, etc. can't compare. The uncertainty, the wonder and terror of witnessing life — born, reborn then savagely killed and consumed as the day goes on – sets canyon fishing apart from all else. From Maine to Hatteras, NC but more in particular from the Stellwagon Bank to below Baltimore Canyon is a submarine Grand Canyon that drops off sharply from 600 feet to thousands of fathoms. Within this mighty wall are nooks and crannies, many mini-canyons and other places the *Makaira* team have found over the years.

As in warm and cold weather systems, the warm oceanic current rams against the great wall like a colossal bus accident. As rich gulf stream water spins off and hits the hundred fathom line, it drives over the rim, injecting life force. I am talking biblical stuff right before your eyes. Why not use a couple of big words:

Phytoplankton and Zooplankton – the bottom of the oceanic food chain and small as the head of a pin — are the canyon grocery store where fish larvae, mackerel, menhaden, herring, butterfish, and squid, and some whales as well as the whale shark come to get dinner. Given the right time, the right water temperature, the exact perfect cocktail of gulf stream water and nutrients hitting the canyon wall and driving it toward the source, life comes to pass.

Given this incredible condition unfolding in front of you, some 90 to 300 miles offshore, here come the finback and beluga whales, orcas and porpoise migrating to these rich waters as far as the eye can see. Blue and white marlin, sailfish, wahoo, dolphin, yellowfin, albacore, bigeye and giant bluefin tuna all join the fray; the feed bag is on. Creation sucker-punches your reality. Sure, the miracle of life is always amazing to witness, but we're not talking about a cute little rabbit being born in the tall grass under a pine tree. We are not talking about a piccolo solo; rather, it's the Boston Philharmonic Orchestra in full force, at full volume, making an exclamation!

The height of my canyon-fishing career heralded the beginning of water temperature surface analysis. Len Belcaro, at that time owner of *Big Game Fishing Journal*, spent hours working with me on his analysis service. The current on the hundred fathom line usually flows at two to six knots. The farther east you travel, the current gets stronger, the side currents greater and navigation becomes more treacherous. Back in the day, *Makaira* would fish for three days and nights without ever seeing another sport fishing boat. We *would* see the Russians, Japanese and later Chinese processing boats all offshore of the American demarcation line (ADIZ).

I beg one small indulgence. Put your feet up, close your eyes and imagine this: you wake up to the deck covered with flying fish. Near the transom of the boat, thirty whales are feeding straight up and down in a big circle — the water fire-engine red with krill. Every offshore bird known to the region swoops and circles. An explosion erupts near the whales with fresh, red blood being pumping up to the ocean's surface where a 600-pound mako has just eaten a white marlin for breakfast. Captain Mike Forman, Capt. Jamie Hummel, and I eat our double egg and ham sandwiches on New York hard rolls, drooling with mayonnaise.

We all agree it is going to be a good day. I do know unequivocally that out in the canyons without skill, without an understanding of where you are and what you are experiencing, you are toast. Oh, and *nobody* ever ate a yogurt on the *Makaira*.

For my entire life to this point, I had been groomed to be the best in the world at something. Africa's prehistoric nature and the true unknown around every corner whetted my appetite for my canyon-fishing career. As I sat in my Southampton, New York home on eastern Long Island, the Continental Shelf looming 60 to 100 miles offshore, I looked at the 12300 chart and the mere six inches of real estate where everybody fished for swordfish, white and blue marlin, and assorted species of tuna, I wondered what life was like right at that moment on the other side of the chart. No one I knew had been there or fished there. A fire was ignited in my belly like a furnace. This would be the start of my canyon-fishing career. The unknown, the unexplored, the unexplained all called to me. The ability to proceed on my own, as captain-in-command, and the ability to shape my own destiny out of the shadow of my father—this was MY sirens' song.

As I struggled to sleep I will never forget my last thought. Is it possible that everything Africa stands for is right off the coast of where I live? The prospect was chilling. I was exhilarated and felt I was plugged into a light socket. What was out there?

30-pound animal shot in Darien Jungle, Panama with local guide

Chapter Ten
SCIENCE IS MY FRIEND

WE BLASTED THROUGH the mid to late 1970s and entered the fast-paced 80s. In America, money flowed like water. Boat sales went through the roof and it seemed like everyone was successful; restaurants, marinas, real estate, boat and aircraft sales all flourished, and so did the commercial fishing fleets with the advent of loads of new technology. Suddenly, the Russians had company! Now the Chinese, Japanese, Taiwanese and others showed up. Thanks to technology, every third-world culture appeared to be harvesting the bounty, not only of the world's oceans but in particular the Northeast corridor.

I received, from a Navy reconnaissance pilot friend, U.S. Navy research on the impact of salinity levels, water temperature analysis, sonic buoy reports and more. The Navy used this for its submarine fleet. This information covered surface current and temperature analyses, salinity and water temperature analysis from the Northern end of Stellwagon Bank all the way to Maryland. Unfortunately, the research could only be accessed via computer and in those days, computers still resembled the size of a building. I finally found a geek in Bend, Oregon who claimed that with enough money he could overlay current, temperature and salinity values obtained by the U.S. Government (which had been legally released to the public) on large plastic sheets that I could overlay on NOAA's geodetic chart 12300, and then do the same on a bathymetric chart which had been released by SubCom Tactical Defense Unit.

The government considered these pathways and the canyons themselves that rise from 500 fathoms all the way into downtown New York City, potential attack routes which the Russians could use to invade the United States. It spent countless millions of dollars on these mapping projects. Obviously all of the information was released because the end of the Cold War made them irrelevant, and no industry could figure out how to use it.

I remember writing a check for $12,000, a seeming fortune. Two months later, super-geek from Oregon flew into LaGuardia Airport and met me in Southampton, New York with a poster-size valise ten inches thick. He stayed at my house for two days. As a pilot who had dedicated his life to canyon research, who used to fly endless grids across the canyon looking for water color changes prior to departing on three-day canyon trips, I felt like someone had delivered to me the holy grail itself!

To the average person this could be a five-second interruption between a mimosa and a Hamptons' eggs benedict, but to me it was life itself. Properly translating the plastic sheets confirmed unequivocally and nonnegotiably to me that the warm core eddies I had been studying and fishing not only existed but were the key to success at my life's purpose. In fact, the evidence proved staggering. I shared this information with one of my dear friends, Capt. Len Belcaro, who published *The Big Game Fishing Journal*. He also published via computer and by fax, water temperature analysis charts of the canyons and the direction of ocean currents of varying equivalent temperatures. While Belcaro became a Tred Barta disciple, I could likewise claim to have become a Len Belcaro disciple; we talked for hours. After inspecting my charts, we agreed we both had a secret that would change canyon fishing forever. God cut Len and me from the same cloth. We were both educators at heart, shared a true love of the sport and both wanted to share our discovery with others. In the beginning, many anglers were just too stupid to listen but things changed.

As a side note, I am convinced that the U.S. Government thought the relationship between current, temperature, and salinity levels were key in deciphering communication between submarines and I personally believe this was part of the early detection system along the Continental Shelf devised by the U.S. Government. That did not interest me at all. But for fishing, I now had the goods and I knew how to use them.

Chapter Eleven
RESPECT EARNED

I MADE A friend named Martin Landey. One day he just wandered down the dock at Indian Cove Marina in Hampton Bays, NY and struck up a conversation. He wanted to know what it's like to fish offshore in our local area. I learned later that Martin had a reputation as a world-class bass fisherman and excelled at run-and-gun type fishing.

The next day, as I left the inlet in my 32-foot Prowler, *Makaira*, I saw what we all called "the maniac in the red Donzi" up tight to the surf. No sane person would bring their boat so close to the shore. "The maniac" turned out to be Martin.

Over time, my crew and I gained great respect for Martin. He fished by himself incredibly hard, and when we left the inlet for the canyon with the wind blowing 25 knots, there was Martin alone in Shinnecock Inlet with eight-to ten-foot curlers casting for bass, dodging the rollers, and completely submersed in white water on the east bar. Being pretty busy getting through the inlet ourselves without losing our lives one morning, I remember my mate offering a passing comment, "That man is an idiot!" I replied, "What does that make us?" As we cleared the inlet, I just had to turn the boat toward shore to see if the man in the red twin-outboard Donzi still floated. As he skirted around the inside reef towards the east, the only thing we could see as the rollers broke and the tops blew off, creating what we called sea smoke, was the tip of Martin's favorite yellow Altenkirch rod. That was my friend, Martin Landey, casting and skillfully working his way in and out the breakers and bars. I could relate: Landey was alone, the sun had not even risen, the inlet had been officially closed and yet, that red Donzi that we saw day after day was meeting his personal challenges.

I next met Martin eating at the Country Deli. I ordered my favorite egg sandwich of two eggs sunny side up on a NY hard roll with melted provolone, mayonnaise and heavy pepper. Why this is significant I have no idea, but I remember it like it happened today. Martin asked the the deli person if they made cappuccino. I am not sure if at that time in my life if I had even heard of a cappuccino. I remember the owner laughing and saying, "Look buddy, this is a working man's deli — no cappuccino." Martin then asked if they had that day's

Wall Street Journal and to my amazement they did. The deli had a raised flower bed built with painted railroad ties by the front door. While living in Southampton, my daily routine in route to my Hampton Bays office included sitting outside the deli and enjoying my breakfast sandwich. Other captains or hunters often joined me. I enjoyed relaxing and the conversations each morning.

One day, who sits down beside me but Martin. A very urbane, extremely educated man, he spoke elegantly but didn't throw big words around. I discovered another side to Martin when he talked about how the yen was moving against the Deutschmark. He wore the best of everything and drove a completely restored gull-wing Mercedes which back then was worth beaucoup bucks.

Over the next couple of weeks, we became pretty good friends. Martin talked about the intricacies of reading the inlet, the breaks, the currents, as well as where and how he could maneuver his boat to make the perfect cast with a surface plug.

One breezy Thursday, we met at the deli at five o'clock in the morning, He invited me to be his guest, casting for bass on what turned out to be a crappy gray day with ugly rain clouds and a 25-knot wind. A cold and dreary type of day when it would have been so easy to just roll over in bed. The moment I stepped aboard Martin's Donzi 32 ZF, off we went across the bay at full throttle. We made our way across the east cut as I scoped out the horrendous state of the inlet. Honest six- to eight-footers had tops being blown off by the wind. We saw nary another boat and even the commercial draggers sat tied to the dock. Forecasts called for 35 to 40 knots that afternoon.

As we entered the inlet I remember thinking, "Don't tell me that I am going to die in Shinnecock Inlet trying to cast for bass!" After all I had done in life, it just didn't seem appropriate. Truth be told (hard to admit even now), I was scared to death. But after watching Martin run his boat for an hour, I began to see his skill, his sense of timing, his passion, and true love for the sport. We caught two stripers that morning: One weighing 28 and the other 33 pounds… caught in raging surf!

As we started to head back to the east, at least 50 people on the back side of the inlet watched us with binoculars. I later learned the Shinnecock Coast Guard station received nine phone calls that morning alerting them to some red outboard in trouble in front of the inlet. The Coast Guard gave their standard answer, "Oh that's Martin Landey. He's just bass fishing."

As we approached the western jetty, rollers created 20-foot high showers of spray as they slammed into the riprap. Martin headed toward a two-foot-wide gap between the west jetty and the rollers at about 20 knots. As I gulped, he threaded the needle like he had done so many times before. On this particular day the urbane man from Westhampton gained my respect and I continue to be intrigued.

Martin Landry (left) and Captain Mike Forman with largest Atlantic sailfish we ever caught at 122 pounds

Chapter Twelve
WELKER AND LYDONIA CANYONS

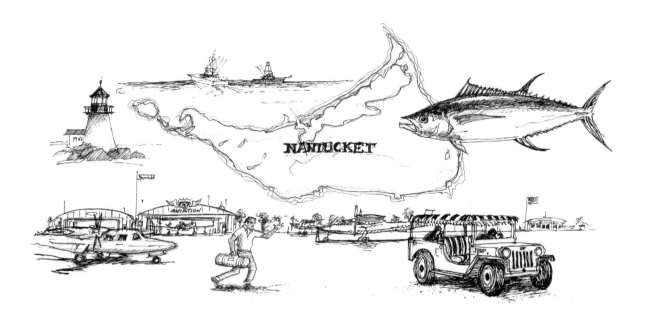

AUGUST IS A most excellent month in the Northeast. All the chores of spring are over and everyone finally has time to take a deep breath after winter. Married couples have completed all the items on their "honey-do" lists. A blanket of relaxation covers the landscape.

My 47-foot Ridgeway, *Makaira*, rests quietly up at the Nantucket Boat Basin while Jamie (Sasquatch) Hummel and Mike Forman go about their separate check lists for our next trip. Jamie Hummel was the son of one of my greatest friends, Jim Hummel. I had known Jamie since he was a little guy. He was always a strong young lad and truly loved the ocean. For the longest period of time Jamie worked Shinnecock Bay for weak fish and blue fish. Jamie at a young age knew the ocean better than most seasoned captains. Jamie was a very quiet man and yet when there was either chaos or a task that had to be done on the ocean he could move with lighting speed with incredible strength and had superb judgement in almost every situation. I would trust Jamie to take a bullet for me if he had to. I considered him then and now a solid lifetime friend.

Mike Forman also came from what I call a waterman's family. His father and I were decent friends. Mike also netted the bays and earned extra income working the bays. Mike possessed what Jamie and I had and that was a sixth sense on how to read the ocean. Mike in many ways was the opposite of Jamie. He could find a dangerous situation before it would happen and implement a safety fix before a disaster reared its head. Jamie on the other hand, was incredible at reacting quickly when a dangerous situation was in progress.

I had a great week working at Joseph T. Barta Associates. I made two deals that generated $162,000 by selling Mobil Oil an early King Air 200, an eight-passenger turbo prop and taking a King Air A-100 in trade. The A-100 is powered by a pair of Pratt and Whitney PT6A-28 engines. It cruised at 225 knots with a full load of eight people, but then could only carry half its fuel capacity based on weight and balance. The King Air 200 is powered by Pratt & Whitney PT6-41 engines. It cruised at 275 knots and could carry full fuel, eight people, *and* all their baggage (the performance icon of the day). Fully certified in both aircraft, I had previously flown both models into a ridiculously small strip at one of my father's summer homes in Sugarbush, Vermont. I mention this because as a salesman, not only did I know the product and had gone to the Beechcraft schools on each aircraft, but I had also attended Pratt & Whitney schools on both power plants. I was sharp, smart, accurate, and one heck of a salesman. But on this particular deal I was deadly. I sold the King Air A-100 trade-in to Voyager Airways in eastern Canada to fulfill a contract with the local government to transport small, rural basketball teams from one province to another —a sweet deal.

The $162,000 was a lot of money back in the late 1970s. I was happy. Mobil Oil was happy. My father was ecstatic. But even with this, my father, as usual, attempted to ruin my weekend with some snide parting comment about something. It was as if he enjoyed attaching a ball and chain around my neck. I always got some comment like, "Have a good weekend. I have a lot of reading to catch up on from Business and Commercial magazine to the Wall Street Journal." He used to search those for tips about expansions or mergers of top corporations. These companies' growth represented good prospects for the airplanes we sold.

So what's my point? Even though I had done my best, made a small fortune the past week, out sold every salesman employed including my father, he just could not just let me go relax on a long weekend. It had to be with a caveat, a jab, and a prod. I remember my inner voice saying, "What a pain in the butt you are. Go take a flying leap." Instead I said, "Yes sir. Have a good weekend." This man I loved so much turned out to be the greatest sadness of my life. To this day I cannot tell you if it made me stronger and contributed to the man I have become, or represents what often is said about me —that I am an arrogant, self-aggrandizing, rude, obtuse, and a self-centered a**. As always I did my best to shake it off and still do. A fact only my closest friends know about me: Before completing a task which requires 100% concentration, I talk to myself. A psychologist once told me that I talk to myself because I couldn't talk to my father. What type of psycho-babble crap is that?

As I walked through Hanger D at Westchester County Airport (HPN), I passed Conoco's Lockheed Jetstar and a Lear 25B owned by a publishing company. Right beside them on the ramp was a Mitsubishi MU-2F, an aircraft we happened to have in inventory.

The Mitsubishi had just come out of maintenance and had to be test flown. This aircraft had the reputation for being one of the hardest corporate aircraft in the world to fly. An unforgiving son of a gun. Rather than having ailerons, it had spoilers and was powered by Garett Air Research TPE-331 direct-drive turbine engines.

Some pilots at the San Antonio training school, which I attended on four separate occasions, described each landing in this aircraft as one terrifying episode after another. It was a numbers airplane meaning you flew it by the numbers – exact power settings and exact speeds for every flap setting. The aircraft had very little feel compared to any of the King Air Cheyenne or Turbo-Commanders.

The Mitsubishi's narrow-cord wing meant the angle of attack at which you flew the aircraft was critical. You literally had to fly this aircraft onto the runway: No gliding, no drifting and it was anything but light on the controls. The bottom line? More accidents and fatalities occurred in Mitsubishis than any other executive aircraft. The industry called it the "Widow Maker." You had to be well-trained, totally focused, and always with the program, never distracted – made all the more difficult for me by my father's comment.

The aircraft had a bulbous tail making it an absolute bear in cross wind. In any other turbo-props, you could literally crab the aircraft in a severe cross wind landing; a technique of using opposite rudder and aileron control to compensate for cross wind. Do that with a Mitsubishi and you'd die.

I greeted the ground crew at Westchester Airport; they used an auxiliary power unit cart for my start-up. A big yellow cord plugged into the aircraft body giving me direct DC current to the engines; a technique used to save battery length but also to prevent overheating. The NiCad batteries had a nasty little habit of bursting into flames during start-ups. The ground crew gave me a thumbs up as both engines spooled up and they unplugged the power cord.

"Westchester Tower 27 Tango Bravo. Hanger D taxi to active." The Tower responded, "Roger 27 Tango Bravo. Taxi to active via Tango and Hotel. Hold short runway 16… you have the front door." Holding short of runway 16 and after completing a precise, exacting and very long preflight check list, I contacted Tower on 118.575, "Westchester Tower, 27 Tango Bravo holding short 16 ready for takeoff." The Tower responded, "27 Tango Bravo cleared for takeoff. Left turn climb and maintain 2500, contact departure 127.3 through 1500."

The beast came alive as I added throttle, sped through 129 knots, rotated and went airborne. The office, my father, and life during the past week literally shed off of me like water droplets on a freshly waxed Corvette. Freedom!

I rolled left, contacting departure control through 1500 feet. "Departure control 27 Tango Bravo VFR direct Nantucket requesting 12-5." The entire crew at the tower knew not only my father but me very well. They always recognized my voice and recognized my Friday departure to somewhere every weekend. Probably because I frequently brought them fresh tuna. They loved me.

Back in those days, FAA regulations were pretty loose compared to today. I heard "27 Tango Bravo, squawk 1200 ident and have a good weekend. Catch 'em up! Everyone in the tower is hungry." I pushed the button on the transponder, a piece of electronic equipment that allowed air traffic controllers to identify and track me on radar my entire trip. I climbed and maintained 12,500 VFR and proceeded to Nantucket.

Long Island's gorgeous shoreline ending at Montauk almost glowed with subtle shades of green. The corn and potato fields sat full of their bounty. As I passed over the great Peconic Bay I could see various sailing schools competing in their regattas. I passed Montauk, Block Island, Cuttyhunk, and Martha's Vineyard, all shimmering like an island oasis. Nantucket Shoals beckoned to me and to *Makaira* that rested in her boat slip. As I descended out of 14,000 I contacted the tower. "Nantucket Tower, 27 Tango Bravo out of 14,000, 20 miles southeast." "Roger 27 Tango Bravo, cleared to land runway 24… winds 20 knots, 220 degrees gusting 25 reported wind shear and turbulence." "Roger 27 Tango Bravo," I replied. Oh good! A tough landing. Just what I needed! I'd have to come in hot, compensate for a bad cross wind, and drive the Mitsubishi onto the runway. Sigh… Just another day in pilot school.

I made a long, straight-in approach encountering moderate turbulence. No doubt passengers would have been scared witless. I added 20 degrees of flaps, lowered the landing gear, and completed my descent and landing check list. This airport was not one of my favorite airports to start with. As you approach the island over the cliffs, you often met tremendous orographic lift as fresh winds off of the Atlantic jammed the walls. It had all of the elements that had killed novice pilots and their passengers from all over the world, but not on this day. As I rolled out on the runway and taxied to the terminal, Mike and Jamie stood on the tarmac waiting. They had rented a yellow Jeep with this cute, very feminine top with little tassels. They claimed it was the only vehicle available on that day. After greetings and salutations, we left for the Boat Basin. But of course, before talking about fishing I had to hear the litany of conquests of the week preceding. All being single and none of us completely out of adolescence, a sacred ritual. At that point in their lives, the boys thought about bigeye tuna and women.

Of course, Nantucket in summer provided a target-rich environment. Seemingly, 50 women visited the island for every male visitor. Ferries delivered load after load of secretaries, nurses and college students, all arriving in the latest summer garb. Life as a single man could not have been better. Politely said, we each enjoyed the rich bounty from the mainland.

Although we had shore side fun together, I held my crew to a very high standard. It had taken the whole week to prepare *Makaira* – food, 1,500 pounds of ice had been blown into below and above deck coffins over at the Fish House with every potential air leak secured by duct tape. We were fueled; rods and reels adjusted perfectly; ballyhoo, mullet and eels ready in coolers; and a new roll of recorder paper was in the Furuno sounder on the bridge. Like an aircraft, every "pre-flight" task was typed and placed on my clip board.

The contrast to *Makaira* was almost laughable where twelve curved butt 80s and 130s covered the gunnels and fighting chair. The buoys, harpoons, gaffs, knives, and coffins made us look like a war ship. We stood out like a sore thumb compared to the mega yachts, magnificent sport-fishing boats, and Trans-oceanic sailing yachts at the marina.

No matter my frustration level with work or my family, as I set foot on *Makaira* everything always became okay. We planned to head off to Welker and Lydonia Canyons, a place which very, very few sport fishermen had ever been.

The next morning's weather looked stellar with winds 8 to 12 knots out of the southwest, inshore seas 1 to 4 feet and seas on the continental shelf 4 to 6 feet. By mid-day all government and private forecasts showed winds light and variable and seas 1 foot or less. One could not beg, borrow, or steal a better forecast. It had us salivating.

On assorted previous trips, both Jamie and Mike had quit, and I had fired them. Sometimes two or three times in a week. It was an ongoing joke. But the arguments were always about the flawless preparation of *Makaira*. Success or failure in blue water big-game fishing is always in the details. You can spend millions of dollars and just one bad knot, one cracked swivel, one maintenance mistake in the engine room means the difference between failure and success. Something as simple as not having fresh rolls of depth recorder paper literally could make you the best in the world or a bum (Today the paper depth recorder has been replaced by Garmin, Simrad and other machines that were not even fathomable during this timeframe).

As a pilot you become very anal retentive. A pilot does everything the same way every time. You process your preflight check list, take off checklist, inflight check list and descent to landing checklist. Why always the same way? No surprises! One mistake, one item forgotten can kill you, your crew and your passengers. I carried these flight principles into my Northeast canyon fishing. Everyone on the dock used to laugh and make fun —right up to the point when we unloaded our catch. Then silence.

Four AM came too soon. The smell of Mike's hot coffee wafted through the salon. That first cup of coffee always felt like an intravenous of amphetamine. Mike's favorite boat breakfast consisted of two eggs over-easy on a fresh hard roll with melted mozzarella cheese and mayonnaise on top. It always tasted like the Ritz and I always wanted to eat five more of them.

As I climbed to the bridge, that damn morning fog, every sailor, yachtsmen or fisherman hates, rolled in giving us almost zero visibility. As you look skyward, for fleeting moments you can see the moon and stars, yet your visibility forward ends about 100 feet in front of your bow. With the radar humming and the range pinging one mile, both engines fired up with a bark. In the still of very early morning, diesels starting up at the dock creates quite a stir in a sleeping marina of wealthy gents and glitzy wives.

I remember asking myself (even to this day) "Where in the h**l have all the men gone?" A perfect sea, an undiscovered canyon where the crush of life unfolds every day. Literally the untamed wilderness awaits and yet, everybody is sleeping, cuddled up in their yachts anticipating their mid-morning mimosas and eggs benedict. A pathetic commentary on the world to my way of thinking. I consider it the "sissy-fication" of America.

Moving through the fleet of anchored and moored sailboats and trawlers in the harbor smacked of a video game with my radar full of targets. I navigated northward around Brant Point, between the red and green navigation buoys of the channel, and once I cleared the inlet, the fog *really* socked in. Traveling at 18 knots in 30 feet of water with no visibility has to be one of the eeriest events in my boating career. You couldn't see forward but you could clearly see the stars above. Clearing Great Point on the northeast side of the island always inspired great angst. These waters give even the best of captains the shivers. As we turned southeast and rounded Sankaty Head Light we passed through Old Man Shoal, Nantucket Shoals (just inside Old South Shoal) and finally got out to the east of

Davis Shoal. My heart is always right in your hand until that point. The rips, tide currents, and the up-wellings generated when the bottom rises from 60 feet of water to 8 feet, can wreak havoc on any vessel, sail or power! It's the place that took great whaling ships to the bottom, upended many a dory, and made plenty of widows in days of yore. I love and hate this stretch of water.

Love? A summer day with no wind and brilliant sunshine makes a magical fishing time for striped bass with live eels. Hate? A night in the fog or in a gale. This part of the Atlantic Ocean can be petrifying. I planned to head southeast to fish Welker Canyon and then move down east to Lydonia. That was the plan. But in this business, everything can change in a second.

The water temperatures in this area of the Atlantic can be some of the coldest on the East Coast; thus the reason for the frequent fog. As we touched the 30-fathom curve, the water temperature climbed from 62 degrees to 67 degrees. The fog lifted like a curtain call for the opera. Bam! Gone!

Looking back, the fog formed a knife edge. The sun now cracked the horizon: A red fiery ball to the east rising above Georges Bank. Beautiful. I made my log book entries that day noting the fog had settled into my eyebrows and as we pushed toward Welker Canyon, the water drops came off my eyebrows and rolled into my nostrils causing a five-minute sneezing attack. Why in heaven's name would I make a note like that in my log book? After about six hours of running, the water went from an ugly, putrid green color to greenish blue. At 80 fathoms the water looked like a glass with fresh blue ink in it, cobalt! The temperature edge between 80 and 100 fathoms soared up to 74.7 degrees. We had a color edge, a temperature edge, and then we entered Welker Canyon.

Welker is a nondescript, very short, narrow canyon. It's unusual because within a distance of less than a quarter of a mile from the 100 fathom line (6 feet to a fathom) you literally fall off a cliff to 3,000 feet! Just slightly farther offshore it plummets to 12,000 feet! It's not a gradual transition like Hudson, Fishtail, or Hydrographer Canyons. It's an absolute shear wall! As usual, we saw no other sport-fishing boat on the way out or at Welker. The radar showed four ships I suspected were Japanese longliners within ten miles. Mike and Jamie put out our 9-rod Porcupine Rig consisting of port and starboard outriggers, three center riggers, and two wing riggers.

This set up allowed us to troll very big lures and baits for bigeye tuna at very high angles from the outriggers. We trolled at slower speeds with the lures closer to the boat than has ever been done before. Previously, to troll big lures on a conventional sport-fishing setup, you need to run pretty fast and let the lures go way back to get them to work properly. The method behind this madness meant to draw the wolfpack into a feeding frenzy close to the boat for solid hookups, for the Barta Throttle Dance, and for savage multiple hook-ups. This system made us the best in the game! We knew what we were doing and it worked, and yet so many wouldn't listen.

As Jamie put out two 16-ounce deep clones — a yellow and green and a pink and blue — on the left and right long riggers, Mike followed up with two single-hooked mullets with two-ounce chin weights on #19 wire on the wing riggers. On the center rigger, we deployed a large Hawaiian kona head rigged on 400-pound mono using a Mustad 7754 triple X Martu tuna hook. On the right and left center riggers were two ballyhoo, one with a large green and white Japanese tuna feather on top and one with a blue and white feather, all rigged with #12 wire using 12/0 tuna hooks. Both flat lines pulled extremely large, 8-ounce jet heads rigged on 300-pound mono. The spread looked absolutely magnificent! Barta/*Makaira* perfection! Next we put out four teasers (hookless lures) across the transom. The outboard two Moldcraft inflatable-bumper teasers dragging rubber flying fish off their tail ends. These teasers dove down into the water below the surface and looked like a school of bonito. The two short, inboard teasers were huge flat head Moldcraft purple and blue chuggers. The back of the boat looked like we had a school of small bonito darting and weaving behind us. Bonito just happen to be bigeye's favorite meal.

Unfortunately, Welker Canyon held no bait. Mike and I got into a yelling match as I told him the recorder wasn't working. And as usual Mike was correct and I had to apologize. There was no bait. There were no birds. There were no fish and there was no life. We did not see a turtle, a porpoise, nor any finback whales —all good signs for bigeyes. I worked every inch of that canyon until night fall without a single bite. With summer evening light around 7 PM, I noticed that the four larger vessels I saw on the radar all took off, steaming east. I had no idea who they were or what they were doing, but at this time of year assumed they must have been longliners. We felt downtrodden, discouraged, and alone. Here we were in a canyon very few people ever fished and doing all the right things. One can only surmise that it was far from the right place and right time.

We had provisions for three days and enough fuel to last if we stretched it. Fifteen hundred pounds of ice lay below and on deck. And yet, we had snake eyes – meaning skunked! As we trolled into darkness, I told the boys to pull in the rigs. We dropped three huge double-hooked squid rigged on 19 din piano wire to three different depths – 90, 200, and 300 feet — in hopes that a swordie would come along. The lines floated out with huge balloons marking their locations; balloons that comically bobbed up and down like cartoon characters. We attached Cyalume sticks to the leaders about 18 inches above each squid. The light sticks glow underwater and attract all kinds of life. Tonight though, we found the Dead Sea. We attached 2-to 16-ounce weights to each line with a very light rubber band so they'd break off during a strike. Finally, I shut down the Cummins 370 turbo diesels. The remaining soft hum of the Kohler generator meant that the day had ended: Time for dinner and a great discussion of the day to come. All in all, a tiring day. Nothing showed on the radar as the great ships had earlier disappeared to the east. Jamie fell asleep on top of the huge coffin in the cockpit, Mike on the brown leather couch inside the salon, and I passed out in my master stateroom. We drifted on a placid sea with naught to be heard except an occasional snore from Jamie.

On Our Way to Lydonia

I awoke to the smell of coffee. I opened the door to the hallway and made a right hand turn into the salon. As I ascended the two steps I couldn't believe my eyes. Everyone lay sound asleep! Obviously someone had turned on the coffee machine and gone back to sleep. I walked into the cockpit to find the ocean absolutely flat like glass. Still pretty dark with about 30 minutes before sunrise, all three swordfish rods and their attendant balloons still held their undisturbed positions.

Suddenly, a very weird and almost surreal observation struck me: Last night, the swordfish rods drifted off toward the opposite side of the vessel! Generally, currents in the canyons flowed from east to west. In this area, it can sometimes run 5 to 7 knots – one reason why many offshore anglers fear this area so. It gets rough quickly and stays rough. In fact, we weren't all that far from the real estate where the story "The Perfect Storm" took place. For a moment I felt dizzy. It seemed like the world I knew turned upside down. When you spend as much time out there as I did back in the day, you exit the world of discotheques, beautiful tan legs, and short skirts… where so many men wore macho gold chains and drove fast, expensive cars. Something was definitely wrong. I woke up Jamie and Mike and we all had our coffee. As I remember Jamie always had his coffee with no cream. Without a word, both of them noticed the anomaly in our drift.

I had spent a small fortune of my own and a couple hundred thousand dollars of other people's money proving warm core eddies not only exist but had significant value on how fish migrated and fed, and where in the warm core eddy to find them.

Being a turbo prop and jet pilot I often flew down the 100 fathom line just off the Continental Shelf 75 miles south of Long Island. I would start at the Hudson Canyon and then fly between 300 and 500 feet to the east making a left turn at Oceanographer Canyon, touching the tip of Georges Banks and back to Francis S. Gabreski Airport in Westhampton where I was based. The flight often revealed extreme water color changes from a pea green on one side and a cobalt blue on the other. Almost every time I saw this condition from the air I would see a tremendous amount of marine life. I saw whales, porpoises, sharks, manta rays, and tuna. I could see giant bluefin tuna migrating eastward. They looked like black Volkswagens moving down the 100 fathom line. The flights were expensive yet back in those good old days the only value of money to me was how to find, track and catch bigeye tuna. If you look carefully at the picture of the warm core eddy, you can see clearly where the warm and cold water butt up against each other and the different temperature variables that exist usually on the northwest corners. It is like a big top spinning on a desk with the warmer water moving in a circular motion very similar to the sight of a hurricane.

Another tremendous trait of a warm core eddy is that it has not only a surface component but a depth component. If you take the temperature from the surface to 200 feet in a warm core eddy you will find the surface temperature is almost equal to the temperature at 200 feet. For example, if the surface temperature is 77 degrees usually the temperature will hold down to 200 feet. Conversely, if you go to the cold water that the warm core is approaching the surface temperature will lose about 7-10 degrees as you go down to 200 feet. You have a condition of warm nutrient rich Gulf Stream water slamming into a wall of super cool water. It is nothing short of a perfect situation.

We checked LORAN and it confirmed that we had drifted seven miles to the north and fifteen miles to the east. Even the town idiot could deduce that we went northeast. How is it possible that in a supposed 6-to 7-knot current steaming from the east to west that we ended up in the northeast?

I apologize to anyone reading this chapter who is not an offshore aficionado or just doesn't understand the facts of how the natural world works. So here's the extremely short version. During my Northeast canyon career, I unequivocally and nonnegotiably proved that warm-core eddies exist. These eddies are offshoots of the Gulf Stream which runs like a railroad track east to west, some 175 miles offshore in the northeast, or about 80 miles from our current position. The Gulf Stream constitutes the largest "river" of very warm, flowing water on the planet, starting down by the Yucatan peninsula and flowing all the way to Ireland. It doesn't disappear in the winter and travels all year long. Think of it as your carotid artery. It is our creator's way of giving life to the world as we know it.

Fact: During the worst January blizzard imaginable, you can catch a wahoo, blue marlin, or any of the pelagic species between 180 to 250 miles off Nantucket, Montauk, Shinnecock or for that matter New York City – if you could get there that is. The Gulf Stream has the same temperature and salinity in the northeast that you'll find in its midst only twelve miles offshore of Islamorada or Palm Beach, Florida during the winter. It's truly a natural wonder of the world and is responsible in great part for man being capable of living on this planet. If you dispute this fact you will lose. From Oceanographer to the Hudson Canyon, the Gulf Stream runs straight as an arrow all year-round. How do I know? Because I have been there.

A quick science lesson: Cold air is denser than warm air. Cold fronts rotate counter-clockwise while warm fronts rotate clockwise. The Gulf Stream works in very similar fashion. When the warm, nutrient rich water of the Gulf Stream (moving west to east) meets the colder, denser, inshore water moving west a clockwise eddy of water twirls like a toy top or tornado, getting larger and stronger as it nears the 100-fathom line inshore.

As this warm-core eddy hits the 100 fathom line all of the sea life — baitfish, krill, squid, and fish pile up on the northeast corner. The massive Grand Canyon-like wall intersects with this monstrous crush of life and thrusts it towards the surface, very similar to wind hitting the Flat Irons in Boulder, Colorado.

Pelagic fish live to eat and reproduce. They don't own Ferraris or condos in New York City. They eat, breed, and survive. That's all. While God allows us to visit this remote portion of the Universe, the tunas and great billfish just couldn't care less. All they know is that massive amounts of food exist at the apex where the warm core eddy slams up against something on the 100-fathom line.

Now that I've set the stage: Mike prepares his world famous egg sandwiches. We reel in the swordfish lines that haven't even had the slightest nibble during the night. As we ate, we discussed the anomalies of our drift. All of us agreed that we must be near a massive warm-core eddy, but it isn't helping us one bit. So, our plan for the day is so obvious it's almost laughable. We'll proceed on a southeasterly heading. If we are right about the warm core eddy, we should intersect a massive temperature edge as we hit the eddy itself. If we then take a left turn due east and follow the warm water to the 100-fathom line, we should find the bait and those eating it.

In the meantime, we're all alone. The longliners don't show on the radar and we've never seen a sport-fishing boat in this area. Plus, we're out of VHF radio range from everybody. Strangely, Mike found an AM radio station somewhere on the coast of Maine. We can hear it due to a phenomenon called "skip." In super-clean, highly ionized air, an AM radio waves (and others) ricochets between the ocean and the ionosphere, an electrically charged layer of the upper atmosphere, allowing us to hear it almost 300 miles away. No matter what he said back then, Mike liked terrible, noisy music called "Rock and Roll." I hated that music. With

Mike down below, I stole one of the batteries out of the radio. When he returned from the head he told me he had lost the signal. "No, really? I'm sorry."

Once again we set out the Barta Porcupine Rig with four teasers. We checked the drag settings on the reels. Once our morning check list had been executed, off we went. Three hours later in 9,800 feet of water, we still had not had a bite. I yelled at the top of my lungs, "Everybody get up here!" We watched the Dytek water temperature gauge change from 66.5 degrees to 67, to 68 —and all the way to 70 degrees. Mike put his hand on my shoulder and said, "Turn left." And so we altered course due east. Within about 20 minutes, air on the flat-calm ocean went from feeling like an air conditioned building to the fresh, outdoor air on an August day. The warmth and humidity almost knocked you over. It felt like the tropics! The water now so deeply blue that it bordered on purple. Pure Gulf Stream water — God's oceanic artery and gift to mankind. The water temperature gauge now read 83.7 degrees. Another left turn headed us directly towards the 100 fathom line. My depth recorder only read down to about 800 feet and after that we looked at the 12300 chart to find our depth. Within an hour we had 800 fathoms beneath our keel.

I don't know how to describe the anticipation except to say all of us were upbeat, happy and we hadn't even had a bite yet. But we had been here before and had enjoyed great success. Then it happened. A piece of grass, four man-of-war jelly fish, then I heard a porpoise blow — and suddenly hundreds of bottlenose dolphin showed up, all steaming to the east. Now, in 300 fathoms with blackback gulls, terns and Mother Carey's chickens, things finally began to look up. Jamie yelled, "Thar she blows!" And sure enough, there on the horizon dozens of finback whales gorged themselves! At last, not traveling but feeding! We could have made the quintessential "how-to" video about where to find fish as we hit the 100-fathom line. There we encountered such a defined edge of putrid green water on one side and cobalt blue on the other that Helen Keller could have followed it.

Our second day brought the crew rampant joy! Day one's skunk would hopefully be off any moment as every single condition that we look for as a sign of fish surrounded us. We had a 14-degree temperature edge, the sounder lit up with massive black balls of bait. To be sure, I asked Jamie to adjust the gain as that damn machine hated me. But Jamie simply confirmed that we were seeing tons of bait. We used 9920 rubber bands on our center rigger lines. The elastic wound around the line and then attached to a brass clip. When we got a tuna bite, the rubber band stretched, and it took so much pressure to break it that it caused six to eight inches of drop-back before it broke, and when it did, it sounded like a .270 Winchester rifle firing. Mike and Jamie remained cockpit bound, looking like two prize fighters about to enter the ring. When Jamie places all of his tuna knives on the coffin, you just know something is about to die. As we were passing right over the top of a finback that had just sounded, the center rigger exploded and we hooked up! Line peeled off the 80-wide. All three of us kept yelling, "Hooked up! Hooked up!" Just as I bellowed from the bridge, "What is it?" the left-long teaser on 500-pound mono was ripped from the transom.

It looked like someone had dropped a grenade off the back of the boat. Water literally exploded so violently that spray reached the salon windows. Next the right long rigger and the right flat line both came down at the same time. Jamie yelled "Bigeye! Bigeye! Hooked up! Three on! Three on!" As trained (and customary) Mike raised his right hand above his head showing three fingers so I could see. I now made a series of hard turns — wheel hard over to the right, wheel hard left, spilling the inboard wakes and allowing the lures on one side to settle into the depths and lures on the opposite side to rise and speed up. The Barta Throttle Dance!

Jamie yelled, "Half gone! Half gone!" Meaning we had lost half the line off the reel on the first hooked fish. I repeatedly yanked the power off and put power on. Turned left, turned right, power on, and power off. Lures and teasers took turns diving and popping out of the water. And the wolfpack attacked. The left long and left wing riggers hooked up. Mike held up his hand yelling "Five on! Five on!" Jamie yelled, "Stop it! Stop it now! Damn you Tred, stop!" We were about to get stripped on the first rods. The curved butt 80 ran out of line and was literally ripped out of the covering board, stopped from flying overboard only by the safety line. Ka-pow! The line snapped. Nothing but a gold spool shone in the morning sun. An angry Jamie started climbing the ladder to the bridge — I think to either attack me or the throttles when three other lines went off. We now had seven bigeye tuna hooked up at one time. Jamie is not exactly petite. Sasquatch kind of describes his figure. However, he turned around on that ladder like a leopard that was just shot eating a night bait in Africa.

The battle raged on. I dropped from the bridge and took over the cockpit controls. Back after the fish we came. In the fray, we forgot one of the yellow and green teasers which one of the propellers promptly shredded. Pieces of rubber shrapnel almost comically floated to the surface. We began getting line back on the first hook-ups.

Ah, what a great life! People say I substituted these adventures for my father's love. All I knew for sure was, I was at peace with two men that I truly respected. In many ways they were my real family.

I hear so often that people say the relationship with their father and mother is incredibly important on how it will shape their lives in the future. Personally I always thought this was hog wash but I see how my father almost single handedly drove me to my success in my fishing and hunting career. I never knew that I ever did anything in my life to gain my father's love but it is quite apparent that the anger, aggressive behavior and sometimes suicidal approach to fishing that I exposed myself and my crew to was simply trying to show my father that I was good enough to be his son and to deserve his love.

My mates, Jamie and Mike were treated by me the way I wished to be treated by my father. I treated them with respect. I complimented them. I trusted them to watch my back. I truly hope a psychologist does not read this book because then I would be committed.

Fighting the Magnificent Seven

Seven bigeye tuna on and only three men to catch them: A feat that is unheard of on any other boat except for *Makaira*. As I stood at the cockpit controls, something akin to lightning flashes punctuated my thoughts. The conflict between me and my father. The conflict of money and position versus living your life in the moment. The conflict of deep-sea currents jamming up against a vertical cliff and herding sea life towards the surface. The conflict of seven bigeye tuna engaged in absolute fights for their lives as they attacked our lures that they mistook for their dinners. And finally, the conflict of them trying to escape as we try to catch them.

The last thought I had before rejoining the fray… was there nothing more to life than one battle after another? Why do I find personal peace only between times of being hooked up or releasing an arrow toward a big animal that could easily kill me? There must be more to it all than that. That entire stream of consciousness probably lasted two seconds.

In calm seas and a current ripping at 6 knots from the east, *Makaira* roared backwards, black smoke billowing from the exhaust. With so little wind and the surface water so warm, the smoke just laid on top of the water like a black vapor trail. I reeled frantically on one of the rods. Mike and Jamie gained line on the rods that were hooked up — both of them almost stripped bare. Once we got enough line back to be in control, Jamie yelled, "Enough! Enough!" *Makaira* went from reverse to forward. Stretching all those lines out, we could hardly hear each other talk in a normal voice as all of the reels' clickers raged. The key now, and the reason why we almost always out fished any and all comers was our method of actually landing seven bigeyes — all between 250 and 325 pounds each —at one time. Most boats would have happily settled for hooking up one or two tunas. *Makaira* hooked up eight and had one break off. Now we wanted to land all seven.

We spent the next twenty minutes alternately reeling on all of the rods while also constantly moving rods over and under each other so the lines wouldn't cross and break. We called it "staggering." As soon as the fish settled down to something less than total chaos, Jamie and Mike hammered drag till the last two fish hooked came alongside. These were the closest with the least amount of line out. We always lost a lot of line during the Barta Throttle Dance. The two closest fish through this entire chaotic process were on the rods on the left and right transom corners. The boys increased the drags to almost 65 pounds. The Altenkirch curved-butt rods bent so dramatically that beneath the varnish coatings, the threads holding the guide feet to the rod stretched and broke. The old Dacron line which retained water in itself pulled so tight that little vibrating water droplets actually flew off the line. Most people can't comprehend the dynamics of 65 pounds of drag.

During the 1970s, Penn 80- and 130-pound-test reels could only generate about 40 pounds of drag. I sent all our reels to Mr. Cal Sheets in California who blueprinted them, changed the drag hands and put the spools on a Dyno so we could actually attain 70 pounds of drag without the reels blowing up or seizing.

Both Mike and Jamie —being right-handed —wore welding gloves on their left hands. You just can't turn the reel handle when pulling 65 to 70 pounds of drag. You need to help the process by taking the line just below the guide closest to you and with a gloved hand, pulling line towards the reel, turning the handle at the same time. This method lets you retrieve line foot-by-foot and inch-by-inch.

I truly loved Jamie's incalculable reserve of strength which he could call on when needed. As he hammered away at his fish, the rod tip almost touched the water — just seconds away from breaking. I begged him to back off on the drag some so the rod wouldn't break. He always listened to me as I was the Captain, but sometimes he moved a little slower than I would have liked — on purpose. Thankfully, he lightened up.

Mike yelled, "Color! Color!" meaning the blueish-black hide of our quarry could be seen. Above my head on the tower ladder hung four gaffs: one flyer — a gaff whose sharp, hooked head attached to a rope and tied to a cleat, breaks free of the pole upon sinking it into the fish, two monstrous straight gaffs by Pompanette, and a small but heavy straight gaff that we had cut down to half its original length. Jamie could swing the mini heavy straight gaff with one hand. Suddenly, Mike yelled, "Wind-On!" The 30-foot section of 300-pound test mono spliced into a Dacron sleeve reached the rod tip. When the leader got to this point, we kicked the reel drag to maximum. Jamie set his rod aside and grabbed a straight gaff. I left the controls and donned my welding gloves that I still have today. They are fabric and leather with canvas tops. I took two wire wraps with my right hand. Then two with my left, each time pulling the leader into my chest. Then I'd release my closest hand and reach farther down the leader and repeat the process, slowly bringing the fish closer and closer to our transom. Meantime, Mike continuously reeled up the slack line I generated so we were always relatively tight to the back of the wire man. Finally, I signaled and said to Jamie, "I have his head! I have his head!"

When you have the nose of a tuna pointed straight at you, you have broken his plane. He can't circle, he can't dig sideways, and when he tries to use his tail to get away he comes straight up at you. It is simply called "getting the fish's head." Fifteen feet —Ten feet —Eight... the bigeye was absolutely magnificent. Its lateral line showed so distinctly that if I didn't know better, I'd swear someone had drawn a black magic marker line across white drawing paper. Metallic silver on the bottom half. Dark purplish black with blue accents above, carrying up to a massive eye that almost seemed to look right through me —as if I wasn't there. The head broke the water. Like a newbie, I yelled for the gaff and as usual Jamie was 10 steps ahead of me. The hook of the gaff went straight into the gill plate of the bigeye.

The cobalt-blue seawater filters out the color red, causing blood to appear black. Mike grabbed the middle of the straight gaff and the two of them hoisted 325 pounds of bigeye tuna over the gunwale. Until my last breath, the thud of these great fish hitting the teak deck is a sound that I will never forget. To me it means the joy of life, joy of death, joy of conflict, and the joy of winning.

I returned to the cockpit controls, Mike moved over to finish Jamie's fish, and Jamie grabbed the next rod with the most line on it, shoved it down on the right covering board and went to work. The gaff went back on the tower railing and crimson blood dripped off it onto my control console. Mike hammered Jamie's fish with extra drag while Jamie reeled feverously to come tight on his fish. A massive spray of water drenched the cockpit. I thought Jamie was screwing around with the wash down pump. Next to the port side of the boat an honest 40-foot finback whale breached just 10 feet from me. "Holy Moley," yelled Mike. The exhalation air of a finback smells like latrine duty at Camp Lejeune. Unbelievably putrid!

The assorted birds homed in on the life and death struggle taking place. In fact, throughout our battle, the birds, whales, porpoises, and man-of-war jelly fish all converged on the scene. We were right in the middle of it. Jamie had color and grabbed the leader. I put *Makaira* in a gentle right turn and wired the fish. This fish proved so tough that on three separate occasions I had to let go of the leader —which I rarely did. Our philosophy called for us to never let go… either take them or break them off. I did a sloppy job of wiring that fish. Our quarry had eaten a horse ballyhoo on #19 wire, and I kept getting the wire caught on the backside of my welding glove. One wrong move and the wire could cut into your wrist severing an artery. You could literally bleed to death or lose your hand. After taking significant verbal abuse from Jamie, I finally got it right. Jamie then threw a pretty lousy gaff shot if you ask me. He hit it too far back and drove the gaff into the fish's heart. Blood gushed everywhere! The 300-pound fish smashed onto the deck and Jamie reached for the Barta baseball bat. This cut-down wooden bat had a core of lead and a rope-loop handle. It always lived on the back of the fighting chair where it could be easily reached. To this day I would testify in court that Jamie loved what was about to happen. The tuna went berserk on the deck, pounding and slapping the floor with its tail. Blood flew everywhere. Two solid hits with the bat, deafening thuds, and the fish lay quiet.

We'd had seven fish on, two lay dead on the deck, and we had five more to go. The boys grabbed two more rods and reeled like maniacs. I charged backwards so they could grab some line, then came forward again.

Mike was a gifted mechanic. He had rigged a brass, direct-drive raw water pump to the engine, just behind the fly wheel. Whenever the engine was running, we had raw seawater coming out of a 3-inch hose. When not in use, the water just poured out the starboard scupper. This allowed us to clean up the cockpit with massive amounts of water in just seconds.

We had 12 short, pre-tied tail ropes that Jamie always kept on top of the coffin in the cockpit. If a fish tail-tied to a cleat went berserk while we were fighting another fish, it couldn't go anywhere or do any damage to us or the boat. At least, that's how it was designed. On previous trips we had literally ripped the aft cleats off the transom! A cleat is a strong metal tie off usually bolted to the transom or the aft sides of the boat to which the vessel can be tied off to the dock. Can you imagine how dangerous it was with a wild, 300-pound fish fighting for its life, thrashing its tail and suddenly it has a solid steel cleat as a weapon to fight back with? After that incident (which surprisingly did not kill anyone), we bolted the cleats right through the hull. Believe me when I tell you, now they are not going anywhere!

One of the great techniques separating us from other crews and a huge key to our success was that we disproved the popular theory that you must always keep the line tight on a fish or else it may spit the hook. When using a Martu-design closed-gap Mustad tuna hook, a tuna with slack is going nowhere. So while other boats endlessly towed their fish around the ocean keeping a tight line, *Makaira* often charged backwards retrieving a ridiculous amount of line while all three of us ran around the cockpit reeling each rod like banshees. When we got down to five hooked fish or less in play, our method cut our fighting time in half. And of course, that gave us 50 percent more time to get our lures back out again and hook up another five fish while the other boats were still fighting their first hookup. I don't remember ever pulling a hook using this method.

We soon had four bigeyes on the deck, all between 275 and 325 pounds. With three fish still on, I loosened the drag on one of the remaining three fish. I moved the boat forward a little faster, purposely losing line on that one rod. With Mike and Jamie fighting I bellowed, "One. Two. Three. Reverse reel!" *Makaira* charged backwards. Jamie and Mike just barely kept up. I remember saying to myself "you can't catch these fish if you are afraid to lose them." With Jamie and Mike gasping for breath, I finally put *Makaira* in forward motion. Mike's leader came up first. Jamie moved in front of me grabbing the leader. I always thought Jamie was a better gaff man than a wire man, but he did an excellent job.

So I took his job and went for the head with the straight gaff. The fish lunged and I just plain screwed up. The gaff landed near its tail and all h**l broke loose. As the fish violently thrashed its tail, the gaff ripped from my hands. I generally didn't gaff very much and now you know why. I wasn't very good at it. I handled wiring much more adroitly. As the fish broke the 350-pound mono leader, a blur passed through my peripheral vision. Mike had run over, grabbed the second straight gaff and slammed it into the body of the fish. My straight gaff fell out and went straight down into the ocean depths — lost forever.

Getting this fish into the boat proved challenging. We couldn't get Mike's gaff out of the fish and it swung around the cockpit slamming into the fighting chair.

Finally, Jamie yelled, "Enough!" When I heard this it always scared me because it meant something was going to die quickly and savagely. Jamie grabbed the death club and literally beat the crap out of the tuna. The cockpit looked like the Chainsaw Massacre. Pieces of flesh pulverized by the bat had flown all over. Five dead bigeyes laid on the deck. I quickly washed the cockpit down and we went to work on the last two fish. They came to the boat exactly, according to our procedure. Bent rods. Maximum drag. Perfect technique in wiring and gaffing. We all high-fived and hugged. We screamed with joy. Seven-for-eight! We did it! No sooner did the last fish hit the deck than I commanded, "Let's get 'em out!" and within five minutes I was back on the bridge trolling nine lures. Lydonia Canyon lay six miles ahead. At the rate we were going and with what we were catching, we might not even get there. A slight southwest breeze sent cat's paws across the water's surface. I went to work looking for our next hook up. Jamie's next effort would mesmerize the finest butchers in the world. His knives flew as he started dressing our fish.

Lydonia At Last

I believe profoundly in a very old adage: Never leave fish to find fish! Despite our recent terrific bite, and despite the plentiful sea life in the area, we had no more hook-ups. Since we bordered on Lydonia proper now, we entered the canyon.

Lydonia – a narrow little canyon approximately 1-1/2 miles long and less than a half mile wide at its widest point — is an odd place because it drops off to thousands of feet. Yet it has no underwater mountains, and the southern corners of the canyon have no supporting flats like most 60, 70, 80, and 90-fathom drop-offs usually support. What also makes Lydonia Canyon unique is its 600- to 700-foot edges that plummet to 3,000 and 4,000 feet within a very short distance, making it quite an anomaly among northeast canyons. Because of this unforgiving topography, very few commercial vessels deploy their lobster gear along the edges of the canyon for fear their rigs might get swept off the edge into the abyss — wreaking terrible financial havoc. Many commercial fishermen I knew also told me that the stretch between Lydonia and Oceanographer Canyons consists of some of the most treacherous water in the North Atlantic. I can't agree or disagree as I just don't know. But I sure have gotten my butt kicked down this way more often than not. Another peculiarity at Lydonia finds many of the current edges have mini-whirlpools on the water surface.

As I crossed 1,500 feet on the southeast corner, the right-long rigger broke the rubber band. A small white marlin — about 40 pounds — hung himself on a 16-ounce deep clone. How the closed-gap tuna hook got through his bill I will never know. The fish frantically tried to jump all over the ocean, but the small fish had zero chance on the curved-butt 130. Jamie winched the fish to the boat. The tackle — so unjust — and the contest so pathetic, we all just laughed. Jamie got the leader, swung the little billfish into the boat, held it over his head and ran around the cockpit like a juvenile chanting, "I caught you. I caught you." He quickly released the white marlin and put the right rigger back into its proper position. The entire event took less than five minutes; a non-event.

But I know one thing for sure: white marlin, blue marlin, bigeye tuna, yellowfin, albacore, wahoo and mahi all love nutrient-rich water. I made a hard left turn to the mouth of the canyon where the chart said the water depth hit about 3,000 feet. Instantly, we all simultaneously yelled, "Hooked up!" Water exploded behind every lure. Teasers got hit again and again. Mini explosions and black backs of tuna rolled everywhere. One fish knocked a line out of the rigger, missed it, and a millisecond later three other fish tried to eat the same lure. Absolute mayhem! A feeding frenzy! Even the greediest insurance salesman would never consider writing the most expensive policy on one of these lures. Jamie yelled,

"Covered up! Covered up! All lines have fish!" One by one we wired albacore tuna weighing 30 to 50 pounds and dropped them on the deck. With the heavy leaders, heavy hooks, and heavy tackle we used there was very little wiring and gaffing, mostly just flipping the fish aboard by hand.

With nine albies in the boat beating their tails against the deck in a vain attempt to escape, it sounded like 300 people with drum sticks beating on the deck – an almost deafening sound. Once unhooked, Mike and Jamie cut the throat latches of every fish so they would bleed out. Using a long knife for this task was extremely dangerous, especially when the fish flapped wildly in their vain attempt to escape. To bleed out, a fish has to be alive. The object is for the heart to pump out the warm blood thus cooling the fish down rapidly. In the long run this makes for much better table fare. It's also very messy. Everything from the salon windows to the transom got colored crimson. The albie blood pouring out the scuppers acted like the bells on an ice cream truck to the blue sharks and the dolphin, mahi mahi, dorado or whatever you want to call them. Although the next hook up was imperative, we first had to manage our fish and ice. With Jamie holding a huge serrated knife (I am talking a 15-inch serrated blade) Mike brought each fish up to Jamie and placed it on top of the coffin. With one whop of the blade he cut the head off like the average person slicing an onion. After the head came off, Jamie reached his hand into the carcass and with a one jerking motion out came all the guts. Then bingo, over the side with the detritus.

The blue sharks' feeding frenzy when the heads and guts hit the water held its own savage beauty. Brutal yes, but beautiful, too. A moment's thought came across my mind: Are we the bad guys? Or just part of the dramatic play that Nature serves up every day? I find it amusing that conservationists and eco-tourists space ride around on safaris in Land Rovers with thousands of dollars of camera gear, trying to save the lions for example, from the brutality of hunting, and get excited to film a lion — the lovely mommy of the pride – running down an impala and sinking her huge teeth deep into the animal's throat, suffocating it, and bringing it to the ground. More photos as the rest of the pride literally eat the bowels out of the animal while it is alive and struggling. Nobody screams passionately at the lion about the feelings of the poor impala. Or how she will not be returning to her offspring who will now likely starve and perish or fall prey to other predators.

Nature is savagely brutal, and every minute, every day, every month, and every year from the top of the food chain down to microscopic, everything that lives at some time is at the mercy of something else. It is the circle of life and most people today don't have a clue about it. In the modern world, especially in my milieu of affluent eastern Long Island, people judge a man by the size of his wallet. Give that man a snare, spear, or a fishing kit and he would probably starve.

The cockpit cleaned and the lures out again, the albacore iced under deck and in top side coolers, we stood ready for the next onslaught. We knew the bigeye were around so the boys switched over to all monster lures hoping we would avoid another albacore attack. Unfortunately, our plan flopped and we caught another 12 albacore. Later in the day – for a change of pace, we caught seven yellowfin tuna — all slammers of 65 to 80 pounds each — really nice fish. At just about sunset, thankfully, the wolfpack returned once more, netting us an additional five bigeye tuna!

Sometimes we have to work hard to get hook-ups and at other times, big fish come in like poetry. This time waxed poetic. Hooking, reeling, staggering, wiring, and gaffing went off like a well-rehearsed ballet. The boys prepared the fish and put them down for their final sleep in the big coffin. Every remaining ounce of ice went in with them. We added three full buckets of seawater until the contents became a giant saltwater-flavored Slurpee!

Mike locked up the top, used two rolls of duct tape hiding every single air leak around its edges handles and then my crew both came up to the bridge. Birds frantically dove in front of *Makaira's* bow as the sun gave up its last hope of being seen and sank into the horizon. Big tuna crashed on the water's surface all around us. My next hook-ups would be spectacular! Mike grabbed the throttles and pulled them to neutral. I looked up at him. Jamie put his hand on my shoulder saying, "Boss we're done. We don't have any space left. The main coffin is locked up."

To say I was peeved doesn't even come close! Birds feeding, the sun going down, the complete spread out. Twelve bigeye tuna on board, a perfect dozen. Every cooler filled with albacore and yellowfin and now we're out of ice? We laid dead in the water until a brilliant thought smacked me between the ears. I said, "OK guys, one more hook-up. Mike, take everything out of the refrigerator, all the meats, drinks and everything frozen." As he descended from the bridge, Mike asked, "Where do you want me to put it all?" I said, "I don't care!" They hadn't even noticed that I had already eased *Makaira* back to trolling speed. I expected a bite, but not the most unusual hook-up I have ever witnessed. We had five fish on after the Barta Throttle Dance. One bigeye tuna (bringing our total catch to thirteen), a 60-pound wahoo — a reel screamer, one yellowfin, a bonito, and an albacore. Highly unusual but it speaks to what perfect conditions we had found. Everything fell into place right here, right now. In fact, it amazed me that we hadn't been attacked by a blue marlin.

We landed the last fish in darkness under the tower lights. We filleted the final catch, putting the valuable and precious meat into individual baggies. All of the food in the refrigerator was brought into the cockpit and Mike prepared a huge dinner and even made sandwiches for the next day. I took a shower in my state room, returned to the cockpit in my monogrammed blue pajamas to find all nine rods had their leaders cut off. Not exactly a mutiny, but it was the crew's way of saying, "Time to go home."

Home… I guess we all missed it. We'd been in Nantucket for about two weeks. I wondered if we could make it home with the fuel we had. After a solid page of math, with a coffee cup filled to the brim and two packages of Devil Dogs on the console, *Makaira* left in an amphitheater of stars and the wonders of nature. During the middle of the night the moon sent a magnificent reflection — a pathway for me to follow back home. We all took turns driving and returned to Shinnecock heroes for a day, or maybe even for a week.

The following illustration is of the "Barta Throttle Dance".

Follow Tred's epic three-day journey to Welker and Lydonia canyons as he encounters Japanese longliners and proves his Warm Core Eddy theory, by viewing the following chart.

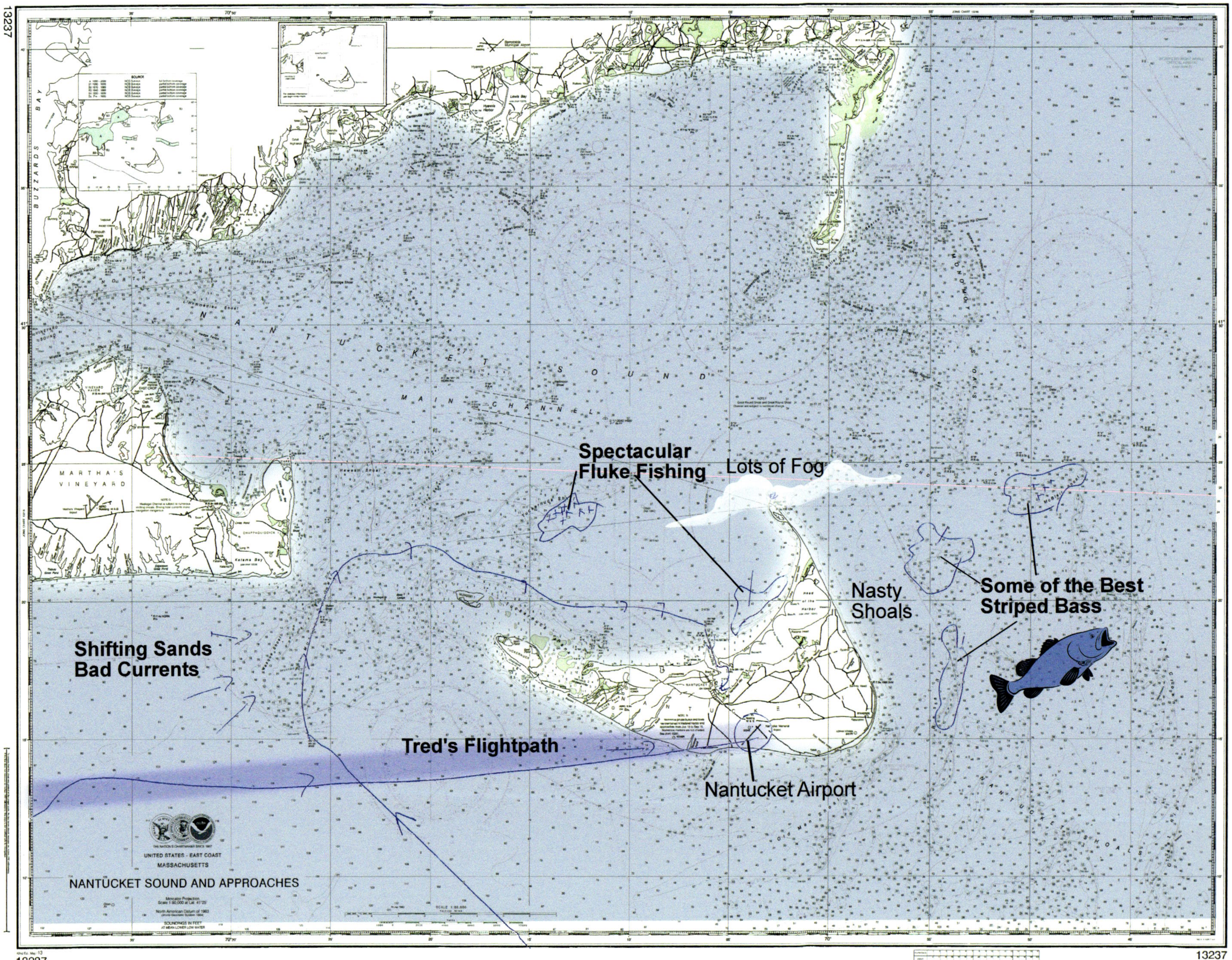
13237
BUZZARDS BAY
MARTHA'S VINEYARD
NANTUCKET SOUND
MAIN CHANNEL
Spectacular
Fluke Fishing
Lots of Fog
Nasty
Shoals
Some of the Best
Striped Bass
Shifting Sands
Bad Currents
Tred's Flightpath
Nantucket Airport
UNITED STATES - EAST COAST
MASSACHUSETTS
NANTUCKET SOUND AND APPROACHES
13237
13237

CHART 4

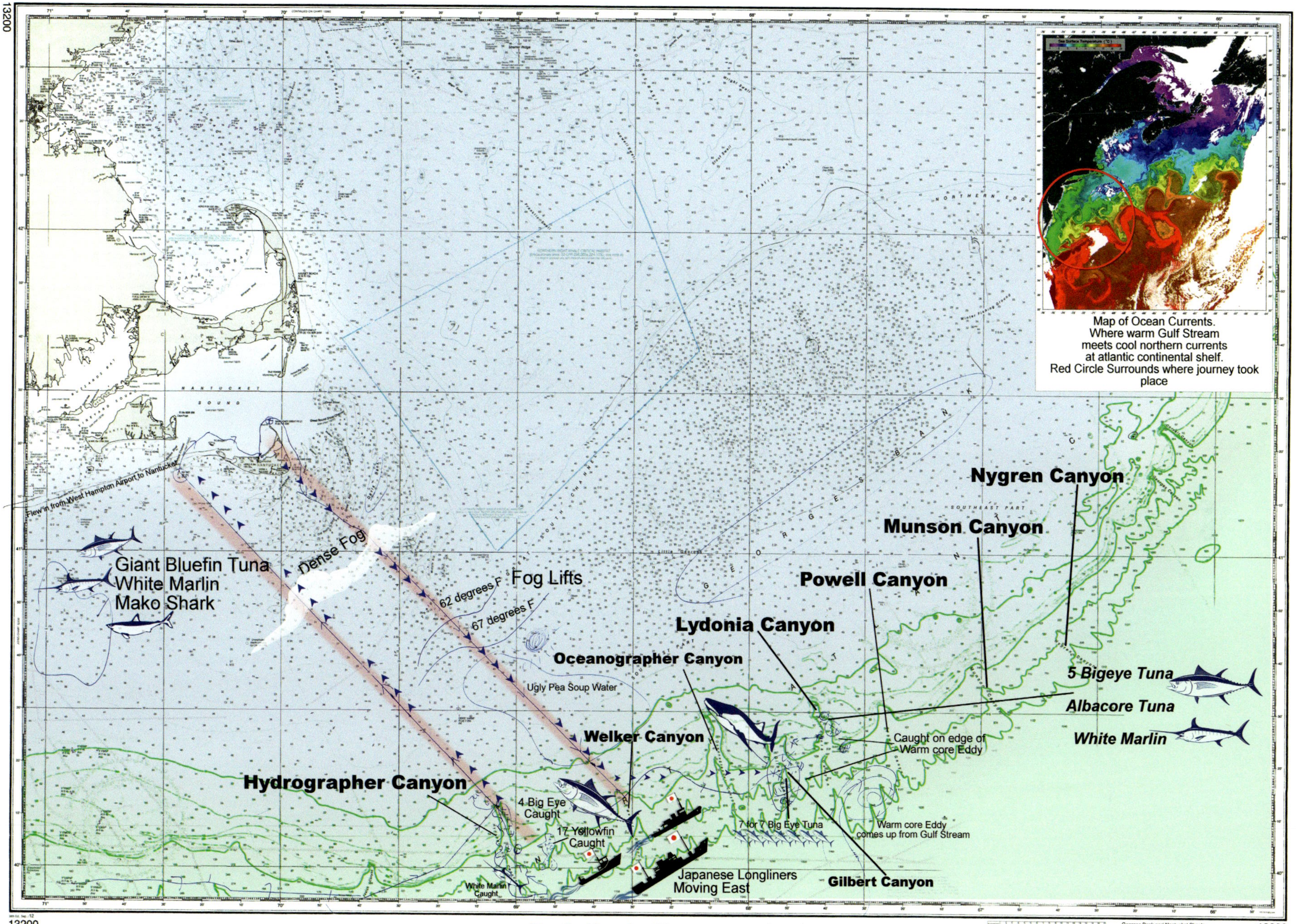

Map of Ocean Currents. Where warm Gulf Stream meets cool northern currents at atlantic continental shelf. Red Circle Surrounds where journey took place

Pacific Publisher's Map Referenced

Nygren Canyon

Munson Canyon

Powell Canyon

Lydonia Canyon

Oceanographer Canyon

Welker Canyon

Hydrographer Canyon

Veatch Canyon

5 Bigeye Tuna
Albacore Tuna
White Marlin

Caught on edge of Warm core Eddy

Warm core Eddy comes up from Gulf Stream

Gilbert Canyon

7 to 7 Big Eye Tuna

Japanese Longliners Moving East

17 Yellowfin Caught

4 Big Eye Caught

White Marlin Caught

Ugly Pea Soup Water

Fog Lifts

62 degrees F
67 degrees F

Dense Fog

Giant Bluefin Tuna
White Marlin
Mako Shark

Trail from West Hampton Airport to Nantucket

Tred's Handwritten comments supplemented for legibility

CHART 5

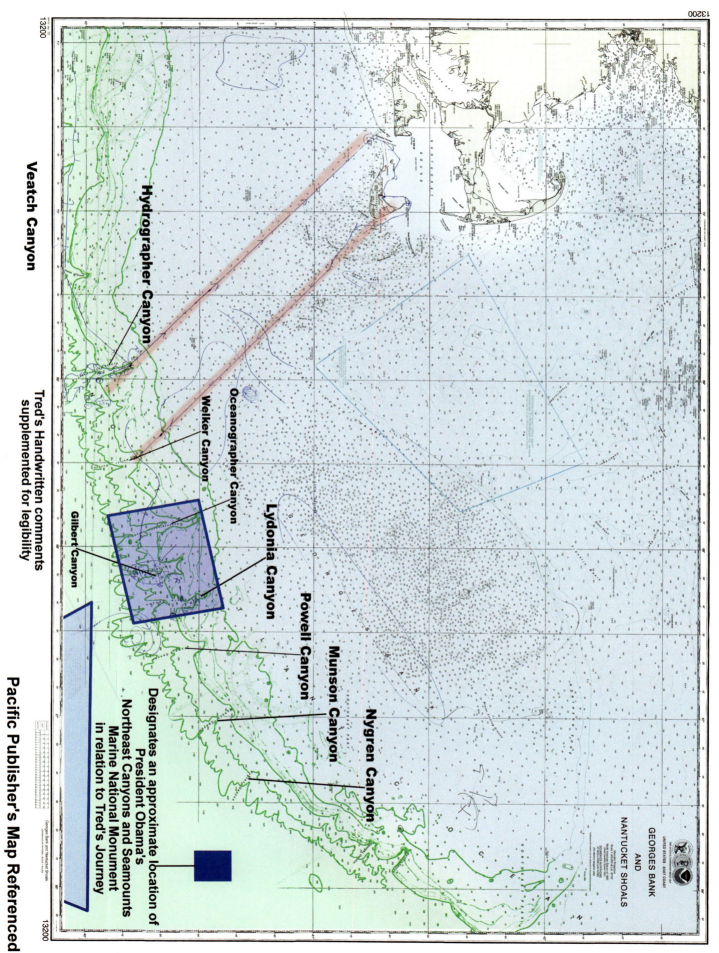

Albacore – Lydonia bites

Chapter Thirteen
OUT OF ICE

BETWEEN THE LATE 1960s and the mid-1980s, the quality of ice coolers was truly pathetic compared to today. A company called SSI led the pack back then. Igloo also had decent products, but nobody made coolers big enough to hold 500-600 pounds of ice plus fish. We could only meet our needs one way: make our own tuna coffin, which we did.

I am going to repeat a sentence four times to hammer my point home to a ridiculous extent. Run out of ice, run home. Run out of ice, run home. Run out of ice, run home. Run out of ice, run home. It's so important, I almost feel like repeating it four more times but I won't. Ice constituted one of the most critical ingredients of our success, because if we didn't have ice then we had to go home.

To stay out in the canyons for three days at a time required guts, stamina, and resources. But it also required ice! No matter how much guts you had, how much you spent, how big your boat was, how great a fishing team you assembled, the bottom line came to knowing how to manage ice. Otherwise, you could never compete against team *Makaira*. And in those days, nobody could. And I must give 100 percent credit not to myself but to Jamie (Sasquatch) and Mike.

To be honest I had enough on my plate just earning the money to financially support these adventures. My love and passion was bigeye tuna and how to catch them, what made them tick, where to find them, and how to hunt them down, etc. On my 47-foot Ridgeway, I spent most of my time on the bridge and very little in the cockpit. The major deck coffin, a large white plastic container, rested athwartships just below the rear salon windows. Onboard, we added an ice and salt slush to keep the fish super cold. This white container stored hundreds of pounds of fish that commercial fish houses purchased from commercial fishermen in its previous life. They were then cleaned and carved and put in these bins for distribution to the hundreds of restaurants and boutique seafood restaurants dotting eastern Long Island. After all, can you imagine the horror if a liberal left-voting conservationist might get a slice of fish that actually looked like a fish?

Jamie and Mike cut large sheets of Styrofoam to fit the sides of the coffin including the bottom. Then they wrapped roll after roll of what we called 100-mile-per-hour tape (actually duct tape) around the entire coffin ending up with a cooler with one to three inches of Styrofoam insulation. They fashioned the coffin lid from a piece of 5/8-inch plywood with a rope handle on each side, also covered by Styrofoam and taped.

Before leaving on a two- to three-day fishing trip, we would go to either Jackson's Marina or Pell's Fish Dock at Shinnecock Inlet and get 200-pound blocks of ice which they fed into a commercial ice chipper. The Shinnecock Inlet was formed by the Great Hurricane of 1938 when it permanently broke through Shinnecock Long Island in Hampton Bays and was named after the Indian Nation. More than 1,000 pounds of chipped ice then blew into our various coolers and coffins through a seven-inch diameter tube. We filled the coffin almost to the top, then added Kosher salt to "lock the top off." A space blanket (shiny surface down) covered the ice. They topped it off with the plywood coffin lid and then taped all the seams.

Salt mixed with ice lowers the freezing temperature, creating a saltwater slush so cold you can't even keep your hand in the mixture for more than a few seconds. You can't stand the pain it is so cold. In the absence of a "brine slurpee," the top of the ice freezes solid, like an ice skating rink. We always carried 100-pounds of salt and 20 rolls of duct tape on *Makaira*.

This box was our lifeline. It held 15 bigeye tuna, 50 to 60 albacore or about 30 yellowfin tuna depending on their size. We blew ice in every single area of the vessel that would hold it: two insulated below deck coffins, a couple of SSI coolers that we kept in the salon (which we also used as a table), and several scattered Igloo coolers. But from the time we pulled into the dock until the time we left with ice, *Makaira* weighed 1,200 to 1,500 pounds heavier.

So now let's go back to our hook up between Welker and Lydonia. We had full ice. None of the coffins or coolers had been violated, by that I mean opened yet, and "Ice Management 101" was about to take place.

In the early days of bigeye fishing, while trying to prove the size of our genitalia based on how many bigeye tuna we caught, we just kept the entire fish on ice. Later in our career we bled all of our fish. Jamie would make a circular incision around the anal orifice, about a half-inch around to allow the guts in that area to be removed more easily. I believe Mike brought a small hatchet onboard. From the engine room he borrowed a small sledge hammer and with a sound similar to immigrant workers slamming railroad nails into the track in the 1920s, he severed the backbone of the tuna with one hit from the sledge. Finally, Jamie cut the throat latch, extricated all of the intestines and cut out the gills. Then we stuffed the carcass back into the coffin.

Later in our career, we found a better way: Jamie removed the head by cutting the throat latch and following the line just behind the pectoral closely around the head severing the backbone and thus removing the head and guts in one cut. Now, with seven heads and gut piles sitting in the cockpit, one at a time Jamie would throw each head and carcass over the gunwale, yelling the chant of the day such as "Ooorah!" It was absolutely primeval. You could describe it as disgusting, unnecessary, over the top, and/or uncalled for, but in my eyes it was a beautiful sight and sound. It was men being men, doing what men have done for millennia. Gather and provide!

Mike then cleaned the cockpit to perfection, of course. We always thoroughly wash out the abdominal cavity with saltwater, both to remove any blood as well as to cool the fish. Lactic acid builds up in the muscle tissue of a fish fighting for its life. The fish actually heats up and if not handled properly can actually burn up — not literally but figuratively — and ruin the meat. Fish buyers inspecting bigeye and bluefin tuna can tell when a fish has been burned by its own body. Usually a big game animal which is wounded and travels a long distance in a short period of time overheats in the survival process. The meat in this condition is often ruined.

As the fish cooled down, the first real challenge of "Ice Management 101" reared its ugly head. We have seven bigeye tuna, all 180 to 220 pounds dressed, about to be placed in the coffin. Of course to make room for the tuna, ice must be displaced. Where do you put that extra ice?

Second problem. If you place the seven tuna on top of remaining ice, what do you do when you catch more tuna? Do you take the first tuna out and dig down to the bottom of the coffin displacing more ice, then lay the tuna on the bottom, putting more ice on top of them and then put the new tuna in and then more ice, etc. — all while it melts like a river runs through it in 90 degree August heat? And of course, if you lose your ice the trip is over. In those days, we couldn't make the vast quantity of ice needed right onboard like we can today.

What would you do? What would the dandy back in Southampton with the wrapped sweater around his neck do?

As if in a race, Mike and Jamie filled up about ten large industrial garbage bags with ice. They placed the tuna on the bottom and filled each cavity with ice and banked ice up around each one as well. The fish were stacked on the bottom with ice surrounding them and they repeated this process, refilling the coffin to the top. Between every two or so garbage bags of ice, they added a thin layer of Kosher salt, thus locking up layer after layer with a frozen ice sheet.

When the ice got to the top of course we had an ice overage. If you get into a bathtub filled to the very top with water, obviously when you get in there will be a displacement of water. We always kept four extra-large coolers on the bridge and the bow. The boys immediately shoveled extra ice into these coolers and locked them down with Kosher salt. With the coffin top now secured with duct tape, the job was finished for the moment. Jamie's kept his fillet knives in a canvas bag. When he pulled out his knife case bulging from the large serrated blades, it meant success.

Being a competitive skier in my early days the feeling one had when looking up at the score board gasping for fresh air to fill my lungs after a downhill run, the name "Barta" appeared in first place was the exact feeling I felt now. It is like having an orgasm. A complete feeling of relaxation and release of tension. We did it!

With the coffin full, the deck perfectly clean, and not a trace of the slaughter that had preceded it, Makaira trolled into Lydonia Canyon at 6.7 knots, lures and baits in the wake, waiting for the next miracle to happen.

Chapter Fourteen
HYDROGRAPHER

SOME FEW, PRECIOUS days throughout a Northeast summer qualify as absolute perfection. During one such period in the mid 1980s, NOAA weather forecasted clear skies with light and variable winds for several days. The offshore area between Maryland and Massachusetts had stellar conditions forecasted. If overlaid on NOAA's Chart 13003, "Cape Sable to Cape Hatteras," Hydrographer Canyon stretches from Baltimore Canyon to the west all the way to Oceanographer Canyon to the east. Hydrographer is a very short, deep and steep piece of the world and should be on any offshore fisherman's bucket list.

I looked forward to this super-high-pressure weather weekend. The barometer smiled big numbers. Meteorologists called for seas less than one foot and winds less than 10 knots. This kind of incredible forecast makes you take a deep breath and devote 100 percent of your effort to the anticipation of the trip to come rather than the horror that Mother Nature can dish out. *Makaira* always sailed in either case, but this was a super gift.

As I finished work at my father's company, Joseph T. Barta Associates, on a Friday afternoon in August, the sun reflected a gentle reddish glow on the cowlings of our twin-engine Cessna 310. After 10 to 12-hour days at the office I was ready to take off... literally and figuratively!

The Cessna sported a pair of Lycoming TIO-540 (350-hp) turbocharged and intercooled engines with three-blade Hartzell propellers. With a very respectable cruising speed of 200 knots at 12,000 feet, I could easily and very quickly transition from New York mainland work mode to Long Island fishing mode. The engines started like Swiss time pieces. One turn of the starter gave me pure energy. After completing my preflight and take-off check lists, it was ground control on frequency 127.25.

"Ground 27 Tango Bravo ready for taxi, hanger D." "Roger 27 Tango Bravo taxi A to runway 16. Watch for Jetstar 37 Tango Lima on same taxiway." As I switched over to the tower on frequency 118.575, I heard those most-beautiful words... "27 Tango Bravo cleared for takeoff. Catch 'em up!" Yes, it flouts FAA regulations to personally communicate messages in this way, but I knew everyone in the tower – for that matter everyone at the entire airport. They all knew that a successful fishing trip for me meant a cooler of fresh yellowfin tuna to share among them.

The noise of our well-maintained engines sounded sweet as I added full power. I cleared the runway, making a left turn, flying VFR (Visual Flight Rules), and climbed to 3,500 feet heading 107 miles "as a crow flies!" Flying over Long Island Sound gave stark contrast to what we considered normal on *Makaira*. Where we experienced relative solitude fishing offshore, I looked down to see hundreds of boats positioning themselves in anchorages and harbors, getting ready for hotdog grilling, inner-tubing and other watersports. Many people anchored up in channels bottom-fishing for blackfish (tautog) and fluke, while many others chased bluefish and striped bass.

Crossing over the Long Island's North Shore, meant time to contact the tower in Westhampton. On final approach, the entire Atlantic Ocean looked like a pane of glass. It beckoned to me, almost to the extent of a siren's call... intoxicating! What would Mother Nature serve up for us this weekend?

I made my final right turn and they cleared me for a straight in VFR approach to runway 24 where I enjoyed a perfect, windless landing.

As I rolled into the FBO (fixed base operator) just to the north of the control tower, I saw my camouflaged Bronco (still sporting a few goose decoys from the last bird trip in January) awaiting me. I drove straight to Indian Cove Marina to meet Jamie and Mike. They were near to completing the preparation work aboard *Makaira*, my 47-foot Ridgeway. The huge handmade coffin in the cockpit sat filled with 1,500 pounds of ice, salted and sealed with a space blanket.

Makaira had also already been provisioned with our standard order from the deli: six pounds each of roast beef, turkey and baloney; three pounds each of Swiss, American and Provolone cheese; two dozen NY hard rolls; two loaves of white bread; five boxes of Twinkies; four gallons of milk; four dozen eggs; three pounds of bacon; and nine microwaveable Hungry-man dinners. Oh, and not to forget the cookies: three boxes of oatmeal raisin, two packages of Oreos, and a variety of crackers, chips, and other snack stuff. Inside the cabin stood four 55-gallon drums of diesel fuel, placed in another monster coffin to keep them from rolling around or spilling. In this weekend's seas which promised to be non-existent, this may have been a little bit of overkill.

Makaira trolled nine rods on seven riggers — over time a system named the Barta Porcupine Rig for obvious reasons. The rods in the cockpit sat ready, every piece of equipment in its place. As the immaculate boat gently tugged at its dock lines and I changed from my office work clothes to offshore khakis, Mike placed a hot cup of coffee on the bridge. I loved that tradition. Before I knew it we were ready to sail.

Today you often hear people talk about Hydro as if it were a mere walk to the corner store, where a 70-foot boat at 35 knots could take its anglers with ease. But in the days that I write about, it was a place only imagined. *Makaira* was alone. No commercial boats. No private boats. Nobody. Our journey to Hydrographer always created quite a stir at the marina. At approximately 173 nautical miles from Shinnecock, one needed extra fuel, perfect weather and beaucoup patience as it was just a long way out, period! I planned to get there by coming in at the Fish Tail (LORAN coordinates 14650 and 43316) and then head east on the 43300 line (named the Bigeye Highway by *Makaira's* crew), then troll down to the east through Atlantis and Veatch Canyons, and then to Hydro. As I said, most boats never visited Hydrographer Canyon. They always had some excuse; the weather, the extreme easterly current, or some ominous report from commercial boats that worked the area. I decided to go directly to Hydrographer; the trip would take about 14 hours. About 100 nautical miles into the trip, we used an Orberdorfer brass hand pump to transfer fuel from the drums to the main tanks. We carried the empty drums to the bow and strapped them down. We now had our salon back.

Shinnecock Inlet struck me as a video game of small boats, all drifting the incoming tide for striped bass and bluefish. The state park on the east side of the inlet held a gaggle of campers and an inordinate number of American flags. In fact, tons of humanity covered both sides of the inlet. Every one of them had an agenda and we had ours. Moving between a stately 11 and 12 knots, *Makaira* glided over a nondescript ocean. An absolute fireball sun met the horizon. In fact, I remember this particular sunset as if it was yesterday… absolutely glorious. Not a cloud in the sky and not a breath of wind. Our blazing bright orange, yellow and red sun literally sank into the ocean.

Darkness approached quickly and we planned to reach Hydrographer by 7 AM the next morning. I'd take the helm until 9:30 PM and then Jamie and Mike would take turns bringing her the rest of the way to the northern tip of Hydrographer Canyon. With my feet up on the console and my crew sound asleep below, I thought to myself, "Wow… I'm free from the grip of my father." I was doing something that I was the best in the world at, pioneering new bigeye tuna techniques in new places, *and* I wouldn't be criticized from first light to my workday's end. Here I was my own man, captain of my own destiny. I was relaxed and in control. My capable crew and I intended to "bring home the bacon." Sure, I loved my father deeply, he was a man's man in every way, but I sure liked getting away from him, too.

Two hours past sunset, *Makaira's* running lights offered the only points of reference in an otherwise totally black environment, almost a surreal, out of body experience. The lights of eastern Long Island long ago disappeared, leaving the turning propellers churning up microorganisms into a glowing greenish contrail behind the boat as our only natural light source. Incredible! The stars were so bright it reminded me of the NY Planetarium. The slightest sliver of moon shared no light at all to mark our path eastward.

I dozed off twice but caught myself. I often slapped myself gently in the face to wake up. Occasionally I'd climb down to the cockpit, quickly walk into the salon, grab an ice cold glass of chocolate milk and some cookies and return to the bridge to eat them. I always reveled at how good an oatmeal raisin cookie tasted dipped in milk and the effort always woke me back up for at least another hour or two.

My biological clock turns off at 9:30 PM. I literally could go weeks at a time if I could sleep from then until 3 AM. At 9:32 PM, Mike appeared on the bridge with a bag of chips. We exchanged good nights and I dove into my fresh clean sheets. Jamie woke me from a deep sleep at 6:35 AM and said, "Ten miles to go boss. Let's mug 'em up." Hands, face and teeth cleaned, I entered the salon. Apparently in the middle of the night, the boys had straightened and vacuumed the salon and everything was in perfect order. Jamie had taken the last watch and usually stayed awake until about 10 AM. Mike, fully rested, would go the distance to about 3PM when he would take a catnap. I regularly stayed at the helm until 8 PM. A grand master plan, but of course it frequently got interrupted when we hooked up. No matter how tired anyone got, we were never too tired to fight fish. As I departed the salon for the bridge, I glanced down at my leather briefcase. It represented the aircraft business, my entire shore side existence and — most significantly — my father's suffocating grip on my life. To this day, I remember just this fleeting moment. I said to the briefcase, "not today!"

One problem with going to Hydro directly is the need to cross a massive flat area of 20, 30, 40 and 50-fathom plateaus. It seems like it goes on forever… like driving through Nebraska and just when you think you are done, here comes Kansas! As *Makaira* finally hit 62 fathoms approaching the northern tip of Hydro, we deployed three teasers and nine lines. We trolled big lures, 16-ounce deep clones, massive Sevenstrand kona heads, 12 to 15 inches long, one two-pound swimming black mullet with a three-ounce chin weight, and all with 12/0 to 15/0 hooks. We didn't come here for small fish! Hydrographer Canyon drops from 62 to 211 fathoms in less than one-eighth of a mile. The northern tip looks like a small fish tail with canyon offshoots heading a couple of miles inshore carrying the 62 fathom line all the way into 50 fathoms within a quarter mile. The 64-degree water was colder than our ideal. The best temperature break for bigeye tuna is 65 to 68 degrees. The water color sucked, too. Its greenish-blue wasn't what we needed. As we crossed the northern tip, the paper depth recorder plummeted, kind of like looking over the edge of the Grand Canyon. Down she went to over 200 fathoms. We called this "going over the edge." My crew and I always hooped and hollered, raising our coffee cups and cheering "Welcome to Hydrographer Canyon!"

We planned to work the western drop off of Hydrographer, crossing from 70 fathoms to 300 fathoms as we moved along the canyon wall. The canyon mouth has a beautiful curve to it. I actually named it the "wine glass." Both sides were caressed with a gentle slope from 74 to 95 fathoms and then (bam!) 562 fathoms right into the mouth itself as it dropped off to 900 fathoms. The very edge of the North American continent!

I often stopped to consider the fact that the quarry we pursued travels thousands upon thousands of miles of pure ocean wilderness… wilderness that 99 percent of humanity has never seen. Then in a very small envelope of time, whether it be luck or a filament of cobalt-blue Gulf Stream water spun off to the 100 fathom line, these magnificent beasts show up at Hydrographer Canyon. In some ways, it's like meeting the last dinosaurs. For a fleeting moment, it makes one feel part of the food chain itself, a sensation so overlooked when buying your tuna at the store wrapped in cellophane.

Noon came without one single bite. Pathetic conditions took *us* all the way out to 1,500 fathoms in search of blue water. We saw a tremendous number of birds: terns, black-back gulls and Mother Carey's chickens by the thousands. We knew that life and death played out somewhere nearby but we just couldn't get in the game. The depth recorder showed massive amounts of bait between 30 and 90 fathoms. We also marked what we thought were bigeye and bluefin tuna. But what would it take to attract them? Where would it happen? When would this bait push to the surface after being carried into the canyon walls of Hydro, and what would it take to position *Makaira* at the right place at the right time during the anticipated feeding frenzy? We were running out of time, running out of fuel, and starting to run out of the human resources for the job at hand. At 3 PM, extremely discouraged, I asked Jamie to take the helm. For some reason, I wanted to lie down for a couple of hours. I told Mike to take a nap and both of us were out like a light lying on the salon floor.

Jamie rarely took the helm, not because he was unqualified, but because he loved the cockpit. At 5:05 PM Jamie interrupted our sleep yelling at the top of his lungs, "bigeyes right rigger!" Mike and I woke up, took sleepy steps into the cockpit, and saw nothing! No line was hooked up, no reels screamed… nothing. I looked up at Jamie and said, "bad joke buddy, we were asleep."

As Mike and I turned back into the salon in disbelief that Jamie would think that was even remotely funny, the right-short MoldCraft teaser ripped out of its the transom clip. The left flat line erupted as a black Volkswagen engulfed a 16-ounce purple and black Deep Clone lure fished on a straight-butt 80 rod and pinned down to the transom on a 130-pound ball-bearing swivel with a heavy rubber band. When the rubber band broke, it sounded like a 30-06 rifle being fired. The right wing rigger and the right short rigger simultaneously exploded. We now had three lines singing and losing line quickly. No doubt about it Jamie had found "*Thunnus Obesus*," the Latin taxonomy for bigeye tuna.

Reels screamed, a sound that a canyon fisherman lives for. The hole left on the strike gaped about 3 by 4 feet. It looked like depth charge or hand grenade had gone off, sending white water into the cockpit. Needless to say, Jamie had our attention now. He had taken us somewhere over the last couple of hours where bigeye tuna may have traveled from the Mediterranean through the Straits of Gibraltar and across the Atlantic Ocean, or gone up as far as the Flemish Cap near the Artic or to Mexico – all in a single season, and now attacked *Makaira* only 12 feet behind the boat.

In the presence of the king of kings. This is what we live for. This is why we breath. As the 80-wide quickly lost line, the right wing rigger exploded. We all saw the breathtaking strike. As the rubber band snapped, the rigger itself shuddered and actually sent the vibration through the entire boat. Like dry-firing a compound bow, you will never forget the sound.

At this point Jamie could no longer stand not being in the cockpit and likewise, I needed to be on the bridge. Looking back, it smacked of "Keystone Kops" hysterical. Jamie coming down the bridge ladder as I went up, like two firemen on a five alarm blaze. How we passed each other on the ladder, I have no idea. I would have thought it impossible.

I grabbed the bridge controls and started the Barta Throttle Dance: Hard left followed by hard right. Hard left followed by hard right then straight line. The uneaten lures danced for their lives. My purpose? To emulate bait fish fleeing for their lives. As I pulled straight away, I pulled back the throttle then added throttle, then pulled the power off and as I started to push the throttle forward again for the fourth time my maneuver worked. The center rigger and right long rigger both came down with a vengeance. As Jamie managed the drags on the rods, Mike stood in the cockpit facing the lures in a spot where I could see him near the starboard transom door, his hand above his head with four fingers raised. "Four bigeyes! Four on!"

Jamie never said much during a hook-up, so when he did, everyone listened. Jamie said, "Line low on the left flat and right wing." Realize that during these turning maneuvers — adding throttle and taking it off — line on the hooked up fish leaves the reels. We were running out of both line and time to get other bites. The wolfpack was on us! As I started to add throttle again Jamie yelled, "No! No! No! You can't do it!" Just as his last "No" left his lips the left teaser was ripped off the boat and the right flat and the left short as well as the left long all came down at one time. Sheer chaos!

Mike screamed — almost begging, "Seven on! Hooked up! Seven on! Tred, stop!" I finally realized that we were in jeopardy of losing the first three fish. Jamie had two rods to clear that were not hooked up as we trolled nine rods. It was Jamie's cockpit. He owned the real estate. He'd paid for it week-by-week in past trips and past accomplishments. Those in the cockpit never questioned Jamie's authority or judgment. Jamie softly said to Mike, "Cut them." Mike reached up with one of the cockpit knives and cut the two unhooked fishing lines. The lures sank into the abyss and the fight was on!

I quickly moved from the bridge to the cockpit controls and we all feverishly moved one rod over and under each other to keep the lines from crossing. Jamie quickly identified the first three rods to be hammered with the drag. These would be the first three fish needing to be caught. We each reeled like the hammers of

Hades getting line back on the reels. Dangerously low line on two rods demanded the use of a maneuver formerly considered unthinkable: As I came back hard in reverse all seven lines went slack. We all reeled like crazy getting line back on the reels in jeopardy. As I pulled forward, the mates moved around the cockpit taking up slack on the other hooked up rods. It looked like world-class sailors trimming sail on one of those big coffee grinder winches!

We slowed the first three fish with 60 pounds of drag. Mike sat in the chair and hooked himself into a bucket harness. I worked the left short rigger rod closest to the controls and Jamie worked the right flat. The Altenkirch rods literally creaked as the wrapping started to explode underneath the guides. We knew the limits of our tackle and pushed it right up to the edge. These fish were big! They all looked about 250 to 300 pounds dressed — with the head and guts removed. I instructed Mike to fight the last fish to bite, the one on the center rigger. Mike started with 30 pounds of drag and I slid my hand over the drag lever, pushing it up to 70. At this drag setting the line hum and vibrates. Water droplets actually pop off the line. It is hard to describe, but the rod verges on breaking in half or the line to break. Strapped into the bucket harness, the pressure of the fish lifted Mike, keeping his rear end from ever touching the chair.

Jamie announced, "I have color," signaling me to put on my welding gloves. The swivel popped the surface and I got a good first wrap. Jamie took over the controls with one hand and held a straight gaff with his other. On the second wrap I popped the fish's head, meaning I turned the fish so it headed towards the surface. If you have the fish's head, then you have the fish's tail. On my third and fourth wrap the fish finally showed itself, a silvery blue with black and blue highlights and brilliant yellow on its finlets. Something flew over my shoulder. Jamie slammed a gaff into the gill plates. When blood streams out in cobalt blue water it is not the brilliant red that will soon cover the cockpit. It's almost black, and that means one thing: Something has died and we are a part of the crush of life. In the blink of an eye, the tuna door opens, Jamie puts a tuna hook in the upper jaw of the tuna's mouth, pulls it onto the deck, stores the straight gaff, ties the fish tight to the rear cleat, and swings three Babe Ruth-type of blows just behind the eyes with our hexagonal wooden mallet filled with a lead core.

The sound is brutal and unforgettable, but it is no more brutal than the tuna attacking our baits. No more brutal than the gulls picking up the remains of torn-apart baitfish. And certainly no more brutal than the mako sharks who hunt the tuna day and night.

While Jamie works the left flat line, Mike takes a 130 curved-butt (the biggest, heaviest and strongest rod in all sport fishing) to the chair and buckles in.

Mike works feverishly with six fish on as he fights with 70 pounds of drag. This fish came incredibly quick. Jamie yells, "color" and no sooner do I get my gloves on, Jamie yells, "we have two right now!" I wire Mike's fish as he gets out of the chair, grabs a gaff and sends it home into the fish. An imperfect gaff placement perhaps, but the tuna is going nowhere. I moved quickly right and wrap Jamie's fish which goes berserk on the wire. I left the boat in about a 2-knot left circle and managed to get the fish controlled. Amidst tons of white water, Jamie grabbed a second gaff from the tower leg and sent it home. Three bigeye on deck and four still on. We've played this drill out many times.

Things calm down some. The fish have spread out pretty well, a decent amount of line now resides on the remaining reels and in the distance, the birds, whales and porpoises are still going berserk. The bite is still on, the door still open. This fight must end and we must get back in the game.

Roaring in reverse, the three of us take line back. I expect the hooks to pull on at least two fish. But, as I go forward we still have them all. One by one we catch and boat them. We have gone seven-for-seven on bigeye tuna with the smallest being 272 pounds dressed, well over 300 pounds whole. High-fiving and hugging in the cockpit, two facts stared us in the face. One, we are in Hydro, and two, we just went seven-for-seven on bigeye. The battle took about two hours and we had about an hour and twenty minutes before sunset.

The teak deck ran crimson red. I headed back to the bite while Jamie carefully removed the heads and the guts, and then took a brass tube and removed the core nerve down the spine. Jamie picks up these leaden fish by himself, first unloading ice from the main coffin so the tuna can stack all the way to the bottom — no easy task. Jamie does it to perfection. The fish sleep. Jamie adds Kosher salt to the coffin to lower the freezing temperature. The success or the failure of this trip ultimately comes down to Jamie and Mike's constant supervision of ice, salt and the resulting saltwater brine. Some 100 nautical miles from home at 12 knots leaves plenty of time for poorly iced fish to lose quality!

We had a tradition aboard, reserved for Mike and Jamie in the cockpit. In some ways savage, but part of the hunt nonetheless and it may have been no different among the cave men celebrating a kill with their wooden spears. One by one, the crew threw the tuna heads overboard usually accompanied by war screams… really cool to hear similar in the Civil War when the Calvary galloped forward with swords drawn towards the enemy screaming at the top of their lungs.

With the cockpit clear, slippery blood hosed out the scuppers and everything put back into its place, I neared the bite again. By golly, Jamie had us on the east wall — exactly where I don't normally fish and exactly where I told him NOT to go. The water on the east side of the canyon a cobalt blue. On the west side a sickly green and ugly. Add to that a four-degree temperature break, from 68 to 72.4. Nearby, no fewer than 15 finback whales fed aggressively; Hundreds of "Stormy petrels" commonly called Mother Carey's Chickens joined the fray. I love the distinctive smell of the fish oil that floats to the surface as a result of the massive carnage and death occurring below. It has a pungent smell like rotting watermelon. Acres of bottlenose dolphin also joined the feast.

With the entire Porcupine Rig out, the yellowfin tuna took their turn at the attack in one of the most amazing bites I have ever witnessed. At times, three 60- to 90-pound yellowfin tried to eat one lure. Mayhem! We became speechless. I finally found my voice and yelled to Mike, "How many on?" "We're full up. Nine on," he replied. Again, one by one, rod over and rod under, the exercise played out to perfection. All nine yellowfin landed in the cooler — three of them bearing the Allison tuna characteristics of dorsal fins that curved, reaching back towards the tail. As the sun started to sink on the horizon, we had one more bite ahead of us and we prayed for bigeye. We ended up harvesting a double, a triple, and a couple of singles just as darkness settled — all yellowfin.

Exhausted, no breeze, a ripping current underneath us and a welcoming night sky overhead, the three of us dined on the coffin table. We nuked two Hungry-man dinners each in the microwave. Somewhere in our tiredness came the realization of how privileged we were to be where we were, when we were, and to have participated in this great event. That night we didn't chum or chunk for tuna, nor did we drop big swordfish squids down into the deep. We just slept. Zero-four-thirty hours would come soon enough. With nobody on watch except our radar proximity alarm, we all slept soundly on a flat-calm ocean.

As expected, morning did arrive accompanied by a light northwesterly breeze that put just a ripple on the surface. The entire ocean sat like a pancake accentuated only by the current rips. We had drifted 14 miles to the northwest while we slept. I ran back to where the bite had been yesterday to find gulls, terns and Mother Carey's Chickens rafting up in massive groups, but no surface activity whatsoever. Most of the birds kept putting their heads below the surface looking for what they hoped was to come. Porpoises and whales must have been busy elsewhere, replaced by migrating hammerhead sharks that seemingly flooded the canyon. I worked a two-square-mile area on the canyon's east side from 97 to 300 fathoms on and off the 100-fathom line.

We had already christened Jamie "Sasquatch" as he was just a big, gentle, soft-spoken guy. All three of us were coffee fanatics. I raised my mug to Jamie and Mike and said in a deep voice, like how I imagined King Arthur sounded,

"Let this area be known as Sasquatch Alley!" To this day it is known as such to those truly in the game.

During the first four hours of morning, we landed six more bigeye tuna with a double header and a four-banger, totaling 13 big eyes for the trip, plus we boated 17 yellowfin tuna. We even picked up a little white marlin which Jamie released. After the release, Jamie came to the bridge and I asked the boys to get the spread out. "We're done! Full up! We can catch no more!" Jamie said, meaning that all the coolers, the coffin, refrigerator and absolutely every other orifice that could contain ice was now packed full of fish.

A canyon fisherman's worst nightmare is losing his ice. Given too much time, that combination of crushed ice, salt, seawater and fish melts the ice down to where you could lose it all. We discussed how long it would take to get back to Shinnecock. I estimated about 17 hours. "How's the ice?" I asked. Jamie answered, "Good but marginal." Jamie felt the 17-hour trip would be too long. Now I had to decide… Do I run for Montauk, Block Island, Martha's Vineyard, Nantucket, or New Bedford, Massachusetts? I chose Nantucket.

In beautiful calm seas, a run to Shinnecock would take about a 17 hours. Montauk was about 40 miles closer. Neither seemed ideal. So, run to Nantucket, Block, or Martha's Vineyard. Nantucket — the closest – sat about 110 nautical miles distant if I went around the eastern side of the island, but about 90 miles if I went direct, through Dead Man Shoals, a very tricky slew of sand bars and shoals. I had done it before and the quality of our catch would depend on it.

We pulled up the riggers, Jamie organized the cockpit to perfection, Mike cleaned and vacuumed the salon, and I announced our plans: "Boys, we are going to Nantucket!" With great smiles on their faces over the adventure to come, Mike and Sasquatch went to their respective bunks and slept without interruption for the next ten hours. We were Nantucket bound. *Makaira* made history that day in Hydro.

44-foot Ridgeway Makaira in Hydrographer

Chapter Fifteen
NANTUCKET BOUND

AFTER OUR TWO-DAY blitzkrieg in Hydrographer followed by ten solid hours at the helm, I found myself in what I call Dead Man's Channel in Nantucket. Muskeget Channel (its real name) sits just east of Wasque Shoal with Martha's Vineyard to the west and Muskeget and Tuckernuck Islands to the east. The official government information says: "Muskeget Channel is an opening six miles wide on the south side of Nantucket Sound between Muskeget and Chappaquiddick Islands. The channel is subject to numerous shifting shoals. Although this channel is partly buoyed, *strangers should never attempt it* as tidal currents with velocities of 2 to 5 knots make navigation dangerous. The currents through the channel are strong, having a velocity of 3.8 knots on the flood and 3.3 knots on the ebb about 1.5 miles east of Wasque Point." Using NOAA chart 13237 of Nantucket Sound and Approaches, I navigated around the east side of Nantucket. To someone born on the island, this channel probably poses no challenge. To someone who visits only occasionally, it qualifies as inspiration for a heart attack.

We were blessed with a beautiful day and the sand shoals, ever moving with the vagaries of North Atlantic weather, definitely had the hair on the back of my neck standing straight up. Jamie and Mike, with spirits as high as they can get, joined me on the bridge. We were young and free and had accomplished things that few people do or even see in their entire lives. Yep… we were pretty full of ourselves, and now we got to lay over in beautiful Nantucket for a couple of days!

Jamie indicated that we had about two hours left on our ice so if we had not made the Nantucket decision, we would have lost all our fish. We made it around the east side of the island and executed our approach to Nantucket Island safe and sound, though several times during our approach, I almost ran *Makaira* aground. With God as my witness, the fathom markings on the chart as well as those indicated in feet, just were not true that day. As I looked down at the sea bottom the charts looked like they lied to me. I will never know the exact approach I did make to the island but I can guarantee one thing, I couldn't do it twice in a row.

We rounded the "NB" buoy at the approach to the harbor and slid easily past Coatue Point, made a gentle turn to port past Brant Point and finally settled in at the fancy town docks called the Nantucket Boat Basin. We docked in the company of mega-yachts from 80 to 200 feet and 100+-foot sailboats; their numerous crews running around in stylish white Lacoste designer shirts replete with the yacht's name, topsiders, and of course, Nantucket red shorts!

The dock master gave us a good slip as I knew him from previous expeditions. I brought *Makaira* to a gentle berth. What a contrast between us and the other stellar yachts in the marina! *Makaira* with its three center riggers, two wing riggers and two 50-foot-long, triple-spreader outriggers, 11 rods in cockpit holders, straight gaffs hanging from the tower ladder, a monstrous coffin in the cockpit, and fuel drums tied to the bow made us a curious anomaly at the marina.

As usual, word that we had arrived spread quickly. My career bordered on celebrity at that point, writing the back page of *Sport Fishing* magazine, being featured in *Marlin* magazine as being one of the top captains in the world as well as being featured in *Sports Illustrated* in a four-page special.

All three of us walked up to the marina office and requested 2,000 pounds of ice. Then the arduous task of carrying 100-pound bags down the dock took place. Many of the local fishermen helped and it looked like an African safari with a line of people carrying big bags of ice on their backs. Jamie drained all the ice water from every cooler and coffin. Because of that, every seagull in Nantucket came to see us starting an absolute riot. The minute before we arrived, Nantucket Boat Basin fitted its reputation as a place of proper conduct and bobby socks. Ten minutes later you could feel the excitement as we unloaded our catch, re-iced and placed the fish gently back in the coolers.

Seventeen big yellowfin and thirteen huge bigeye tuna covered the entire deck. The dock had standing room only. Jamie had done a spectacular job with the ice. The fish were primo. The last fish was loaded and our catch, once again, rested safe and secure.

During mid-summer, Nantucket becomes a playground for the rich and famous. Punctuated with palatial estates on the southwestern part of the island which transitions from verdant green farmland and underbrush then catapults down gigantic rock cliffs to a rocky shoreline. The beauty of this island simply takes your breath away. The island's neat as a pin with white picket fences, upscale retail shops of every description, and superb restaurants. Everyone in the Northeast who owns a large yacht always makes sure to have a visit to Nantucket on their social calendar.

Two cultures coexist here: one of working people, mostly fishermen and service personnel, and summer visitors. The *Makaira* crew was welcomed by the local fishing community. As I recall, Jamie and Mike made a smoking-hot deal with five of the local restaurants, selling our catch at record prices! My crew were happy with money in their pocket and a lot of it. So, for the next two days, we enjoyed some of the best fluke fishing known to man. We had a great time relaxing together. One of the most hilarious moments of the trip was Sasquatch, Mike, and I renting single-gear, beach-cruiser bicycles with little baskets on the front. If you could see Sasquatch on a bicycle you would fall to your knees laughing. We rode all around the island, each of us having close calls hitting tourists. Looking back, this was unbridled fun. If I only could have shared it with my father.

The weather during our stay remained picture perfect. The island enjoyed a gentle breeze, different than the type you have offshore. It had the smell of low tide and the fragrances of salt, land, flowers, seaweed, and fish oil that the crews of the sailing ships of yore must have adored when coming back from their whaling trips. We caught some real big door-mat fluke, and each night we cooked our catch at the marina, providing tuna appetizers to the entire dock from our offshore catch. Without exaggeration, we were superstars.

A fat cat making millions of dollars a year screwing people on Wall Street, basking on his 90-foot yacht could never become us. Just as much as he knew it, I knew that I couldn't be him. I was living my life the right way for me.

The next morning, after refueling with what I called "golden fuel" (man alive was it expensive!), we ran back around the east side of Nantucket heading to Shinnecock. The chart read 115 nautical miles to the inlet. We eventually tied up at Indian Cove Marina, whence I grudgingly flew back to the office and went to work. Our next canyon trip would be in six days. Mike and Jamie could have two days off, and then spend four days prepping for our upcoming trip. Life was truly good.

Chapter Sixteen
CANOE PADDLES REQUIRED

FOR A SHORT while prior to my father's stomach cancer being diagnosed, Dad was OK and vicariously enjoyed traveling with me in pursuit of some of the largest fish on earth.

I had heard from many people that Prince Edward Island — in particular, North Lake — qualified as the finest giant bluefin tuna fishery in the world. I heard it from the world famous Murray Brothers, fellow Long Islanders, pioneers in all sorts of fishing techniques, and manufacturers of some of the finest fishing chairs and equipment. I also learned (through scuttlebutt) that you needed a special invitation from the Canadian government to fish there. True or not, I also heard of alleged huge payoffs to Canadian officials to allow you to enter the fishery as an American citizen.

I became absolutely convinced an inside deal was needed. Some anglers told me that the season was extremely short — lasting only a few weeks as the area marked the northern most part of the bluefin migration. Every single time I tried to pin someone down for information on how I could go there, I felt the response was extremely guarded. I called the Bluefin Hotel in North Lake and a nice chap answered the phone. In a Prince Edward Island accent, the gent said he knew of a man who fished for giant bluefin tuna but he didn't know if he had a fighting chair on his boat. He told me he fed his dogs bluefin tuna all winter. In any event, before I knew it I was in touch with Captain Morgan who owned a lobster boat. I didn't ask any more questions about permits, licenses or anything. I just chartered the boat over the phone, sent the man a certified check for three days of fishing, and planned the trip for the middle of September. I could not believe that after all I'd heard it was so easy. Nonetheless, I would only believe it when I actually boarded the boat and went fishing.

In the early and mid-1970s Prince Edward Island and the Port of North Lake produced some of the largest giant bluefin tuna in the world. And contrary to what I'd heard, there appeared to be no major regulations concerning the fishery, no particular sport-fishing presence in the area, and certainly no marketing or promotion of the fishery. Looking back, I believe a very lucky few kept this fishery a well-guarded secret.

When it came to giant bluefin tuna fishing, the Murray Brothers – then of Palm Beach, Florida — unequivocally held the exalted status as the movers and shakers in the sport. They had invented and reinvented the sport more times before breakfast than I could in a lifetime. I had fished next to them all through the northeast, but unfortunately we also bumped heads in philosophies on Block Island, Nantucket, and Montauk. Frank Murray, viewed me as a snot-nosed kid but with a lot of passion. As time passed, he grudgingly viewed me as *the* canyon-fishing expert for my knowledge of bigeye tuna. I learned to accept the entire family as the absolute experts in giant bluefin tuna. The Murray Brothers had their retail tackle and fighting chair business based in Florida. Most of my fishing centered out of Shinnecock Inlet in New York so once they moved south from Long Island, we kept apart for a long time.

On a mid-September day, Dad and I planned to fly from Westchester County Airport directly to Charlottetown Airport located on Prince Edward Island; a fairly routine flight that afforded us some time to work on a new airplane leasing company.

An investor wanted Joseph T. Barta Associates to be a 50 percent partner. My father had me in mind to run the company, but I was totally against the idea because I believed I would make considerably less in this new venture. I didn't even attempt to hide my reasoning and told Dad. Dad came back at me with, "You're only thinking about yourself." I told him I agreed wholeheartedly. That was exactly what I was thinking and the conversation ended quickly. It wasn't any real big deal.

It dawned a glorious September day. I fueled our King Air 200 and as always, followed the factory ground check list. The ground crew pumped 300 gallons in for the flight at hand. I climbed into the King Air and reviewed the flight plan which my co-pilot had laid out. Our flight plan called the trip 555 nautical miles, a 2-1/2 hour flight. The aircraft held 486 gallons of fuel and had a maximum takeoff weight of 12,500 pounds. It cruised at about 270 knots with a range of 1,500 nautical miles. The flight distance posed no problem at all. We had a spectacular tail wind of 80 knots at a flight level of 210, pilot talk for 21,000 feet. It was nice not having to worry about the weight and balance with just three people on board and two curved-butt 130 rods and tackle. Ignoring fuel management also gave me joy.

Dad showed up looking like *his* flight plan took him to the Breakers Hotel in Palm Beach. A touch embarrassing to be honest. He wore his old-style white buck shoes, pleated white yachting pants, and a highly starched Brooks Brothers shirt. Of course he had the power-broker brown leather briefcase with the Wall Street Journal neatly tucked under his arm, and a ridiculous Scottish-type chapeau. I – on the other hand — came ready to fish! Khaki pants, a blue fishing shirt with *Makaira* embroidered on the left pocket, topsiders, and a standard dark-blue fishing jacket that everyone seemed to be wearing at the time.

The flight went well, and with the great tail winds, went by unusually quickly. Clearing customs in Charlottetown took no effort at all. I remember being asked by the customs agent what I was going to do in Prince Edward Island. When I mentioned I was attempting to catch a giant bluefin tuna he asked what I was going to do with the fish if I did catch one. I told him I was probably going to release the fish so it could fight another day. I remember he just couldn't quite grasp the concept and said, "Why would you fight something so big and then let it go. It seems so stupid!"

The biggest stumbling block to chartering in Prince Edward Island at the time turned out to be a real dearth of big-game fishing boats. None were on the entire island near as I could tell. Our particular fishing guide was only available Wednesday through Friday and I don't remember if I ever asked why. Anyway after being picked up at the airport in a friend-of-a-friend-of-a-friend's pickup, we headed down Route 2 through some incredibly beautiful countryside.

Prince Edward Island qualifies as one of the most beautiful places I have ever seen in my life. Everything shone a rich, beautiful green. The landscape was punctuated by one church after another with every church the family center of that township. Oh, and every building gleamed! Maintained to white-painted perfection. On the very northeastern tip of Prince Edward Island, sits the town and harbor of North Lake. North Lake had a small inlet with an interior lake harboring a fleet of New England-style lobster boats and ground-fishing vessels. I'm telling you that if you want a gorgeous drive, take Route 2, which turns into Route 16 at St. Peters Cable Head and Goose River. It couldn't be prettier. As we passed St. Margaret's Bay we passed one of the quaintest churches. Little anchorages riddled every turn in the road and each one had four or five lobster boats. I felt like I had walked into an oil painting.

As we neared our destination. I remember thinking to myself, "People who take such magnificent care of their boats, houses and churches must live under a wonderful fabric of moral code." Needless to say, evidence abounded that the residents here were very thankful for what they have and take care of it all to a very high standard.

Father's staff had rented us a quaint cottage in the town of Campbell's Cove which abuts the provincial park of Prince Edward Island. The rented cottage was a very simple three- bedroom house of about 900 square feet. It sported a wood stove in the middle of the common area and a stack of freshly cut cord wood on the porch. I'd sum up our accommodations as old yet immaculate, the type of place that made you wonder who stayed there before you. In my case, I wondered whether other giant tuna fishermen from other parts of the world may have rested their heads on my same pillow.

After we settled in we ended up in North Lake to do a little bit of sightseeing. After an hour of walking around we met a local fisherman just coming off his lobster boat. He informed us our captain had mentioned to him that he had a charter and he would meet us at eight the following morning. Dad and I spent the rest of the day touring the island. Every district had delicious fresh pies for sale. Each town looked absolutely immaculate. As a matter of fact, one of the best parts was between the main city of Charlottetown to North Lake, all the way across the island, I didn't see one piece of trash anywhere… not even a candy wrapper. This place got lost in time. I felt a pretty strict Christian conservative vibe about the place.

The next morning Dad and I waited at the dock. Along came a pickup truck with — of all things — a barber chair in the back. Three men hopped out of the truck and carried the barber's chair to a 36-foot, single-engine wooden lobster boat. The barber's chair slid over the top of a stanchion, not in the cockpit but rather, on the gunwale. They secured the stanchion with a large metal strap that went across the back of the transom and wrapped around the inside of the cockpit wall, finally bolting to the deck. I freely admit to being absolutely flabbergasted! The chair had the angler literally sitting over the water. If that wasn't enough of a shock, the metal chair boasted some kind of coffee basket on the armrest and the footrest was a wooden milk crate placed so a person could actually use it for fishing.

Now I understood why you could only fish on Wednesday, Thursday and Friday. The answer was simple. They needed the fighting chair on Saturdays to give haircuts in the local community. On Sunday no one on the island seemed to work due to it being a day for prayer, church, family, and community service. Coming from the Hamptons, I never realized anywhere in the world still had such a simple lifestyle!

On our first day fishing, our crew consisted of the lobsterman, the town barber, Dad, and myself. I had brought two curved-butt 130s loaded with Cortland black Dacron line with 70 feet of 300-pound mono attached with a Chinese splice. My large tackle box contained 19 din piano wire, hooks, swivels, crimpers, and everything you might need to go giant bluefin tuna fishing. Luckily, I had brought my tackle box because the boat had not an ounce of tackle anywhere. I began to really worry when I noticed we had no harpoon or gaff either!

If you are a fisherman, please sit down. You won't believe this.

On board, I found two Old Towne canoe paddles with lead sheathing attached to their leading edges. When I asked their purpose, the Captain told me if we caught a fish, we would drag it into shallow water and literally beat the fish to death. In my entire fishing career, I had never heard of a technique quite like this. When I asked them how many fish they had caught using this method, he answered, "Not very many. Most of them got away." Add to the paddles and the end game, the boat had no bait on board. Eventually, I had so many questions, and got such ridiculous answers every time I asked that eventually I just stopped asking. Dad and I went with the flow. Our charter had claimed lunch included, and yet I could not find one molecule of food on board.

It was chilly and overcast as we headed out from North Lake, with no depth finder, LORAN, or radar — literally no electronics! But we did have a small wood stove forward between two bunks. Did you hear that? Yes, a wood stove, and a small bundle of kindling next to it. The stove sat on two red bricks and the exhaust chimney went out the front deck where a one-pound coffee can sat on top of the chimney so no salt water would put the fire out. I always thought wood boats and wood stoves didn't really go together well. Disbelief!

Shortly after leaving the dock, we stopped in what appeared to me as a non-descript piece of water and our professional crew unraveled two hand lines with six hooks each — white strands of a rope tied around each hook. After two jigs each, both hand lines came up loaded up with Boston mackerel eight to 12 inches long. The entire bait catching operation took maybe two minutes. As they reeled up the hand lines on two coffee cans I asked if we had enough bait. They replied, "More than enough!"

I handed our mate (the town barber), a 12-foot long, doubled #19 wire leader attached to a Mustad triple X tuna hook. He took one mackerel, drove the hook through the chin of the fish and out the other side. Then said, "Let's go fishing." Upon seeing this I said, "Do you mind if I rig the bait?" "No problem," he replied. Using a needle and waxed thread I rigged a perfect mackerel daisy chain using six of the mackerel. The hooked bait — rigged to perfection — had the hook coming out the anus of the bait and sewn to the tail. We traveled at least another six minutes from where we caught the mackerel. The captain pulled us back from our 8-knot cruising speed to a 2-knot trolling speed.

With all the time and effort I had put into making this a perfect trip with my father, I started to get angry. This entire operation seemed to be a farce and I could swear they acted out this comedy just to make fun of us. We trolled in no more than 70 feet of water. Everywhere I looked I saw sand bars. We were so close to the beach that I could actually see a man reading a newspaper. I think with a good set of binoculars I could have read the headlines. What a joke!

Three hours of empty trolling passed before I asked, "What is for lunch?" The mackerel leftover after making the daisy chain had been sitting on the deck, neither refrigerated nor on ice. The mate reeled in my daisy chain, cutting two mackerel off the top and put the rig back out. Taking the two mackerel, he walked down to the wood stove and commenced cutting the mackerel into two inch pieces, adding onion and slices of potato. He then announced proudly, "Lunch will be served in 30 minutes." And so it was. He handed both Dad and I each a fork. The captain and mate each had a fork, too and so we passed the pan of mackerel, onion, and potato stew around until it disappeared. To this day, I count that as one of the finest meals I've ever had.

Twenty minutes after lunch, I noticed a brown streak coming towards the boat. It looked exactly like the propeller of any vessel getting too close to a mud bottom and kicking up silt. The streak kept getting closer and closer. In the back of my mind, I kept thinking, "Harbor seals." Moments later a black Volkswagen bus emerged from the depths and engulfed not only the hooked bait but all four mackerel on the daisy chain in one bite! I had the strike drag set at 22 pounds and line screamed off the reel. We had hooked up to one of the largest bluefin I have ever seen! Dad climbed into the barber's chair. I had brought a Murray Brother's bucket harness and with the clips crisscrossed on the reel, the battle began.

I never found out how shallow it was exactly, but as we fought the fish, it became very evident to me that a safety line from the back of the bucket harness to the aft cleat would be a good idea, so I made it happen. Dad struggled under about 55 pounds of drag. The stump puller rod I brought bent right over. I must grudgingly admit that our captain did a magnificent job of handling the huge fish. We fought the fish for 35 minutes with the leader out of the water for more than half of the fight thanks to the incredibly shallow water. Everywhere the fish went it left a contrail of silt. The good thing about that, though… the tuna couldn't dive! It had nowhere to go. What a surreal adventure!

I steered the back of the fighting chair so my father could face the fish, and the pedestal issued an awful squeal every time the chair turned. Out came a can of 30-weight Rotilla engine oil which the mate poured over the stanchion collar quieting things down quite a bit. The fish started to tire so I called for an official release — meaning the top of the leader touches the rod tip. Not surprisingly, this meant nothing to our crew. The captain headed towards a very narrow channel which lead between two sand spits. I swear it looked like he planned to beach the boat. As he passed through this extremely narrow maybe 40-foot wide channel, the giant bluefin tuna followed us closely. We had very little line out. The captain then turned right around the last sand spit, added throttle and the giant tuna beached itself on the sand bank. Sand, seaweed, and mussel shells flew everywhere as the mighty fish tried its best to get back into the water.

The captain backed up to the sand bank as the barber fishing mate threw me an Old Towne paddle. He jumped off the boat, yelling for me to follow. We ran down the sand spit with paddles in hand and beat the tuna into submission. The captain tossed a rusted meat hook up onto the beach and we placed it through the lip of the tuna and, with both of us covered in mud, got the fish farther up the sand where it expired. I didn't know whether to laugh, cry, or yell for joy. In my entire fishing career, I had never seen anything like it. Next, we threaded a hefty anchor rope through the gill and out the mouth of the tuna and towed the giant fish off the sand bar and back to our dock in North Lake which, even after a full day of fishing, stood less than a mile away.

Standing up on the bridge, the captain announced proudly, "Good job. That's how we do it in Prince Edward Island!" As we closed on the dock and the lobsterman's mooring, the captain said, "Do you want to weigh that thing?" "Absolutely," I replied.

Apparently it cost $100 to weigh it — a lot of money in those days, especially in Prince Edward Island. A butcher located somewhere mid-island had a large Chattilon balance beam scale on which he weighed cows. With the $100 in hand, the scale headed our way. A nearby construction project required another $50 to have one of the local excavators bring a backhoe to lift the bluefin tuna up to the scale. What a total circus! The scale mounted to the backhoe and the tuna to the scale. Up and up they raised the fish. Finally, the great fish's head left the sand and tipped the balance beam — reading 962 pounds! What an incredible giant — at the time, the largest ever caught on rod and reel.

We had chartered the boat for three days, but after seeing the operation that caught this fish, quite honestly I feared for my father's life. This had turned out to be a dangerous adventure. The bolts attaching the fighting chair to the transom as well as its supporting angle irons were already very loose. The technique of beaching a fish and then beating it to death with canoe paddles also did nothing to allay my safety concerns. On the other hand, 962 pounds! A BIG fish.

Ultimately, over time, this fishery grew up. As the Murray Brothers and other great fishermen brought their own boats to North Lake and the years passed, several anglers caught fish over 1,000 pounds! This wild tuna trip has always been a favorite story of mine to tell, and to this day I have never seen something like this again. So here's to canoe paddles, the beautiful island of Prince Edward, and the people who live there.

As we flew back to Westchester County Airport, I still could not believe how big the fish was and the techniques used to catch the fish. Now, some 40 years later, the giant bluefin tuna fishing era has caught up with North Lake. Some boats have caught and released up to 60 fish a day by chumming them up right next to the boat. Every technique imaginable has been used, trolling, chunking, and even kite fishing. Still today, some of the largest bluefin tuna in the world come from North Lake, Prince Edward Island. I can guarantee you one thing though, no one today kills their fish with canoe paddles.

Follow Tred's swordfishing trip with his father, Joseph Barta, by viewing the following chart.

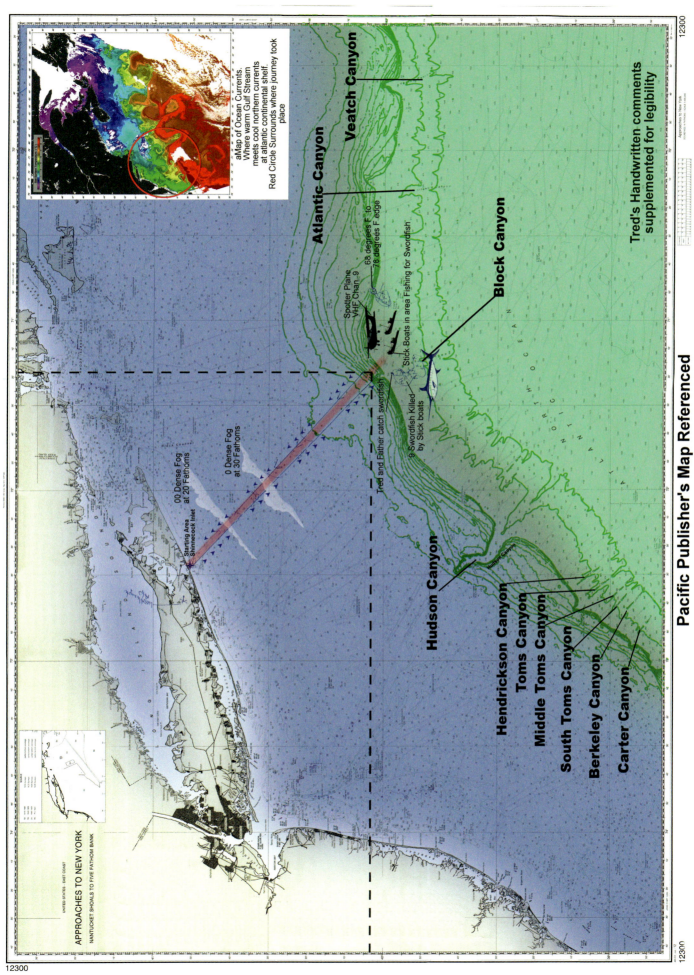

Chapter Seventeen
WHEN THE EARTH STOOD STILL

MY FATHER, JOSEPH Barta, allowed me to call him "Dad" in private but required me to call him "Sir" in public. He divorced from my mother, Judy Barta, several years earlier. There was a great schism in the family during their divorce as family members took sides during the dividing of assets. The battle for assets had to be court examined. To me it became a very ugly and unfair process.

Father had financed the "Ball Boy Company" which manufactured tennis teaching aids for instructors of the sport, founded by my mother. This company required hundreds of thousands of dollars in capital and a manufacturing facility in Bronxville, New York. My mother was extremely active in promoting her career and the businesses in which she was involved. They required her to play tennis, ride horses and in many ways, be seen in the industries that she represented. It is important to know that I really never saw my parents as parents, as the real disciplines of life were taught to me by other means.

The truth be told, I don't remember my father as a father or my mother as a mother in the sense that most people do because in truth I was hardly ever home. I obviously loved my family and my mother was truly a great woman in her own right. However, as I write this, it's hard for me to remember any tender moments from either of them. I do specifically remember a common conflict in my youth that other peoples' parents were always there to support them when they fell and to hold them when they needed help and love. All I remember is being criticized and pushed to the limit of everything I did so I looked at my parents like aggressive athletic coaches.

My pseudo-uncle, Eric Bergmark, who obvious to me, was my mother's lover previous to the divorce, was her business partner in Ball Boy Company. I know that profanity is not becoming of a gentleman but this entire thing was an effing mess. It was dirty, and to be honest it felt like the show "Dallas". On the other hand, my father was madly in love with Leona Impastato, my father's secretary and confidant at Joseph T. Barta Associates. She was everything my mother wasn't: soft, kind, caring, nurturing, and supportive. I had worked for my father for almost ten years and in our office I worked 18- ¾ inches from his desk. There was nothing I did not know.

Ball Boy Corporation never made a profit and although it churned a lot of money it never paid back to my father the massive amount of capital that he'd invested. Giving full credit to my mother, I believe she worked extremely hard at making a go of it. My mother was very smart and not lazy. But she had no business sense, and despite doing all the right things at the right time, she just could not make any of her ideas profitable. All of us have met people like that.

My mother pretended not to be spoiled, but the net is we always had live-in maids, the grounds taken care of by others, and the help did the cooking and laundry. I am not painting a bad picture of my mother, but she did not have the distractions that most women have and could focus all of her attention on her business. Yet the truth be told she never made a dime and neither did Eric. Obviously my father did what he did because at one time he loved my mother and wanted her to succeed in her dream.

The mainframe of the Ball Boy Corporation was the ball-throwing machine and the rebound net, invented and brought to fruition with Eric's brilliant architectural and engineering background. This was an electric machine on wheels that threw tennis balls across the net at different speeds and varying trajectories. If you were practicing hard, down-the-line backhand hits and were weak at the shot, the Ball Boy machine could be positioned to duplicate that shot time and time again.

Most of the family businesses were fun in my father's absence. I remember going to the Ball Boy offices and fishing for carp on a river that ran through town near the office. My recollection of my father's brokerage and my mother's tennis school and real estate developments are however fleeting memories.

We lived in an 8,000 square foot, stone mansion comprised of manicured lawn tennis courts, stone dunking pools, a formal rose garden equal to any castle's in England, thousands upon thousands of dollars in maintenance vehicles including tractors, lawn cutters, blowers, and a team of four people who came with the property as maintenance staff. Two lovely women handled the daily operation inside the home.

My mother rarely cooked and was lousy at it. My father hated this fact. My favorite helper was Alba May. I believe she was an angel and I loved this woman deeply. The estate had hidden passage ways and dumbwaiters. When I was punished at the dining room table and sat for hours refusing to eat my green beans, Alba May would come to my rescue. She would send up chocolate cake with a cold glass of milk via the dumbwaiter after the conflict was over. Alba May was one of those women who literally set the standard of what I appreciate today. She was kind, supportive, and proud. She loved her family and she loved me like I was her family. So it hurt me terribly at the dinner table when my mother used to ring a bell and ask the most trivial requests of Alba May. Alba scurried from the kitchen to the dining room to meet my mother's request such as "can I have a little more tartar sauce" or "more ice in her water glass". This type of behavior turned my stomach. It enraged me. It was not how I wanted to live. My father didn't buy the act either.

In any event the divorce got ugly. Finally, my father bought a mini-mansion in Chappaqua and married Leona. My mother and sister remained at odds in my life. Leona was a wonderful woman, and rather than whip my father on the tennis court, she preferred holding hands with him in public. My mother thought this extremely demeaning as it apparently diminished her womanhood. Leona loved dining with my father and enjoying a good meal. My mother gobbled a meal down, calling it only fuel. Her seemingly favorite activity was berating, embarrassing, and emasculating every man she came in contact with.

At this — the best time of my father's life – he developed incurable stomach cancer. After his diagnosis, Father and I planned to go fishing, so we flew to Suffolk County Airport (FOK), which was renamed in 1991 to Francis S. Gabreski Airport. The approach to the airport was a piece of cake. I flew the King Air A-100 single pilot while Dad remained in the aft cabin during the short flight from Westchester. We loaded our gear into my camouflage-colored Bronco and drove to Indian Cove Marina. Father, a mate and I were heading for an overnight fishing trip in the canyon aboard my 32-foot Prowler named *Makaira*. At departure time, we couldn't find the mate as some crisis in his family caused him to get drunk the day before. Here we go... just Dad and me.

A lot of people back in the day said that I was reckless, stupid, arrogant, and ignorant. When the fog was close to zero visibility, you'd find many of them drinking hard liquor around noon. I wasn't afraid of the fog. To me, it represented an opportunity to hone my navigational skills and literally be able to fish because of that well-honed skill set rather than sit on the dock drinking and criticizing those that went.

Indian Cove Marina conveniently nestled on the Shinnecock Canal (4700 feet long) just before the great Peconic Bay Canal lock system (250 feet by 41 feet) which allowed you to pass from Shinnecock Bay to Peconic Bay. The lock system built in 1919 gave fishermen or yachtsmen complete access from Hampton Bays, New York to Montauk and onwards to Block Island, Martha's Vineyard, Nantucket, and eastbound. If you wished to visit the Connecticut coast, New York City or the Hudson River, the locks saved you from needing to travel all the way around the south shore of Long Island, Montauk and then back into Long Island Sound, saving a great deal of time. In severe weather most yachtsmen were afraid to run Shinnecock Inlet. A terrifying inlet in a blow, many have died there over the years trying to use it coming and going. Consequently, when they deemed the weather too hard, scary, or rough, most people would go fluke and sea trout fishing in a magnificent Shinnecock Bay instead.

On this particular day, Shinnecock Inlet roared from a storm that mixed the ocean up like an egg beater. A blanket of fog covered her with 1/8-mile visibility. People and their trucks lined the inlet shores waiting for someone with enough guts (or stupidity if they had no skills) to take the Atlantic on and enter the arena via Shinnecock Inlet. They wanted someone to die similar to people wanting to see people crash in a Formula One race or someone fall to their knees in a prize boxing fight.

The north and south outer jetty LORAN numbers are ingrained in my mind to this day. Dad and I pulled out of the Indian Cove Marina into a terrible wet fog that formed water droplets on our glasses and eyebrows. Yet, you could feel the warmth of the sun as it tried to burn off the fog. In short order we crossed the East Channel, wrapping its way around a large sand bar that separates the Atlantic Ocean from Shinnecock Bay. Through the inlet we went, intercepting Dune Road on the west side of the inlet and Meadow Lane on the east. The inlet's fog horn bellowed above the crashing ocean surf, punctuated by the lonely moaning sound of the Shinnecock sea buoy. This combination literally scared the crap out of 98 percent of all offshore fishermen. Only a handful of stupid people would venture out onto the ocean on this particular day.

At the time, I wished I could paint some particular drama, an act of heroism on my part, especially as captain in command, in front of my father but couldn't. I picked my way through just another moderately rough inlet covered with a blanket of fog. We set course to the Fishtail Canyon, also referred to as Block Canyon, on heading of 165 degrees and 64.7 nautical miles, cruising at about 27 knots.

As we passed 20 fathoms, the dense fog line setting atop the flat-calm ocean came to an abrupt end. Suddenly, brilliant sunshine washed over *Makaira*. It turned out to be a truly spectacular day on the ocean. The sea reminded me of a carpet in someone's living room; soft and inviting. It felt almost like a fairy tale. The entire Shinnecock fleet, with but a few exceptions, lay in their boat slips for the day, making fun of those who ventured out. We almost had the ocean to ourselves.

Dad and I wanted to try to catch a swordfish, either by day-time baiting methods or by night-time drifting with monster squids at depths down to about 600 feet. At night, swordfish would feed just above the thermocline — a moving temperature gradient that only the unknown controls.

I spied a stick boat from Nantucket on the horizon. A New England stick boat — usually a converted down-east lobster boat — sports a tall mast steadied by four main stay cables. One cable attached to the bow, one each attached to the port and starboard gunwales, and the last cable usually fastened to the bridge top. On top of the mast, a crow's nest — a metal cage with a steering wheel and one set of controls — allowed the Skipper to pilot the boat with much improved visibility down into the water. Most of these rigs sported a single engine diesel. Many modern sport fishing boats rely on massive turbocharged diesels to propel them at 30 to 50 knots or more. Attached to the bow of a stick boat, a 20- to 60-foot pulpit jutted out over the water like Pinocchio's nose. When fishing, a man out on the catwalk would thrust his harpoon into the back of a sunning swordfish or a giant tuna, much like the whalers of yore.

A spotting plane usually guided the stick boats to the fish, and on this particular day Neptune himself landed Dad and me in the middle of three stick boats doing their jobs. Two spotting planes circled above. I assumed they took off in the early morning out of New Bedford, Massachusetts. When the plane spied swordfish swimming lazily on the surface, the pilot threw a green dye marker out of the window, marking the general direction for the stick boats to concentrate their efforts. As two planes circled above and three stick boats scurried from one spot to another marked by the spotting plane, Dad and I entered the arena. I actually knew one of the boat captains who lived in Nantucket. Recreational fishermen usually frowned upon spotter planes. However, when they went to the Long Island's east-end restaurants, these same fishermen were quick to order a delicious swordfish steak that most likely came from one of these stick boats.

In *Makaira's* cockpit, a curved-butt 130 and a curved-butt 80 wide sat in their rod holders with 14-inch squid rigged on double #19 wire with two opposing 7754 Mustad open gap hooks ready to hit the water. Upon seeing a swordfish on the ocean's surface, I instructed Dad how much line to let out. With his thumb as the brake, Dad shifted the drag lever into freespool, and all things going correctly, I would pilot *Makaira* so that the squid would end up directly in front of the swordfish.

In the vernacular of our sport, this was called "surface swordfishing," one of the most difficult endeavors in which a sport fishing boat could engage. Ninety-five percent of the time the swordfish wouldn't strike the bait, and if it did, usually either the hook got fouled during the strike or the bill got in the way while it attempted to eat the bait. To the uninformed this must sound ridiculous. But rarely did a classic hookup would take place.

As I trolled the periphery of the three stick boats obviously working together, Dad and I made our first pass on a swordfish easily weighing more than 500 pounds. The coordination between us was flawless. The double-hooked squid slowly passed just under the great sword, triggering it to strike our bait with breathtaking ferocity! What happened next was almost comical. As the swordfish used its massive bill to strike and kill our squid, the bait came flying out of the water some twenty feet directly in front of the sword's mouth. Obviously the swordfish hit the metal leader. The squid was chopped in half and the bait reduced to a big softball which no game fish would dream of eating. Dad reeled the bait in preparing to fire a second bait to it, but by then it had sounded and we could no longer find it. The spotter planes working with the stick boats monitored VHF channel 9 and so did we. During the next four hours the fleet killed more than nine swordfish as the ocean continued being flat as a pane of glass, ideal surface swordfishing conditions.

Small dories launched and collected the harpooned fish and the stick boats' gear. Lime green and orange buoys attached to the end of a rope that in turn attached to the lily (the harpoon tip). The dories would collect the swordfish. One such dory sat dead in the water with four swordfish tied to its gunwales, waiting to be picked up.

If one had told this story back in Shinnecock, which lay in a blanket of fog all day, you'd be laughed off the dock, criticized and ridiculed beyond belief. The net was these people had no clue of what went on right on their Atlantic doorstep. They had neither the guts, skill or the vision to be great. They only lived and carried the vision to fail.

To sportsmen, seeing one swordfish on top per day was in essence a success. Only a few in the world got blessed with the experience to see eight to

10 fish on top in a day. By 6 pm, Dad and I had seen 16 swordfish and baited seven. And still we hadn't hooked up with one single fish. At dusk, we circled to bait our last fish before darkness.

My father was fairly weak from his stomach cancer chemo. The last time they opened him up for a biopsy, his WWII commanding officer came into the hospital room while I was at Dad's side, reached out taking my father's hand and said, "Joe, you're a dead man walking. Your cancer will kill you and the doctors give you two weeks at the most." Dad did not whisper or show any emotion. He merely said, "We all have to die sometime." The end of the day was always Dad's worst time as he ran out of steam. And so it was with our last pass the 80 wide buckled over, line peeling off the reel with about 35 pounds of drag and we hooked up. "Swordfish on! Swordfish on," I yelled.

I got Dad in the fighting chair, buckled him into the harness, and went to battle. Within the first 15 minutes of the fight I used every technique available to try to pull the hooks. Swords are notorious for getting fouled hook. Their mouths are very soft, and often if you don't test the waters early you'll lose the fish hours later. By some amazing feat this fish remained hooked. After about an hour's fighting time, Dad was whipped. So I tied the reel to the fighting chair allowing my father to rest and just turn the handle when the fish gave up some line. Later, in darkness with the tower lights on and going into three hours of fighting time, we had color; you could see the fish's sword and body below us. I had grabbed the leader on three separate occasions but couldn't hold on. Dad threw up, his vomit ending up on his pant legs and the rod itself. Four or five buckets of seawater later, Dad was cleaned up.

On my last wiring attempt, I popped the fish's head up. He was coming right at us. I yelled for Dad to help gaff the fish. My father, completely exhausted, simply couldn't get out of the fighting chair. I triple wrapped the leader with my right hand (potentially, a suicidal move). With my left, I held a Pompanette straight gaff and slammed it into the underbelly of our trophy. I yelled to Dad for a tail rope and for the first time in my life I heard my Dad say, "I can't." When my father said, "I can't" I felt so ashamed. He was a man who had more guts than anyone I knew. A B29 war hero. It was only because of his cancer that he was weak. I exploded with anger and yelled back, "You can and you will!" To this day I am thankful for what happened next, because if it hadn't I might have cut the fish off. I would not have my father fail in front of me even though my entire life he cruelly set me up for failure time and time again.

The next thing I knew Dad gave me a tail rope. I cinched it up. Using a block and tackle, the rope tied around the tail, I attempted to pull the fish up to and over the gunwale. I couldn't do it by myself and Dad was sick and finished. I remember sitting on the gunwale telling myself "use your head and make this work." I affixed another block and tackle to the overhang of the bridge. We now had two lines to the tail and two block and tackles. I grabbed the forward V-bunk cushion and placed it under Dad, had him tie the rope around his waist and wedge his feet against the engine box. As I tightened up on my rope I counted to three and asked Dad to trust me and instructed him to thrust back with all of his might. The V-berth cushion would protect him from getting hurt.

I figured the swordfish would offer a lot of resistance while being dragged over the transom, so I placed a large plastic sheet over the gunwale for the fish to slide over. On the count of three Dad pushed backwards. I pulled like heck and between the two of us, the great swordfish came up and over and slammed onto the deck with a magnificent thump! The fish laid in the cockpit as a gladiator of the sea, its black eye as big as a soft ball. We had done it! I iced the fish down with proper care while Dad laid down on the large couch in the salon — out like a light.

On the radio, I heard about the dense fog blanketing Long Island all weekend. My choices were to stay the evening — the prudent thing to do — or run back home in darkness and fog, and face Shinnecock Inlet on an outgoing tide. Funny... even to this day I'd have made the same decisions with barely a second thought: I just ran. Four hours later we tied up at Indian Cove Marina. I covered Dad with a second blanket and passed off to sleep myself laying on the salon floor.

The night proved extremely short. I awoke to a crowd of people gawking and crawling around the dock for a first glimpse at our fish. I tried to give Dad all of the credit. That evening everyone dined on swordfish steaks. No one believed we fished in sunshine all day. No one believed the stories of stick boats and spotter planes. It was a marvelous trip and one that I will never forget. It proved to me that you should always follow your heart, your instincts, and hone your skills, because one day you'll have to use them.

I will end this adventure by merely saying, "Congratulations. I love you, Dad." Dad died in my arms from stomach cancer just two weeks after this trip. Fortunately, I was not only groomed but had already started to take over my father's business. Life marches on.

"Uncle Eric" and Tred (Joseph Barta in background). Tred in training for biathlon team.

Year Tred won U.S. Junior Championship.
Drafted to University of Colorado and trained at Fort Richards, Alaska with U.S. Junior Biathlon Team.

Chapter Eighteen
MY FATHER'S DEATH

THEY DIAGNOSED FATHER with colon cancer at 61 years old. I consider it a tragedy that my father taught me more about life while dying than while actually living. Looking back, it seems a travesty but true.

Besides being a B29 WWII hero, command pilot, and later taking over the B29 training school, my father was the toughest man I ever met. The best way to describe him would be grace under pressure. The stock market could be tumbling with the potential of losing a small fortune amassed over time with hard work (not luck) yet he never panicked. I always thought it must have something to do with his experiences during the war. Getting stories of Dad's past in the war was like pulling hen's teeth. But one day while having a couple of cocktails at the revered "Quiet Birdmen" — a revered organization of pilots — Dad described one of his missions in detail. I listened in awe. Father made a bombing run with twenty-two B29s in tow. They would drop their payloads on my father's cue. Deep behind enemy lines, they took fire from enemy fighter planes as well as fire power from the ground. He described it as a slaughter. Out of 23 aircraft, they lost 14 birds, each with crews of 7-12. Dad continued to describe the turbulence from the flack and the emotions he felt as his squadron suffered being cut to pieces. My father's aircraft was named "*The Miscarriage*," appropriate since my mother had four miscarriages before I was born. It somehow seemed appropriate because I wasn't born yet.

During this mission, Father endured tremendous damage to his aircraft, the tail partially shot off, the outboard starboard engine and the inboard port engine lost, the fuselage shot to h**l and four crew members dead or dying — their bodies ripped apart by enemy fire or pierced by shrapnel from artillery. Father didn't turn back, nor did those who followed him. He dropped his payload of bombs on the target, destroying it. Halfway through the mission he finally received friendly air support, many of those also losing their lives. As Father spoke at the table that day, the four other airmen became emotional. I will never forget my father's face; stoic, serious, but completely in control. If ever a man could have filled John Wayne's shoes, it was Dad. Matter of fact, to me, he *was* John Wayne.

On the way back to his home base, limping back on two engines, Father refused to land until all the other birds sat secure on the ground. On his final approach, my father lost a third engine and barely made it back to the airfield. The landing was rough, but routine to him. His B29 would never take to the air again. It was literally shot to confetti. The entire bay was filled with men's blood – an absolute nightmare with one airman completely cut in half by shrapnel, his body resting in two pieces. After the fire team extinguished his smoldering aircraft and the remaining living crew reported for debriefing, my father insisted on carrying every dead man off the aircraft himself. He described picking up one of his best friends underneath the arms and carrying him to the ambulance. There was only half of his torso in his arms. He then returned to the aircraft and brought the other half to the ambulance. As he described the blood that covered him, he did it in the most amazing way I've ever heard; almost like a sermon in church. It wasn't filled with horror, but rather with love for his fellow man. I remember it as one of the most incredible moments of my life.

How could anyone be so tough? How could anyone be so pure to his command? How could anyone be so outwardly unaffected by what had happened? Unadulterated grace under pressure. If it hadn't been for the other "Quiet Birdmen" present that day (and perhaps several stiff bourbons), I probably would never have heard that story.

I believe that incidences like this shaped me into the captain that I became, not only in boats but in aircraft. It beckoned to me to explore canyons never visited. It allowed me to fish in weather most people deemed unfishable. I guess the persuasive attitude my dad had about life made me live my entire life for just a sliver of his respect and love. I know it sounds crazy, but at times in my life while growing up, I actually dreamed of being one of the men that my father carried off the aircraft. I obviously do not want to be dead but to be held in my father's arms with the respect and reverence he had for his crew was something which I believe I never received until very late in life.

Father fought the good fight against cancer but it was not a battle to be won. In a last attempt to save his life, they opened him up and discovered he was riddled with cancer, "A dead man walking," and yet he carried on as if nothing was out of the ordinary. In agonizing pain at times, he made fun of losing most of the hair on his head.

Hours before Father died, we had a bedside conversation. I wondered at that time if he might say, "Son, I love you." But he didn't. What Dad said was, "Son, never give up and never say never." He told me all things are possible, that I had the right stuff, and that I would always be successful. Wow! On his death bed he *almost* said he loved me — or perhaps he did in his own way. News of my father's death spread quickly on eastern Long Island. His burial at sea inspired every boat in Indian Cove Marina in Shinnecock, Long Island to offer help.

On a day with a fairly flat ocean and a leaden, gray sky, 13 boats followed as I captained *Makaira*, then a 47-foot Ridgeway, to the east along Long Island's seashore. Ultimate respect gets shown all Birdmen and seafarers by turning to the east, where the sun rises and each glorious new day starts. I requested the U.S. Air Force send a command pilot in one of their modern-day squadrons, and to my amazement, they granted the request immediately. A high ranking officer in uniform joined us in the funeral procession. All of the boats circled just offshore of Southampton, maneuvering our vessels transom-to-transom. Aboard *Makaira* were my mother, sister, and respective family members. I asked that they all stay in the salon with the doors closed while I committed Father's ashes to the sea. As the ashes gently fell from the urn, the pilot saluted. My father had been reduced to a jar of ashes, and yet his spirit and lessons have stayed with me my entire life.

To this day, I look up to him for strength and wisdom. I always hear the same thing: "Never give up, never say never. Do the work and do it well." Often in private, when things seem like they could be no worse, with no hope in sight, I see my father calmly saying, "Do the work, it will work out".

To this day, I know of no greater man, no greater hero than my father. God rest his soul.

Tred's father, Joseph Barta, with his beloved Rolls Royce in 1987.

Joseph Barta with sailfish and striped marlin in Cabo San Lucas, Mexico.

Chapter Nineteen
TO SET A WORLD RECORD

IT'S PATHETIC TO think that most people who knew me during the days when I thought of nothing other than setting IGFA world records, are either dead or senile. Thirty-six years ago I became obsessed with catching the biggest fish on certified ultralight line, to prove I was the best in the world.

Now later in life, I've had it explained to me that I was, again, trying to get my father's love and attention. The only thing he understood was being #1! So for example, when you do break a record, and you catch the biggest fish in the world in one of the various line classes, nobody can argue that you are #2 or #3! You hold the world record. I truly don't believe my father caused all of my burning passions. I do know that my quest for world records taught me incredible patience and reinforced my "Never give up" attitude… and it cost me a ton of money each year.

Every sport has different levels of greatness. You may be considered a great baseball player in high school or college, but until you join a major league team, you haven't gone as far as you can go. Then again, when you get on a major league team you're just another player until you are the best on the team. Carry this logic on until your picture is in Cooperstown, in the Hall of Fame, next to Babe Ruth! No matter the sport, you always have different levels of accomplishment. You can be a Triple-A shooter in skeet and trap, but still be 200th in the world. To be the absolute best skeet or trap shooter takes a lifetime of work and a quadrillion hours of practice. I tried to be the best American biathlon skier in the world; I was good but failed at becoming the best. Considering this view of the world, meeting all the requirements such as catching big fish on ultralight line — possibly resulting in a world record for a particular species, in a specific line class, judged and verified by the IGFA World Record Committee — had tremendous interest.

For approximately 10 years, I dedicated 95 percent of my income to setting world records on ultralight line. Considering I came from a well-to-do family (though not incredibly wealthy), it's quite amazing that I got as far as I did. To call me self-consumed would be an understatement. Marriages and relationships all took second place to my passion; an absolutely sad but true statement.

The art of setting a world record of very big bluewater species on what would appear to be sewing thread, requires a fairly detailed explanation. The IGFA awards world records for all species cover two main categories: Conventional tackle and fly rod. In the conventional tackle arena, the line classes consist of 2, 4, 6, 8, 12, 16, 20, 30, 50, 80, and 130 pounds. When you catch a fish and apply for a world record, you must submit a sample of the line you used when the fish was caught. Back at IGFA headquarters in Dania, Florida (worth a visit, by the way), that sample gets stretched to its breaking point on an IGFA certified and maintained scale called an Instron machine. If the line breaks at or below the specified line class in which you entered the fish, and you followed all the other rules, your name goes into the World Record Book! For those of you who are interested in knowing what those rules are, visit *IGFA.org*.

As absurd or boastful as it may sound, very few people in the world can develop the very fine feel of the rod and reel required for ultralight tackle fishing. I have been paid to teach multi-millionaires this aspect of big-game fishing. No matter how much money they spent, none of them had what it takes. It is like trying to teach a fat old man how to be an Olympic gymnast. It can't be done. Visualize a six-pound-test line tied to the tip of a lightweight fishing rod. The other end attaches to a six-pound weight. Now imagine lifting the weight off the ground with the rod bent over almost double. If you lift the weight slowly, you can probably get it off the ground. If you lift it quickly, the line will break. Why? The weight weighs six-pounds, the line is six-pound test so why would the line break? The reason is simple. The rapid force upward against a static object creates more than 6 pounds of pressure.

When fighting a tuna on six-pound line, the fish may weigh 10 or 20 times the line test. It's moving between 20 and 40 miles per hour. The fish probably pulls well over 100 yards of line into the ocean within the first minute of being hooked. Also, with no guarantee the fish will swim in a straight line away from the boat, it's likely forming a loop or curve in the line as well. Now add the 6 to 7 knots of boat speed to the equation. As you can see, a great many variables all place dynamic tension on that six-pound line!

That begs the question then: How is it possible to catch a 65-pound tuna on 6-pound test line? And especially when the fight took in excess of three hours! This is one of my world records which still stands today, so I assure you that it *can* be accomplished!

Setting such a world record also requires a team effort. I couldn't have done it by myself. You need a captain with very particular light-tackle boat-handling skills. You need mates with exceptional talent in wiring, gaffing, and killing the fish. Of course, first and foremost, the angler must keep that fish on the line. Six-pound test line means you can exert six pounds of pressure on that fish before the line breaks. Sewing thread breaks at about 4-1/2 pounds.

Let me take you on a journey, in my case not hypothetical, on just how to land a big fish with ultra-lightweight tackle. Say you're trolling a squid on six-pound line. If you set the initial strike drag at 5.8 pounds the line will snap about 4 seconds after hookup. Why? The dynamic shock to start the drag and spool of the reel spinning on a savage strike with the fish moving at 20+ miles per hour in opposite direction. The boat moves forward at 6 knots trolling speed and the fish suddenly yanks the line in the opposite direction with the resulting pressure far exceeding the line test. Fish gone. Ten years of experimenting taught me to set the strike drag at 1.5 pounds on six-pound test. The fish needs an extremely sharp hook (putting less pressure on the line), and I retrieve line at an extremely fast pace. Every time the fish turns to the left, right, or submerges, additional water pressure pushes on the line. Since it changes constantly, you cannot measure the water pressure exactly, but after breaking off hundreds and hundreds of fish, I know of only one technique to keep the line from breaking: Backing off the drag even more. Here's another math factor. You've filled the spool of your reel completely with line and you've set the drag at three pounds. When the spool becomes half empty, it now takes 6 pounds of pressure to get the same line off the reel. The drag has doubled even though you haven't touched anything!

Indeed, the varied dynamics impacting catching big fish on light line can stagger the mind. We have: The speed of the fish, water pressure against the line, the spool increasing the drag without us touching anything as line departs (changing again constantly as we reel line back in), the unpredictable movements of the fish itself, jerking, twisting, turning, all while it tries to get free from our clutches. We have the possibility of seaweed snagging on the line and being dragged through the water, the pitching and yawing of the boat as it negotiates waves – all of these dynamics contribute to the staggering odds against catching this fish! Yet, somehow one must calculate all the variables with split-second timing in order to not break off the fish. I sometimes repeat a prayer in my head: "Oh fish, you are so strong and my line is so weak! "

But the drag helps to even the odds somewhat. For example, if I attached a line from a fishing rod set at two pounds of drag to your belt, and then you swam away into the ocean, before you traveled 50 yards, you'd be exhausted! If you doubt me then try it. Despite all the mathematics, the dynamics, the almost infinite variables, the act of catching monstrous fish on light line comes down to something unquantifiable… to feel. Consider how hard to hit a golf ball on a putting green in order to compensate for a fast or slow course, for dry or wet grass, or for the dip or rise in the green itself. No one in the world can tell you how to do that. They can explain what they see and feel, but they can't tell you how they did it.

Obviously, the prime objective of light-tackle fishing is to not break the fish off. I have spent days upon days with divers submerged in a swimming pool trying to figure out how hard or deep two pounds of pressure can drive a fishing hook into a block of balsa wood. I can tell you it can drive the proper hook completely through a large block. I mention this so you never underestimate what a small amount of pressure can do, not only immediately, but over time.

By the time I perfected my light tackle methods, I had already contributed all I could to the sport regarding my knowledge of the canyons and bigeye tuna. Being either the genius or monster that I am, I needed my next task to be more difficult. I was driven to own an IGFA world record for bigeyes. I knew where to find them and how to hunt them down. I had the appropriate team at hand to get the job done, and I wanted a bigeye tuna record more than anything else in the world.

I had already broken off some 90 bigeye tuna on 12- and 20-pound test. I couldn't get it done even though I'd had several battles lasting more than four hours. To my way of thinking, that meant that if I could keep a fish on for that long, then sooner or later I would succeed. Sooner or later the fish would make a mistake or I would just get major lucky. I got close enough at times to know it was possible. Unfortunately, others disagreed with me, and to be honest — that really hurt. In fact, I had a hard time finding professional mates because they simply didn't want to spend hours upon hours fighting fish, being yelled at by me, and having no fish to sell at the end of the day. I became pretty demoralized.

At the time, Hank and Mickey Altenkirch, owners of Altenkirch Tackle on the Shinnecock Canal, Hampton Bays, New York represented the latest technology and the greatest perfection of fishing tackle in the sport. I truly loved Mickey as a man, and I considered Hank a good friend. Sure, I spent a fortune in their shop. But besides that, Mickey never lost faith in what I was trying to do. At one point, he was the only person who believed in me.

On July 26, 1980 the forecast for the canyons called for light and variable winds at five knots or less from the southwest and seas less than two feet. A dear friend, Herbie Lipke, met me at Indian Cove Marina at 4 AM. I had taught Herbie a tremendous amount about canyon fishing over the previous three years and he loved the sport. Herbie owned a glorified salad bar restaurant in Manhattan. I stayed at his condo often when I visited New York City and likewise, Herbie and his friends stayed with me at my Southampton house. He knew how to wire and gaff. One day, Herbie said, "I want to speak with you." He informed me that this would be the last trip and he no longer wanted to fish when I was using nothing but ultralight tackle. The investment of money and time, with no tuna to show for it, and the negative emotions borne of constant failure had reduced canyon fishing with me to something he no longer wanted to do.

This scenario played out again and again by most of my friends as well as fellow dock rats. The consensus deemed Tred Barta an idiot and obsessed. I went too far and I was no longer fun to be around. It was a very lonely and sad time for me. To make it even worse my father kept making statements like, "Have a good weekend playing with your tuna, Tred." Something deep down inside of me insisted my goal was possible even though nobody in the entire world had been able to do it – yet the IGFA 20-pound line class for bigeye tuna was vacant. When a dream costs you your friends, money, and ends up in constant failure on top of it all, it breeds devastation!

Herbie and I left the marina at 4:35 AM and we ran to the southwest corner of Block Canyon (LORAN 14650 and 43315). The run took three hours on the button. Herbie slept down below as I drove *Makaira* from the tower. At the end of July, I knew where the fish were. I knew that if I trolled from morning until dark on the southwest corner of Block Canyon, between 80 to 500 fathoms, concentrating most of my time in 200 to 300 fathoms, that we would get a bite. Herbie got the 20-pound test Altenkirch rigs set up the way I liked them. Since I was going for a world record on 20-pound test I only trolled six lines: Three green machine lures on the right-long, center, and left-long riggers. Two monster chin-weighted mullets swam on the port and starboard flat lines. A sixth rod was trolled down the middle. Not having a single bite the entire day got us pretty discouraged by 2 o'clock in the afternoon. Especially since we saw tremendous life on the southwest corner of the canyon.

A group of ten finback whales worked the area. Mother Carey's chickens by the hundreds danced on the water eating the whales' feeding leftovers, which caused a large oily slick. Oil slicks from feeding frenzies that lay on the surface of the water always mean success. Terns and black-back gulls followed small schools of bonitas that we did our best to avoid. Our goal was a record bigeye tuna on 20-pound test.

My friend, Herbie, suddenly went ballistic! Three boats — four to six miles inside of us — were loading up on albacore and yellowfin tuna but I refused to move. Herbie finally broke. "I love you Buddy," he said, "But this is the last time!" Every fiber in my body told me I was in the right place. I knew I would raise the wolfpack, trolling six 20-pound international reels with Cortland white Dacron attached to a swivel and a 14-foot wire leader, Triple X Mustad Martu-design tuna hooks and 300-pound mono. Mickey Altenkirch at that time used Fin-Nor guides, and he made his rod butts himself by hand. Cal Sheets in California, had "dyno-ed" the spools and blueprinted and calibrated the drags, setting them at four pounds. Very few people in the world were this advanced with their tackle.

Then it happened! The right long and right short were engulfed by world class bigeye tuna like a bomb had dropped. Holes formed in the water from their strikes. Both lines hooked up and the 20-pound test proceeded to disappear from the reels at an alarming rate. For a change, I wasn't trying to catch multiple fish. Just one very special fish! I came off the tower, yelling to Herbie to cut all of the other lines, keeping just one fish on. As if on cue the left short rigger, left flat line, and left long line all hooked up! What a cluster! Before I knew it, the left long rigger had crossed with the right long with both lines breaking simultaneously. The right short completely spooled and the line broke off the reel, sounding like a .22 rifle firing in the cockpit. IGFA rules strictly mandate that only the angler can touch the rod, so I constantly yelled at Herbie not to touch any of the rods. With three lines broken off, a fourth in jeopardy, I picked up a potential world record on one of the rods. I can't even remember what one it was. I do remember it had a fish on it. I reeled frantically and the line broke. As I reached for the only rod left with a fish on it, it also broke. I screamed at Herbie to straighten out the boat more just as I heard a big thump on the side of the boat. My heart sank. Herbie had run over a lobster pot without seeing it. With all five fish lost, I turned to Herbie and said, "Let's go home." I realized at that very moment, in many ways, what everyone said about me was true. I put my arm around Herbie and said, "I'm sorry. This is my dream not yours. You are right and I am wrong."

We started to tidy up the boat and get ready to ride home on a flat calm sea with all the rods lifeless in their rod holders, I throttled up and as I accelerated I remember just passing about 15 knots, the center rigger jolted and vibrated through the tower. I turned around and to my amazement one line, the center rigger, did not break and was untouched during the entire ordeal. It still had a lure on it and it was out. To claim complete and utter amazement on both our parts would be a vast understatement. We had totally forgot about the sixth rod after losing the five fish. Herbie again took over the controls. I strapped up on what felt like a big fish and the battle started. I had a great advantage as I hadn't lost half the spool of line I normally would while clearing the other rods. We had just one, heroic rod hooked up! I started the battle with practically a full spool.

The first run proved breathtaking. More than half the spool of line dumped into the water. Herbie spun the boat in the direction of the fish and we ran alongside it at 18 knots. Incredibly, the bigeye stayed on top of the water. When we got three quarters of the spool back, Herbie took off the power and the great fish sounded. As line peeled off the reel I kept pulling back the drag to compensate for the algebra that I knew to be true. During the first 30 minutes of this fight I must have made a hundred drag adjustments. When I had water pressure created by big loops of line in the water I tried to compensate the best I could. When the great fish sounded I tried to be extremely quiet on the rod and wait him out. When I had a huge amount of line back on the reel sometimes I'd end up at 15 pounds of drag. Herbie violently backed the boat up so I could retrieve line, then drove forward in big right and left gaping curves to move forward on the fish. Going into the second hour, I knew our game had ended. A solid quarter-acre of porpoises, hundreds of them, swam right across my line. One touch from their sandpaper-like skin and my dream would be lost.

All tuna — including bigeye — can fight for hours in a "death circle." When a tuna runs all over the ocean, making power run after power run, left and right zigzags on top, the fish isn't hurting. I often claim that God is my co-pilot. Some people think that the belief in religion is the elixir of the weak. Others feel, as I do, that there is something to it. I only knew one thing at that moment; I still had my fish on and that was a miracle. Somewhere around 90 minutes into the fight, another special moment happened. The great tuna started to circle, meaning it was hooked well, starting to tire, and this now became a battle of wits, technique, and strength. It would also take some skillful boat handling and after all of that — either luck or faith just might get you through. The great fish circled to the right with one-quarter of the spool off the reel. Each time the bigeye passed 12 o'clock, I tried to increase the drag and get a full pump on the rod, reeling down to the water on the down stroke. After 15 minutes of this maneuvering, Herbie screamed that he saw color. I finally saw what he was yelling about — a large 800- to 900-pound tiger shark who sensed the tuna battle. My line suddenly went slack, my heart fluttered, and almost stopped beating and my whole world stopped. I reeled frantically, gaining huge amounts of line. Obviously the tiger shark, wanting my tuna had chased it towards the surface. I finally felt the pressure of the tuna again, the steady thumping of its tail and the movement of its head. The shark? Nowhere to be seen. I told Herbie to make a very dangerous maneuver which I have used on other occasions while fighting giant tuna. Rather than follow the fish in its right hand death circle I had Herbie pull away and turn the boat in the opposite direction. Often this maneuver ends up with a pulled hook. I wanted to break the fish's plane, to pop its head to the surface, and then for the fish to regain its balance, it would have nowhere else to go but up. It worked!

Finally, we had color! The white Cortland 20-pound line, certified to break at 18 pounds, 5 ounces came off the rod tip like cars speeding on a highway. We had turned the fish from a right hand circle to a left hand circle. We absolutely had control! It was now up to me to exert maximum pressure on the fish without breaking the line. Herbie could make no mistakes. He wore two cotton gloves that had soaked in the water so they wouldn't slide on the leader. Two straight gaffs lay on the left gunwale. We were in a left hand circle and you could actually see the swivel on the leader. In ten years, I had not gotten this close. On the rare occasion when you beat a fish to submission, it literally gives up. It has no more will to live. With the last circle of the bigeye tuna, it laid over on his side. In one of the last turns, Herbie grabbed the leader and made perfect wraps on his left hand, then his right, then his left. We had complete control. Herbie reached down with the short gaff and slammed the hook into the gill plate. The fish laid still. As far as I could tell, the earth stayed still. I placed a tail rope on it and it took both of us to pull the fish up onto the deck where it lay lifeless. With both of us on our knees by the fish, Herbie reached out and held me in his arms. We were both estatic! I had accomplished a tremendous feat. My goal took 10 years to reach with more than 110 break offs and hundreds of hours of fighting time. A goal that defined me for the rest of my life. I don't know for how long, but we both sat silently on the deck and stared in amazement at what we had done.

Without broadcasting a word on the radio, and not looking for any praise from anyone (very unusual for me), both Herbie and I took *Makaira* on a flat calm sea back to Shinnecock, around the east channel, across Shinnecock Bay to Indian Cove Marina. As I crossed the bay, I smelled the heady aroma of barbequed burgers in the air. I saw families with their inner tubes and rafts enjoying the summer and it all seemed so far removed from the way I lived my life — like borderline culture shock. How I yearned once again to merely go to a barbeque and have fun.

Upon tying up at Indian Cove Marina and removing the great fish from the ice-filled coffin, I called Altenkirch's store. Mickey picked up the phone. I will never forget these words: "Mickey, it's Tred. I did it." What I heard next was very unlike Mickey. He yelled to Hank, "Close the store now!" In the store at that time was Skip Tolleffesson, owner of the Lobster Inn and another very dear friend. Minutes later Skip, Mickey, and Hank were at the marina as we weighed the tuna on an electronic Chatillon scale, certified by the IGFA only two weeks prior. It was the end of the day and all of the boats at Indian Cove Marina had returned from off shore and the surrounding bays. The marina was full of people. The same captains and mates who had criticized me over the years and labeled me as a "Finely Skilled Fool." To my true friends this represented a time of true triumph in my life. However, those who are my greatest disbelievers I think they were actually disappointed as it proved to them what true victory looked like. A victory that this group of people would not realize.

Many hands enthusiastically helped slide the great fish to the scale. Eddie Laursen climbed up the ladder with the scale and turned it on. He bellowed the weight, "215 pounds!" Everyone clapped except Mickey Altenkirch. With his arm around my shoulder, he yelled at the top of his lungs, "And the new IGFA world record!"

I say it today from my wheelchair not one bit differently than I said it then, "Never give up, never say never."

Tred Barta and Herbie Lipke with IGFA world record Bigeye tuna.

Chapter Twenty
WALKER'S CAY AND THE BARTA BLUE MARLIN CLASSIC

IN 1995, THE "Go-Go" era neared its end. At the upper end of the food chain, money flowed like water. A rising tide floats all boats, and thus it went with the economy. Gold chains, fast cars, businesses looking for write-offs, and moral values, in my opinion, hit an all-time low. At the time, money also ruled everything in the sport of bluewater fishing. I had recently moved from eastern Long Island to Jupiter, Florida. My boat docked at the Jib Club just inside the Jupiter Inlet.

It didn't take long for my outrage to grow. I found tournaments where "Sportsmen" slaughtered and sold giant bluefin tuna. Anglers commonly used 200-hundred-pound test line, and all of the tournaments had astronomical Calcutta's rewarding dead billfish on the dock. A group called BBC (Bahamas

Billfish Championship) held a series of tournaments each year in the Bahamas where hundreds of thousands of dollars hung in the balance. The BBC started in 1968 and I believe the BBC tournaments, at that time, exemplified the polar opposite values to my personal beliefs. I struggled at that time wondering what our sport really represented and what responsibilities we had in exchange for enjoying it and everything that came with it.

As a Christian man, I have learned that calling people names and saying unkind things about abhorrent philosophies only makes the speaker look bad. So let me just say that things I personally observed at tournaments fell way short of having any type of moral compass by which I live my life. With that, I let your imagination unfold before you of what all transpired, I witnessed owners who were gamblers, not fishermen. I also observed mates and captains who became intoxicated with the vices of their owners. I cannot say this more politely, but as I write this I am still enraged. During this time, tournament lawsuits ran rampant. I actually knew attorneys who made their livelihood traveling the calcutta billfish tournament circuit. Many of the tournaments hired observers — and some of them got paid off to cheat. I even know of an instance where an observer accepted an invitation to visit a young lady below decks for the purpose of receiving sexual favors. The whole thing disgusted me and seemed like the decline of the Roman Empire. Over time, many of the calcutta gambling tournaments have cleaned up their act. In the few tournaments where I participated personally, I counted 10 to 15 marlin, not gutted or filleted, but in a pile rotting in the sun before being towed out to sea to be unceremoniously dumped.

Children and wives never attended most of these tournaments because the stakes were too high and the morals were too low. What I found amazing was most of the boat builders and very good Christians went along with the whole pathetic scene because it all boiled down to the almighty dollar. Almost every angler, captain and crewmember who participated in these calcutta events considered me an annoying jerk, a holier-than-thou elitist. I chose this period – with all of this calcutta tournament crap going on, to start promoting family values — getting families involved in our great sport of fishing.

One of my keystone slogans has been "Families who hunt and fish together, stay together." The status quo in tournament fishing so angered me that I decided the time had come to try to teach all who would listen that Nature teaches us patience, reliability, honor, moral code, and the ability to show the best of humankind; families can spend quality tournament fishing time together to *everyone's* benefit. I wanted our children to know that when someone shakes your hand and looks you in the eye while saying, "I trust you," it cements an unbreakable bond. My goal then, and today, is to teach kids nothing is more important than your word, and that when great people get together, all things are possible. I often use the example of "trust" by citing a 12-year-old girl with a shotgun walking behind her father in a Nebraska corn field. The father taught her well and *trusts* there is no ammo in the chamber; the muzzle is always in a safe position; and the safety is on.

I honestly didn't understand why people who so loved the ocean and everything living in it, couldn't embrace a 100-percent catch-and-release tournament. No cash under the table, no obscenely large winner rewards, no observers, lie detector tests, camera requirements or lawyers. A tournament where if you said you released a fish, then so be it! Your word was your bond. Children and wives could fish and could be helped if needed. Without cash involved, cheating disappears. I felt certain that the greatest fishermen in the world would come for the ideals and camaraderie. To me, the concept of drag-'em and snag-'em — the art of pulling artificial lures — represented the nadir of aptitude and pinnacle of laziness. I've actually met fishing mates incapable of rigging baits. It made my stomach turn. I believe the art of rigging baits must not be lost like so much of today's knowledge. Many parents no longer teach their children how to change a tire on the family car, cook a meal, sew, or develop basic carpentry, plumbing and electrical skills to repair their own homes.

Another sore point: In Palm Beach, Florida and environs, conduct over the VHF radio plummeted to an all-time low. Once when fishing out of Jupiter, a father and son who had rented a center console, hooked up to a blue marlin while surrounded by a fleet of professional charter boats and elite sport-fishers. They had absolutely no idea what to do and asked the fleet for help. I will never forget this day as long as I live. Some of the best captains from Palm Beach called the father a bozo and berated him on the radio. One of the most famous captains back in the day, whose name I will not mention out of some ridiculous courtesy, said, "Hey buddy! Why don't you go back where you came from?" I was embarrassed by their behavior. The Corinthian spirit no longer exists.

Fortunately, one of the great captains of all time, Captain Ely Brown from Jupiter, Florida aboard his 37-foot Merritt *Do Say*, talked the man and his son through the marlin catch and release, step by step. I noticed the professional fleet dared not attack Captain Ely Brown. I joined Ely on the VHF several times. Since I was fishing nearby, I pulled in all my lines on *Makaira* and pulled up alongside the father and son to help coach them on the catch and release.

Clearly, their marlin weighed a good 125 pounds. Finally, I instructed the father and son to cut the fish free. The entire fleet ganged up on this father and son deriding them about how the fish was probably a 30-pound sailfish. I quickly defended their catch on the VHF-radio and to my surprise, not one of them said another word.

At that very moment, I had an epiphany: I became determined (and had the courage) to form the Barta Blue Marlin Classic, a tournament with the sole intent of bringing honor back to sport fishing. The simple rules leveled the playing field. We had divisions for junior anglers including both boys and girls in two age categories, small-boat, outboard, professional anglers and charter captains. You could fish this tournament against people of your own skill level. However, it had no Calcutta, no monetary prizes, and no side-betting. People would fish this tournament for the camaraderie of their fellow anglers. This event promised honor-system scoring (your-word-is-your-bond) and 100-percent release of all billfish. If the swivel never reached the rod tip, then you didn't release a fish. My vision called for a 30-pound test, dead-bait tournament, specifically designed to accommodate kids and women. It prohibited the ridiculous 130-pound unlimited tackle so commonly used in the tournament scene of the time. It presented an opportunity for all participants to renew their bait-rigging skills which had been replaced by fancy, double-hook artificial lures. Ultimately, the bait box competition became one of the most popular events at the tournament!

The Barta Blue Marlin Classic awarded plaques and trophies to winners and every penny raised via auction items, entry fees, etc., benefited the IGFA Junior Angler program. I had written concept articles on the subject in *Marlin* and *Sport Fishing* magazines for years. In the fishing world, I became the laughing stock of all of South Florida for my tournament vision. People claimed nobody would fish my tournament; it was a stupid idea; doomed.

Amazingly Bob Abplanalp and his son, John, very wealthy men and owners of Walker's Cay, Bahamas contacted me, asking me to come to Yonkers, New York to meet. Bob established and owned a company called Precision Valve Company and invented the first mass-produced aerosol valve in 1949 which today still goes on everything from perfume, deodorant and hair spray, to olive oil, paints, and anything else that comes in an aerosol can. Talk about the largest cash cow ever developed! Next time you pick up an aerosol can, now you can think of my friend, Bob Abplanalp, who made your life easier! Bob arranged to send a corporate jet down to pick me up in Palm Beach and bring me to Yonkers. I had left my car on Singer Island, home of the famous main charter dock at Sailfish Marina. As I approached my truck to leave for the airport, I discovered all four tires had been slashed — my vehicle resting on its rims. A note left on the windshield said, "It will never happen." Reading this note to Bob over the phone infuriated him and he decided to fly down from New York the following morning to meet with me.

Let me explain the history of Sailfish Marina. Originally, a single charter-fleet dock was built just north of the Lake Worth Inlet (Palm Beach) in the late 1940s. Almost 40 years later, in 1977, Palm Beach inventor and entrepreneur Alex

Dreyfoos purchased the marina. Someone unknown to me built another charter dock just south of the marina. Dreyfoos purchased it, combined the two and formed The Sailfish Marina & Resort which became synonymous with big-game sport fishing in Palm Beach. It sits a mere two-hour cruise from the Bahamas. It had the reputation as the "Yankee Stadium" of sport fishing. In 2004, the property sold to American Financial Group.

That same evening, I received a call from Steve Moynahan, owner of HMY Yacht Sales, the largest Viking Dealer in the world. He claimed he had read my tournament article and wanted to meet me. My tires were slashed, people made fun of me on the VHF, and I felt like I didn't have a friend in the world until two of the most influential people in the industry wanted to meet with me the next day. Something was happening. What, I didn't exactly know. Emotionally I had been very down but suddenly I sensed a glimmer of hope.

The Abplanalp family loved sport fishing and owned a 54-foot Whiticar called the *Sea Lion II*. They maintained this vessel at the manufacturer, Whiticar Boat Works on Old Saint Lucie Blvd. in Stuart, Florida. Under the graces and charity of Whiticar Boat Works, I maintained my boat, *Makaira*, there as well. The next day I met with everybody concerned. Steve and his partner looked into my eyes and told me I better have some tough skin. Steve handed me an envelope and enclosed was a check for $50,000. I couldn't believe it! Here I had a check for $50,000 for the promotion of a fishing tournament that didn't even have a rule book yet. Petrified, I didn't know what to do. He caught me totally caught off guard. I asked Steve why he was so generous. Steve put his arm around me and turned me towards the marina. He pointed to a family of six just boarding a Viking yacht he had just sold. He said to me, "Tred, *that* is the future of boating, not what's going on now." Bob and John Abplanalp met me in Palm Beach. Then we flew to Walker's Cay, Bahamas in his converted twin-engine, Grumman Goose sea plane. We sat on the Walker's Hotel veranda with his entire staff. There we worked on dates for the first Barta Blue Marlin Classic.

Walker's, being one of the closest Bahamian island resorts to the United States and an easy run even for outboard boats, normally enjoyed having every marina slip and hotel room fully booked all spring — the island's private airport jam-packed with aircraft. Spring represented the height of their season. So if we wanted kids to fish the tournament, then it had to be held when school let out. Unfortunately, that fell right smack in the middle of the most lucrative time for the Bahamas. Bob announced, "Tred, I am hereby blocking off the entire island for one week in April. There will be no reservations, no hotel rooms sold, and there will not be a boat in this marina except for your tournament boats." Talk about scared! Can you imagine the pressure I felt?

"Walker's Cay — legendary diving and deep-sea fishing resort. This 58-acre island has exposure to the Atlantic Ocean on the north and east part of the cay and Little Bahama Bank on the south and west. It's also close to Matanilla Shoal giving it special fishing conditions. It boasts a 2,800-foot air strip and its own electric generating facility," said the travel brochure. All this made it a spectacular place for the tournament. Five other investors popped up that week. They wished to remain anonymous, but the net came to $100,000 in seed money!

Tournament brochures got printed, rules formulated, and advertising was placed in *Marlin, Sport Fishing, Big Game Fishing Journal*, and *Florida Sportsman* magazines. A dear friend, Pete Ryan, one of the best giant tuna fishermen of the day, helped me with a great deal of the logistics. Pete owned a 50-foot Post named *The Sneaky Pete*. He helped me arrange how the marina would lay out. The marina could hold 109 boats; whether or not we had any boats remained to be seen. Captain Danny Azzato, another dear friend from Oakland, New York, owns Fish and Wildlife Unlimited taxidermy. Danny has thousands of molds of virtually every fish species, in stock, cast from the actual fish to capture every detail. Danny quickly agreed to provide all of the tournament trophies.

Then I met with the IGFA who at that time sensed the revolt in the family fishing frenzy. Of course, they agreed to join us, especially as they stood to gain as the recipient of the tournament money. The general plan: Get sponsors to donate product and services. Auction those items off at the tournament. Promote the event via hundreds of printed T-shirts. As it turned out, boatloads of product, given on the basis of my vision of family fishing, traveled to Walker's Cay via the Abplanalp tug and barge.

In a show of unity and class, almost everyone at Sailfish Marina on Singer Island boycotted the tournament. Let's frame this discussion if I may. An entire industry, supported by millions of dollars of gambling money, and generating potentially monstrous payoffs for the best captains and mates fishing the calcutta/kill tournament, felt threatened by family values! In their myopic view, their future, their financial well-being and "the way we've always done it" all hung in the balance. Instead, they could have taken the more enlightened view of kids being their customers in 15 or 20 years and if they didn't learn to enjoy the sport now, then when the time came later...

I was asking great offshore fishermen to join my tournament for a measly $500 entry fee, for the right to win a trophy, receive a hand shake, and to top it off, with no opportunities for mates, captains, and owners to gamble. Bring their boats, big or small, inboard or outboard. At stake? The greatest trophy of all; Being named the best fisherman in the tournament and given a pat on the back.

Certainly some mercenary types didn't see the allure. In my eyes, the greatest benefit of this tournament was demonstrating to our children that despite how big business and society operated in today's world, we could still live with our word as our bond and have our peers trust one another.

Right up to the week before the tournament, the fishing industry boycotted my event. Lure manufacturers didn't like naked, dead baits. South Florida marine businesses didn't like the event being at Walker's in the Bahamas. Captains and mates didn't like losing potential revenue through charters or winnings. Some of my closest friends, (those without spines), caved to peer pressure and no longer spoke to me. Many in the marine and fishing communities viewed me as a cancer, someone who wanted to change the sport, and who would hurt the income of captains and mates.

A few days prior to the Barta Blue Marlin Classic, I found myself sitting with the Abplanalps on the Walker's Hotel veranda overlooking the Little Bahama Bank towards Palm Beach. We discussed the terrible weather forecast; high winds, torrential rain, and funnel clouds were expected to pummel both the Florida coast and the island.

Sure enough, the day before the tournament, only three boats sat at the marina docks. Two of them lived there! Make that four if you count "Big Daddy" Joe Flanigan's unique houseboat that also lived there. A big tent had been erected, flags and banners flew at the weigh scale on center dock, even the airport staff decorated their office! The entire vacant island waited for what appeared to the forthcoming worst nightmare any of us could imagine.

It appeared that even Nature herself had sabotaged the inaugural Barta Blue Marlin Classic tournament. I resigned myself to the fact that no one was coming and I would be the Judas Goat and the laughing stock of the industry. They called for 6- to 8-foot waves in the Gulf Stream. My only hope? A weather window around 4 o'clock which called for diminishing winds and clear skies in Palm Beach.

Many of us have seen a dark, steel-gray weather front sweep across the Florida Straits into the Bahamas. We know what it looks like. That's what greeted us on the day before the tournament — one of the darkest lines of weather I have ever seen appeared headed straight at us from the mainland. Employees ran up the hill at Walker's calling out to each other, "Rain is coming! Rain is coming!"

The wind picked up, whipping the pennants wildly on outrigger halyards through 25 knots of wind. Maybe it's the clearing front we were all waiting for. No matter: It signaled to me that my tournament was doomed. As Bob and John looked out at the front approaching us, we all commented on the severe white water hitting on the bank. It looked abnormal. Bob put his arm around me and said, "Tred, I am so sorry." I remember feeling terribly upset and dejected.

Walker's Cay had previously been hit by hurricanes, each time sparing the small hillside church above the marina. I looked down on the church in total disbelief. My intentions were good and righteous and so many people had given so much. Why was this happening to me? As I left Bob and John, I started to walk down the hill to secure my boat, I heard Bob yell. Bob was always soft spoken and I personally never heard him yell before so it surprised me. At the top of his lungs Bob yelled, "Barta get your a** back up here!" I had no idea what I had done wrong and came running. He handed me a large pair of binoculars and said, "Do you see anything unusual about this storm?" I raised the binoculars and God be my witness, as far as I could see that the white tumulus spots on the horizon weren't waves but were boats! Everyone had left from Miami to Vero Beach at the same time in boats big and small. What an incredible sight. As the boats filed in to Walker's Cay, Bob told me he had never seen anything like it. A line of a hundred boats filed into the marina. The docking process took hours. I believe the count totaled 125 boats, making it the largest billfish tournament in the history of Bahamian sport fishing. Not an inch of space was left in the marina and some 18 boats had to anchor out front.

All of the local natives selling their fresh conch salad chipped in to help ferry people to their boats and back again. The entire population of Walker's and Grand Cays came alive. Never had such a number of boats descended upon the island. Some of the finest blue marlin fishermen from eleven different countries flew to the tournament: South Africa, Australia, Guatemala, Ireland and England to name a few. Families came from North Carolina. Some of the biggest names in our sport showed up: Dr. Guy Harvey, a Jamaican marine wildlife artist and marine biologist came to support the catch-and-release billfish event. Marine artist, Don Ray and sculpture artists Pierre Pierce and Hanes Hoffman also attended.

The marina absolutely buzzed with activity, crews rigging ballyhoo, mullet and Spanish mackerel. Normally no fishing was allowed in the marina or on the marina bulkhead. As I walked to the marina with Bob and John, we saw hundreds of kids fishing on every crevice of that island. Every single rule in place was broken that day. Under the tent that evening, I gave grace and thanked everyone for coming. I think the kids loved it the most, though. Not only were they here on their families' boats with mom and dad, at a billfish tournament where they usually didn't get invited, but they could explore Walker's Cay at will! Such independence. "Just look both ways before crossing the airstrip!"

Apparently several boycotts and several attempts to close the tournament down failed. All of the mucky-mucks from the IGFA came, including two of my favorite people: IGFA employee Jim Brown, our score keeper/radio operator, and IGFA president, Mike Leech.

The weather for the first day of fishing looked good. We established a 60-mile radius rule stating no fishing farther than 60 miles from the head pin of Walker's channel.

At 9:02 AM came the first call with a hook up! Angler Brad, a six-year old hooked up with a blue marlin in the junior division. No one could believe it. The captain spoke into the radio that Brad was in his father's lap, the rod leaning on Brad's grandfather's shoulders, and mom was guiding the fighting chair. Instantly, the entire tournament entered stasis. At 9:42 AM, with screaming and yelling in the background, little Brad got on the radio and yelled, "Blue marlin release!" Nobody cared about IGFA rules or even how big the fish was. Nobody cared that the captain hooked the fish from the bridge rod. Everyone cared about a young boy battling a blue marlin in his father's lap with grandpa and mom helping.

Fifteen minutes later another boat off Matanilla Shoals called in a white marlin hook up by Melissa. The young lady fought and released the fish all by herself. With 105 boats in the field all trolling dead bait, the billfish bite really turned on at about 11 AM. Nine boats hooked up throughout the day. Poor Jim Brown finally announced on the radio, "Hey everyone! Don't worry about calling in your fish on time. This is an honor scoring tournament. Your word is your bond." Somewhere around 2 PM, Captain Jimmy on the *Sea Lion II* (the Abplanalp's boat), called in a blue marlin hooked up by a junior angler. The entire fleet rooted for the *Sea Lion II*. After just over two hours, Captain Jimmy came back on the radio announcing the marlin had pulled the hook with the leader only four inches from rod tip.

Tournament control immediately responded, "Did the mate touch the leader?" Jimmy responded, "Went to grab the leader and missed it by an inch." To my surprise and joy, the tournament went absolutely crazy congratulating the *Sea Lion II* angler. At that moment, I could hardly control myself. The Barta Blue Marlin Classic had succeeded in my life's dream. That junior angler, at that minute, learned honesty and a moral code.

The entire tournament exuded the word "trust." Under the tent that evening, I brought all of the junior anglers to the podium. I explained that although that fish wasn't caught, the excitement of the fight, family and friends working together, and the honor of the entire crew doing the right thing was much more important. The number of white marlin, blue marlin and sailfish released that day totaled 44 fish. Are you sitting down? Fully 82 percent of the fish were caught by junior anglers under 12 years old. The buzz on the dock was contagious. The captains of some very fine blue marlin crews stood mesmerized by these facts. An eight-year old boy sitting in dad's lap hooked up a blue marlin on 30-pound tackle. He let the fish go against light drag and things settled down in the cockpit. Just relax and take a deep breath. You can catch the fish with no problem. It's easier and less stressful when you don't care whether or not you lose the fish — a fish ostensibly worth tens of thousands of dollars in a Calcutta/kill tournament. No backing up with black smoke billowing from the exhausts. No one yelling and screaming. No burying the transom in a huge wave flooding the cockpit. Just take your time, have a good time and catch him. We found that with patience and light drags, kids could catch these fish all day long.

Junior anglers got trophies for the top fifteen dolphin, wahoo, tuna, and any other pelagic fish. I found it heartening to see professional captains walk up to the weigh table representing the family that owned the boat. It put a smile on everyone's face. Here comes a hot-shot captain on a huge custom boat walking to the weigh table with a proud 7-year-old girl, mom, dad, grandma, grandpa and a peanut dolphin in tow. Finally, Jim Brown announced to the gathered crowd, "7-year-old Heather — dolphin — 4 pounds 2 ounces!" and the gallery exploded with cheers, clapping and profuse congratulations to Heather. For that moment, she was the star of the event! Heady stuff! The air filled with happiness for all the anglers.

The next morning the weather dawned a little bit iffy, but everyone left for fishing anyway. We soon got a "distress call" from one of the bigger Hatteras boats in the tournament. Over the VHF we heard, "We have five junior anglers on board all under eight-years old. Three of them are sick. We are coming back to go bottom fishing inside the reef." What should I do? A stillness came over the tournament. I asked the captain, "Where will you be fishing?" He said, "Right behind Walker's, on the grass flats." I thought for a moment, starting to panic. This tournament was for everyone. I called Jim Brown and other members on our tournament board on the VHF. "Hey everyone, it's Captain Tred Barta. I propose an amendment to the rules of the Barta Blue Marlin Classic which hereby opens up to junior anglers any of the waters inside the reef for consideration of one trophy per junior angler per species." The short silence seemed to last decades. What to expect? One by one each board member approved and signed off. Each approval got funnier and funnier. The first board member said, "Approved." The second board member came back, "Here ye! Here ye! All who hear my voice. I hereby amend article 32.6 of the Magna Carta to approve your request." Every board member added a new twist to the approval.

This tournament... I watched in awe as it evolved into what I wanted it to be; a family tournament. As the day progressed our fish totals surpassed 100 billfish released. Are you hearing me? One hundred billfish — most caught by children! The biggest Bahamian tournament in history and we had released more billfish in two days than any other tournament in history. All on 30-pound test and dead bait, to boot. Our rules allowed trolling two teasers, but they had to be dead bait, meaning no artificial lures. That night, money flowed like water at the auction. One-hundred percent of all the monies made at the live auction went to the IGFA Junior Angler program.

In the middle of the auction, five very strong mates escorted me off the stage. When I returned, a package with the name "Captain Tred Barta" sat on the podium to be auctioned off. Everyone who knows me understands that as a man's man, I hate the color pink more than any other. As far as I am concerned the entire world going "pink-less" wouldn't bother me one bit. All of a sudden over the microphone I heard, "Let the bidding begin." I opened the package and to my horror, one of my monogrammed dress-white uniforms, along with a hat, captain's bars, and belt greeted me — all dyed hot pink! They pulled a curtain up around me and being a good sport, I put the outfit on. I can't tell you how embarrassed and angry I felt wearing that outfit. Of course the crowd loved it but it literally tortured me. The bidding started at $100. When sold, I had to wear the outfit one entire day. The bidding hit $700, $900, $1000. People were yelling and screaming as they stood on chairs. The bidding got up to $5000 to wear that outfit all day fishing. Just when I thought the bidding had run its course, my dear friend, Tom Malone, a successful tort lawyer who owned the 70- foot Striker *Justice* stood up. "I bid $10,000, and anyone who matches my bid of $10,000 may extend Captain Tred's wearing of the uniform throughout the tournament to the award ceremonies." This meant I would have to wear that damn pink outfit from 6 am until 11 pm if someone matched his bid! More than any real man could handle. At the time, I enjoyed notoriety for my signature drink: chocolate milk. As I held a glass up, Steve Moynihan stood up on a picnic table and shouted, "SOLD!" Mr. Malone bellowed at the top of his lungs and I heard the swinging anvil crash the second time. The crowd noise deafened me. Twenty thousand in cash raised for the IGFA Junior Angler program just for me wearing hot pink!

True to my word, the next morning greeted me with hoots, hollers, and wolf calls as I wore the pink uniform. I took the ribbing of my life. I left the marina, driving from the tower of *Makaira* in this pink getup. The comments lasted all day. At 2 PM on the final day, Jim Brown announced over the VHF that all our efforts had raised $123,000 for the IGFA Junior Angler program!

The Barta Blue Marlin Classic existed at Walker's for seven years. Seventy sponsors, countless volunteers, thousands of participants, and ultimately, we raised over one million dollars for the IGFA Junior Anglers! In addition to the million dollars, the tournament gave $250,000 to Grand Cay, which built a brand new school and equipped all of the students with computers, arguably one of the biggest accomplishments of my life.

I have always said "Never Give Up, Never Say Never." Sure, I am dyslexic, have ADD/ADHD, and many disabilities to work around, but one thing that you can never underestimate is passion. The Barta Blue Marlin Classic absolutely and unequivocally changed the fabric of our sport. Today if you got caught killing a blue marlin and letting it rot on the dock in the sun just for the money, even the fat cats would lynch you.

Bob Abplanalp died in 2003. In 2004, Walker's Cay suffered two back-to-back hurricanes, Frances and Jeanne. Those hurricanes devastated the island leaving nothing but rubble — and the beautiful little chapel. After all of the devastation, the absolute totaling of the island and its structures, the little church where I prayed on my knees for the success of the tournament remained unscathed.

I and many others believe frigate birds are the souls of great fishermen. They use Walker's Cay in the late afternoon as their resting perch. Some fifty to one hundred frigates rest along the shore vegetation. As you leave for the fishing grounds in the morning they follow you as if to say, "I remember you. Please remember me." I find something very peaceful and calming about a frigate in flight. Quite simply, all great fishermen should go on the wings of a frigate when their time comes.

See the following chart of Walker's Cay.

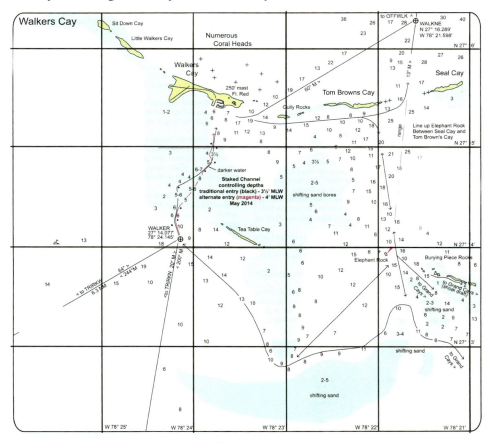

Chart 8

Walker's Cay and The Barta Blue Marlin Classic

Captain Tred Barta wiring blue marlin off Walker's Cay.

Barta Blue Marlin Classic in Walker's Cay
From left to right: Bob Abplanalp, Tred Barta, and John Abplanalp

Barta Blue Marlin Classic in Walker's Cay
Kids who participated in the tournament

Barta Blue Marlin Classic in Walker's Cay
Dock on Walker's Cay during the tournament

Barta Blue Marlin Classic in Walker's Cay
Tred (in pink) with Omie Tillet who gave the prayer and designed the "Carolina Flare" on boats.

Chapter Twenty-One
THE BARTA BOYS AND GIRLS CLUB BILLFISH AND INSHORE TOURNAMENT

WITH WALKER'S OUT of business due to the hurricane damage to the island, we had no tournament. Enter a dear friend of mine, Jim Bailey, a fervent and loyal supporter of the Barta Blue Marlin Classic tournament and with whom I have had business dealings buying and selling corporate aircraft. Jim wanted to revitalize the old "Captain Fanny Mae Tournament" held in North Carolina and he knew I had the recipe for tournament success.

While I enjoyed going from being a tournament pariah to having seemingly fifty-odd other fishing tournaments vying for my support, Jim had supported me in the past, and I trusted him in business and as a friend. Jim flew up to meet me in Southampton, New York in a Beechcraft King Air with a young lady and her husband. Jim suggested the young lady, Cynthia Barber, would make a great tournament director and, with the help of her husband, David, would handle the local tournament groundwork. Cynthia and David turned out to be just fantastic people. They care deeply about the proposed charity, the Boys and Girls Club of Coastal Carolina, located in Beaufort.

I had followed the Boys and Girls Club closely for years. I had also fished the North Carolina coast for marlin and tuna for many years. I knew first-hand of the great devastation hurricane after hurricane took on the southern Outer Banks. The town of Beaufort (pronounced Bow-furt) started life as an Indian fishing village before Europeans "settled" in the town. In 1723 the Europeans incorporated the town, then called Fishtowne, but later changed it to the current Beaufort. Another town spelled the same way in South Carolina is pronounced Bee-you-furt. Should you care, you can remember them by Bow sounds like O and North Carolina has an O in it. Bee-you-furt sounds like U and South Carolina has a U in it. Or not... Initially, Jim Bailey put up $25,000 of his own money to start the tournament. One day in the dead of winter, Jim, Cynthia, David, and I sat around a table with Jim's $25,000 check and the tournament became a reality.

We designed The Barta Boys and Girls Club Billfish and Inshore Tournament to be similar to the Barta Blue Marlin Classic: A dead-bait, honor-system scoring, no calcutta, your word is your bond tournament. We needed no observers and participants should expect no personal gain of any kind. The tournament resurrected the art of rigging natural baits. It encompassed several different categories so that the playing field remained equal for everyone. I demanded an amateur division, pro division, small-boat division, and a women's division. Only circle hooks would be allowed and it would join the prestigious North Carolina Governor's Cup Tournament Series (which does not follow all of the IGFA rules.)

Many locals, especially those closely involved with "Big Rock" (a big Calcutta/kill tournament) weren't exactly thrilled to hear about another tournament coming to the area. As with the Walker's tournament, many people felt success required dead fish on the dock, especially dead fish on the dock for money. I have always professed that you can never win in life if you're afraid to lose. Here came yet another opportunity to put money where my mouth is. This tournament — almost a duplicate of Walker's Cay — restored my faith that many good people still believe in family values, a prayer before meals, and saying the Pledge of Allegiance. We have become so liberal that any tradition now gets deemed passé. For example, I believe in honoring our military rather than denigrating it, so we always have the honor of a U.S. Marine Corps color guard from nearby Cherry Point Marine Air Station. It's always been important to me to honor the people who have laid down their lives for our freedom. It's an integral part of who I am and a value I want to teach our children.

Every year the 54-foot party fishing vessel *Captain Stacy IV* takes 40 boys and girls from the Boys and Girls Club bottom fishing for the day. Many of these kids have never been on a boat and quite a few have never fished. These kids don't care if they catch a prize fish, a shark, or a jellyfish. To hear their stories and to feel their excitement, whether the fish was caught by themselves or one of their friends, energizes the staff, donors, and the 70 tournament volunteers. These kids march down the dock to the tent (covering the entire village parking lot) singing a new tournament song each year, which is like giving me and the staff a powerful vitamin. Their need and enthusiasm keep us going.

I became paralyzed in the tournament's fifth year. Recovering at Craig Rehabilitation Center in Denver, Colorado prevented me from attending the event. A video hookup let me speak to the tournament crowd from a large TV screen. Halfway through the broadcast, I no longer saw or heard anything on my computer screen. Everybody at the hospital panicked, not knowing if I was transmitting or not. So I just kept on talking! I later found out they could hear and see me even though I couldn't see them. I talked about my cancer; how I lost faith and got it back; about how much the tournament meant to me; and how I wanted to return at least one more year.

I told the tournament group that if I died, I wanted them to continue the tournament. The next year when I was flown to the tournament in Don Quadlbaum's private airplane, I received a hero's welcome! The Chief of Police gave me an escort from the Coastal Carolina Regional Airport in New Bern to the tournament. Beaufort Mayor Ann Carter gave me a key to the city. These things never made me feel more important, but rather made me very thankful I was still alive and gave me a renewed purpose in life.

Every night before dinner, I say the evening prayer under the big tent. Sometimes I ask to be placed on my knees for the prayer, which believe me is not very pretty and surely isn't easy. Usually two men in the color guard grab me underneath my arms, lift me out of my wheelchair while another volunteer holds the microphone. Daniel Montoya, my aid, keeps me from falling head-over-heels and makes sure my pants do not fall off. It's quite the juggling act with multiple people aiding me. From my point of view, I always find this humorous.

I remember one year my pants did almost fall off. I could see in the faces of the crowd that everyone suddenly prepared to be horrified. Daniel reacted immediately, laying me on the stage, pulling my pants up, plopping me back in the wheelchair, adjusting everything and after the prayer, the entire gallery under the tent gave me a standing ovation.

Every year we have a sponsor's dinner at The Boathouse, a great supporter of the tournament. This invitation-only event affords me the opportunity to thank our biggest donors like Volva Penta, Walker Napa Auto Stores, Anheuser-Busch, RAJ Distributors, Nationwide Insurance, Murphy Brown (Smithfields), Outback Steak House, Transportation Impact, Grady-White, and Albemarle boats. In 1934, the property on which The Boathouse sits was purchased by the Mace family, founders of Beaufort Fisheries, Inc. For the next 75 years the company processed menhaden on the site. At these appreciation dinners, people dress elegantly, but that sure doesn't make them stuffy. These very kind and caring people give money, materials, and do absolutely anything to make this organization run like a well-oiled machine. They care deeply for the children. Not boastful about their wealth or position, they just represent a room full of the kind of people the world should be, and it gives me hope about humanity. I am honored to know them and to have them be critical spokes in the wheel.

It excites me to see captains bring children to the Weigh-In Station with their pinfish, wahoo, tuna or dolphin catches and to get their photos taken by a professional photographer and the congratulations of their family members. Some of the young children catch fish too big for them to carry so it makes me smile when they are pulling and dragging a big dolphin to the Weigh-In Station. We have an "Act of Kindness" award; recognition highlighting sportsmanship like a child giving up its chance in the fighting chair so another less privileged angler can catch a fish.

Awards night is always fun and very busy. Tables sag under the load of trophies. Parents need to be herded — often acting more out of control than the kids. While certainly proud of the fish they caught, the children take even more pride in their shiny new fish-mount trophies.

In recent years, weather has continually harassed our tournament. But if we have a day blow out, fishing inshore. I remember one awful day, a beautiful 70-foot Spencer custom Sportfisherman fished two feet from the seawall in the port of Morehead City, trying to catch pinfish! The kids didn't care, being thrilled to be included on the boat!

We learned and grew over the next 13 tournament years. To date, we've raised more than $875,000, well on our way to the pledged one million dollars.

Let me share a few tournament highlights I vividly remember.

In 2005, the second year of the tournament, we released 115 billfish in 12 hours (2 days with 6 hours fishing each day) — over 85 percent released by kids 12 years and younger. It proved unequivocally that when you have no money on the table, truly wonderful things can happen. It also proved there's more than one way to catch billfish. You can back down, spin around, hammer them with heavy drag and heavy tackle or you can take your time and enjoy the fight without exhausting and hurting the fish.

Each year, we enjoy having 250 to 300 kids fish the tournament, with 97 percent under the age of 16. We even awarded the wrong person as winner once, but we admitted our mistake and ultimately made everyone happy.

Duane Reynolds is the Executive Director of the Boys and Girls Club of Coastal Carolina. The club has programs for children 6- to 18-years old. The after-school program runs daily from 2 to 6:30, the summer program from 7:30 am until 6:30 pm and costs only $25 a week plus $5 if the child goes on a field trip. All tournament money raised goes to the general operating fund of the club. In addition, we arranged for a company named Thomasville Bus to build and donate a 64-passenger bus via our tournament. James P. Bailey's family established a scholarship fund which provides $2,000 a year to the Boys and Girls Club Youth of the Year. Our annual tournament artists have included Pierre Pierce, Danny Azzato, Carey Chen, Hanes Hoffman, Guy Harvey, and Larry Carter. Sponsors have donated substantial auction items: Casa Vieja Lodge donates fishing trips in Guatemala; Mark Tupper donated a fishing trip worth $5,000; Napa Auto Parts donated a four-by-four ATV worth $14,000; and noted marine artist, scientist and philanthropist Dr. Guy Harvey has donated some of his signature line of jewelry... to name a few.

Once, the boat called *Good Time* lost an engine during rough weather. We got the call that they had hooked up. After about 30 minutes, Captain Mark Beckham called in. We heard kids screaming in the background. He said, "Savannah Beckham released her first billfish, a white marlin!" We conveyed how happy we were for him and Savannah. His reply was, "I am the proudest dad on the ocean right now." It brought tears to our eyes. It took them five hours to get back to the dock. Tradition calls for anyone who catches their first billfish to be thrown into the water. Even though Savannah returned at 7 pm and the weigh-in station had closed, her father and I gave Savannah the official "Billfish Bath in Taylor's Creek!"

Another time, a 48-foot Viking, *Real Time* was in rough seas and suddenly discovered water coming in. Owner Rick Sykes called the Coast Guard and in the meantime, the boat sank. The US Coast Guard, British and American Navies were conducting joint-forces operations not far offshore. All three responded to the distress call, as did the U.S. Marines at Cherry Point Air Station, by sending its beloved HH-46 Sea Knight rescue helicopter — affectionately known to all as "Pedro," that plucked a small child from the sea. Luckily, and thanks to all, everyone aboard survived without so much as a scratch!

More than eighty sponsors support the spectacular annual event in Beaufort. The town loves the tournament, as thousands of people come and patronize the businesses. Restaurants are packed; the stores are busy; men, women and children enjoy being in the tournament, come to the auction, or just want to enjoy the evening events, making it a win-win situation for the entire town. I am proud to be a part of this tournament and it gives me great pleasure to give to the community.

After I am gone from this world, plenty of people will judge my life. I believe — if they judge it correctly — the number one thing I accomplished is changing the tournament attitude about conservation. I feel I have redesigned not only the tournament landscape, but gave people the courage to follow in my footsteps.

Tred with the kids who participated in the
Barta Boys and Girls Club Billfish and Inshore Tournament.

Chapter Twenty-Two
A New Reality

ONE DAY IN May 2009, I woke up at my usual 5 AM at my Longbow Ranch in Eagle, Colorado. I showered and shaved with special unscented soap. In total darkness, I put on my chambray shirt, blue jeans, and pulled on my cowboy boots. I buckled my belt. The buckle was made from the largest Colorado big horn sheep ever shot. The scrimshaw image of the large ram had faded over the years from rubbing against my Carhartt vest and jacket.

Even though I owned this beautiful Colorado ranch complete with a large barn to accommodate seven horse stalls, an indoor professional riding arena (120 feet by 66 feet), and all the trimmings, another section of the barn to house tractors, 4 wheelers, hunting and fishing gear, I still made my coffee in a blue camping kettle. I sat on the entrance stairs to my house with perhaps the best friend a man ever had, my beloved dog, Ahi. Ahi, a part Australian Shepard rescue dog, always slept at my bedside and literally never left me. We were inseparable. While sipping my coffee and watching the first silhouettes of light, I reminisced about much of what has been written so far in this book. Now I invite you to walk in my boots as a new reality took over my life. My wife (now ex-wife), Anni, always eked out every ounce of morning sleep that she could. Anni was definitely not a morning person and as you might guess, ranch life always starts early.

The house had been completely remodeled since we purchased it. Well-designed with beautiful furnishings, it could easily have been displayed in *HGTV* or *Gardens and Guns* magazine. We added on a 1200 square foot trophy room with a cathedral ceiling and beautiful thick wood beams. The reclaimed wood flooring came from an old barn floor which we pegged to the subfloor with old style flat-cut pilgrim nails.

Huge windows opened up to the magnificent views of Coffin and Bear Mountains from my trophy room as well as from the front porch. On the other side, great sandstone cliffs turned a lovely green as the aspens cut their leaves after the long, cold winter. In the fall, it felt like walking into a postcard of what Colorado should look like, printed by the Department of Tourism. Simply breathtaking.

Longbow Ranch sat atop a small knoll. The "Back 40" spiraled up another few thousand feet to the top of a high alpine meadow. Although the property encompassed only 17+ acres, it abutted hundreds of square miles of national forest with a well-deserved reputation for being arguably the greatest mule deer hunting block in Colorado. Two- hundred to 230-point deer (world-record statistical terminology) fed and bedded on our front field.

In the depth of winter, several elk herds would descend from the high country in search of food. In the harshest winters, Colorado's Department of Wildlife issued special permits for us to feed the elk hay and later reimbursed us for the cost.

You accessed Longbow Ranch via Salt Creek Road. The ride from Eagle, Colorado to the ranch wound through some of the most beautiful countryside in the state. Fields of hay and alfalfa grew on both sides of the valley and wintered hundreds of horses and cattle.

Ascending from Brush Creek Road onto Salt Creek Road you came to a dead end some 1,500 feet higher at the Brazington Ranch, one of the top properties in all of Colorado. I had permission to hunt on most of the properties – all privately owned — on Salt Creek. Black bear, mule deer, elk, beaver and all of Colorado's small game thrived there. This life was a dream come true!

Ahi and I walked through the uncut grass down to the barn, wetting my boots and legs of my pants with the morning dew. The massive barn door opening made a horrendous squeak that everyone hated but I loved what it meant. As the great door slid open Ahi always crouched down ready to pounce on some unsuspecting field mouse or barn rat. I took one step into the barn, hitting the light switches and Ahi raced off at 300 miles per hour on the heels of a terrified rat. The rat raced down the concrete hallway in front of the stalls and tried to put its brakes on to slow down and escape through a small hole in the rear barn door. Ahi didn't stop, slamming into the door. I heard some growling and dying rodent noises. Ahi proudly brought me his trophy barn rat.

The day held great promise. We had already bagged our first animal and the day had barely started! Our barn, with its professional arena, was a show stable. The stalls had wrought iron gates on rollers and each horse had its name engraved on a brass plaque, a hook for the horse's bridle and halter, and a lead rope next to their stall. We had a beautiful outdoor area that was 194 feet by 90 feet. Disposing of the rat in a large metal trash can, Ahi and I took a walk down to the lower pasture to collect my horse, Badger and Anni's horse, Trogdor.

Ahi never missed an opportunity to trot around the large watering trough in the lower pasture. On his watch, there would be no coyotes or foxes permitted into the area. Salt Creek had several cougars that hunted on the various properties. In addition, there had been several sightings of lynx and bobcats. What a marvelous place to live. As I came to the pasture gate, both horses showed up making collecting them easy as usual. While holding two lead ropes, Ahi and I walked back to the barn and tied the both horses off to a hitching post outside the barn door. Badger was a black and white Indian Paint and had won several awards for roping and ranch chore competition. Trogdor was a magnificent trail horse and a safe ride for Anni. Trogdor was a woman's horse and loved Anni. The two of them had a love affair wonderful to see. Behind the barn, I brushed and curried the horses, blanketed and saddled them. Both of them took a bridle smoothly, just like butter. Leaving the barn door open with the sun just cresting over the sandstone hillside east of the ranch, I led the menagerie up to the main house.

Amazingly, I found Anni ready to go. We mounted up and climbed steeply up the hillside behind the ranch. We rode behind two neighbor's ranches, ascended a side hill which gently rose to a trail that lead up a small pass and traversed over to a trail head that ultimately brought us to a point high above our property, where an alpine meadow offered an exquisite view of Longbow Ranch.

We rode early this morning because I was leaving for Alaska the next day to shoot my TV show. This episode of "Best and Worst of Tred Barta" on NBC Sports took me in search of black bear. I'd be packing all afternoon for the two-week trip. I just wanted to get this ride in with Anni before I left for Alaska.

The ride felt more like an accommodation by Anni than something she really wanted to do, though it turned out to be spectacular. The horses performed perfectly. We rode some truly rough terrain, pausing several times to look below at Longbow Ranch as it glowed in the morning sun. The ranch house, barn, and the entire property stretched out before us. Ahi ran between the horses' legs as usual. We returned to the barn without incident and Anni scurried off to begin her day flying to Mexico on vacation.

I washed both horses using a squeegee to roll the water off their hides. When I released them to the pasture, of course they both immediately rolled on their backs and made sure both sides of their bodies were scrubbed in dirt. I always found this comical. You can really only keep a horse clean for a very short period of time.

I spent the morning working at Barta-Iso Aviation and the afternoon finishing up my packing. Life was good. Business was good. My TV show was good. I was happy and full of hope — my life firing on all cylinders.

I noticed while walking into my office that my left leg seemed numb, like when you sleep on your arm during the night and when you wake up your hand and arm feel numb. But as you move it, the feeling goes away. I couldn't lift my left foot higher than my opposing right knee. My lower back felt sore, too. I thought, "Something's not right…" I convinced myself it was a pinched nerve or charlie horse, but as I went to sleep that night it did not get better.

The next morning, I drove to my doctor in Grand Junction for several cortisone shots in my lower back. Later in the afternoon I drove to Vail for a MRI. They found what looked like a pinched nerve in my lower back with some swelling between the vertebrae, but thought the MRI inconclusive. By lunch, I could barely drive or even lift my left foot off the pavement. Anni had already left for a one-week vacation at her timeshare in Cabo San Lucas, Mexico. I started to fear something serious was on the horizon.

My Alaska journey rapidly approached. But how could I possibly film an outdoor TV show when I could hardly walk? I became nervous enough that I called the crew and postponed the Alaskan bear hunt for one week. That created quite a stir as both Danny Kirsic and Dave Abbott, the cameramen, had already flown to Vancouver from their homes in Tennessee and Georgia. I was supposed to be on my way to the Denver Airport myself right then. I had a difficult decision to make and I felt terrible about inconveniencing everyone. Not only would the cameramen lose two weeks of pay, but Larry Larson of Wild Alaska Cruises and Sportfishing would lose the revenue on a two-week charter on his mothership. This was not the norm for Tred Barta nor what I stood for.

The next morning, I awoke with horrendous pain in my lower bowels. I couldn't urinate and could hardly move my left leg. All alone at the ranch house with Ahi, I struggled to walk downstairs to the kitchen and down another staircase to my truck below. Sweating profusely, I called Dr. Palic at the nearby Palic Clinic in Edwards, a well-known chiropractic doctor and just a twenty-minute drive from the ranch. He had been working on me all week. I called his emergency number and he agreed to see me immediately.

To this day I have no idea how I managed to get into the truck but I did, but I admit to something I never felt before… panic! I believe I blacked out at the bottom of Salt Creek Road because when I opened my eyes my truck sat parked on the side of the road – in Park. I don't remember pulling off or parking. I fearfully drove onto the I-70 highway towards Edwards. Halfway there I started to feel like I was going to black out or completely lose control of the truck. This was definitely no charlie horse or pinched nerve. In the middle of I-70 I turned my truck sideways in both lanes and put it in Park. I laid there knowing that if I wasn't flattened by a 16-wheeler, someone would stop or call the police. I tried to dial 911 but the phone slipped out of my hands. The door opened on my passenger side and I remember looking up to see a highway patrol officer and flashing lights. I remember being conscious and asking to be taken immediately to Dr. Palic who was waiting for me. The conversation seemed disjointed and he said he couldn't do that unless my truck was broken down. I remember the following in a blur: I'm not even positive exactly what happened. The man in uniform knew me from my TV show. He picked me up out of the pickup truck and placed me into his squad car. We passed cars and trucks like they were standing still. The speed limit was 75 miles per hour and we blasted by them. I can't imagine how fast we were going.

I remember hobbling into the doctor's office with my arm around the officer. Dr. Palic came around the corner and saw me. I heard his assistant yell out, "should I call an ambulance?" Dr. Palic shouted, "we don't have time." The patrolman and the doctor carried me to the doctor's personal vehicle and we drove to the Emergency entrance at Vail Valley Hospital. I seemed to know everyone at the hospital. I was well known in the valley for my TV show and my mini-celebrity status, and I'd been featured quite often in the Valley newspaper.

I had an excruciating pain in my groin and with bandage scissors they cut off the left leg of my jeans. I can't remember the details of the next couple of hours but I do remember the intravenous drugs dripping through an IV in my left arm and slowly, the pain drifted away. I looked down at a Foley catheter that had been inserted to drain my bladder. Two nurses and three doctors worked frantically on me with a terrible urgency in the air. I could no longer move my left leg and had no feeling at all.

A black horror swept over me. The greatest fear any man could face. What was happening to me? Why was it happening? Why couldn't I feel my left leg?

People were running all over the place. I heard a doctor yell in the hallway outside of my room, "Get the f..king helicopter on the way!" The terrible weather — fog, rain or snow — had all of the passes shut down to flying. I remember yelling, "What's happening to me?" I tried to get out of bed and to my horror now I couldn't move my right foot. People were yelling. A helicopter touched down on the helipad. Two pilots came running to the stretcher I was on yelling, "No go! No go!" A nurse threw her arms over me with tears rolling down her cheeks which I will never forget. I had no idea why she was crying. They loaded me into an ambulance.

It was dark, cold and lonely. I awoke to machines on my chest and an oxygen mask over my mouth. One of the people in the ambulance talked on a cell phone with Denver Hospital. The other apparently continuously monitored my vital signs to prepare the Denver Hospital for my arrival. Anni was still in Mexico. I think she yearned for time away from me and the ranch. I didn't want to disturb her. Nonetheless, I asked someone to tell her that I was in trouble. Seeming chaos surrounded me as I arrived at the Denver Hospital — kind of like TV shows such as "ER," except this time the drama all centered around me. By the time I arrived, neither leg would move. The paralysis had moved up to my hips making it impossible to walk.

I had my stomach muscles and could sit up. Everyone ran around me like I was dying! I thought perhaps I was experiencing an out-of-body experience. I felt like a medical dummy in a training hospital. I finally yelled out at the top of my lungs, "Stop! Someone talk to me!" The doctor put his arm around my neck and told me that I had become paralyzed from my waist down and they were trying to stop its progression. All kinds of blood tests, an emergency spinal tap and I don't even remember what else. I lost all track of time.

Apparently they were taking me to the operating room to cut through all of the vertebrae in my back — literally splitting them in half — to allow extra room around my swelling spinal cord. Anni had numerous connections with the Vail Valley Hospital and with some doctors specializing in this field. As I headed to the operating room Anni walked in. How? She was in Mexico and now she was in the hospital? I didn't understand. Apparently she had gotten the first flight out of Mexico. I don't know what day it was, but the specialist that Anni spoke with at the hospital stopped the surgery. Later, experts determined that the operation would have killed me.

As I write this, I am crying. I just can't hold back the tears. I knew my life would never be the same and I honestly didn't know if I wanted to live as what I had now become. Everyone kept telling me how tough I was, but honestly it all meant nothing to me.

A stroke had been ruled out. After several highly sophisticated blood tests were taken, they diagnosed me with a one-in-a-million case of Waldenstrom's Macroglobulinemia, a non-Hodgkins form of blood cancer that thickens the blood, which ultimately blew up my spine. The problem over the next two weeks was that the cancer was ascending towards my head and no matter what, they couldn't seem to stop it.

I'll save you reading volumes of medical jargon, but eventually the paralysis stopped just below my chest. I remember one very kind, older doctor. I asked everyone to leave the room except him. I looked into his eyes and asked him for the truth. He told me, "Tred, you will never walk again. You will be paralyzed for the rest of your life and if we don't get a grip on what is going on, you will die."

I remember laying in that lonely hospital room and saying to myself, "I will die like my father did." One of the most helpless, darkest places I have ever been. Little did I know that this moment would be absolutely nothing compared to what lay ahead. I stayed in the hospital for more than two months, during which time they pumped me full of several chemo drugs, the worst being methotrexate. It was slowly killing me. Both of my kidneys stopped functioning properly. I became so weak that I could hardly do anything.

Anni's two brothers and son, Ian, were incredibly supportive. Anni stayed with me and never gave up. Unfortunately, I am now divorced from Anni and many of the good feelings have been replaced with bad ones. But at that time in my life Anni rose to the occasion as most wives would and no matter what, will always deserve every bit of my thanks and admiration. She was a hero and no one could have done better. An orderly pushed my wheelchair out to a Koi pond in a courtyard just outside my hospital room, all my many intravenous bottles following me on a rack. I spoke to my business partner John Iso, telling him that I honestly didn't think I could live anymore. I reached the absolute lowest point in my life. I left the hospital bound for the Craig Rehabilitation Hospital where my 60-day training schedule on how to live the rest of my life as a paraplegic began. This school taught the handicapped skills necessary to live and to give a person hope. To some extent the rehabilitation training worked.

The chemo made me weak and terrible incidences of bad blood counts interrupted my training. I probably only benefited from maybe ten days of actual training. At one point, I had to endure pheresis, a process where all of the blood in your body passes through a machine which vacuums it through a filter and then pumps it back into your body.

During one of these sessions, the main line — placed in my chest – blew, and I watched my own life blood not only spray all over me, but pump out all over the floor, too. I had been through so much that even though it horrified everyone else, I found it humorous. To this day it seems funny.

The net: Vail Valley Hospital, Denver Hospital, flew off to Swedish Hospital, Craig Rehabilitation Center, and then had a major relapse that threw me back into Swedish Hospital, (actually attached to Craig Rehab). The doctors gave me about a week to live and I figured that was about right as I had no more strength in me. I didn't want to die, but I prepared myself for it. I had lived my life with purpose, with the belief that something greater exists in the world than myself, though I never completely bought the vision of flying off to the clouds of Heaven. I had lived my life the best I could, with a code of honesty. I thought I had helped others as much as I could. Although I probably needed loads of forgiveness, I felt I had been a basically good person and my life stood for something. I remember the exact day I told Anni I wanted to go home to die at our Longbow Ranch. I wanted to spend my remaining time on my porch with my dog, Ahi. Ahi had visited me quite a few times at the hospital. Of course, the hospital didn't want to release me, but I continued begging Anni to take me home. While everyone was out of the room, I reached down and tore the chemo drip and a saline solution intravenous tubes out of my arm. All kinds of alarms went off when I pulled the tubes. I'd had enough of that room. It was dark and had death written all over it. Everyone wore latex gloves and their touch made me cringe. I wanted out! Anni worked very hard to prepare a bedroom on the first floor of the ranch for me. Against all odds I couldn't wait to get home.

Earlier that day, in the courtyard with my arms outstretched over my head, I pleaded with God to allow a merciful end to my life. I remember feeling a warmth and caress by what I felt to be God himself. It came in the form of something extremely soft; maybe it was an angel. Actually, I have no idea what it was, but it was something. I questioned why I had to suddenly leave the world when I had been so young and healthy. I wanted more time to hopefully inspire others.

I checked out of the hospital to go home without truly knowing what would become of my life. I looked back at the times I only had one arrow left in my quiver, or one more chance at a world record, or one more yard to climb to the top of the mountain. I knew that right at this moment, I was still breathing, still alive. I had something left in my tank, though admittedly the needle read "E."

My incontinence posed one of my biggest psychological blocks. I had been a rugged, outdoorsman and now I had a catheter for my urine. I had to wear disposable diapers and had no control over my bowels. How could I go anyplace, do anything, or be around people with this problem? Would I need a nurse my entire life? All of these questions went unanswered as I got into the van for the ride back to Longbow Ranch.

The drive home was somber yet exhilarating. Vail Pass looked vibrant and beautiful. It had been almost four months since I last set foot on Longbow Ranch. In the fall the entire landscape blazed with yellow aspens and magenta buckbrush. As we pulled in past my horse, Badger, Anni opened the van window. Badger looked at me and I knew I was home. Ahi ran alongside the van. Finally, home with my longbows, horses, and my beloved dog — weak but alive.

Anni did an incredible job preparing my downstairs bedroom, making it warm, loving, and inviting. My book collection on hunting and fishing sat in a wall unit next to my bed. I slowly transferred into bed and the night became a blur. In short order, it became quite evident to me that I could not live in that regime. I awoke the next morning with no real hope. The first couple of weeks at home, I'd drink my coffee on the porch with Ahi at my side, knowing that I could not live wearing diapers and being incontinent.

Eventually I was introduced to Dr. Alexander Urquhart at the Shaw Vail Valley Cancer Center. He reviewed my case and begged me to try one more chemo, but I refused. I also met with Dr. Reggie Franciose, who had been a military medical doctor and an expert in triage. He shot guns, trained with the local SWAT teams, and was my type of man. We got along very well.

I begged for a colostomy operation at Swedish and Denver hospitals. This would reroute fecal material from my large intestine out my abdomen. By using a plastic wafer and a collection bag I could take care of my waste products myself. In short, I would not be incontinent. I also requested a suprapubic cystostomy (catheter in bladder) along with the colostomy, but no one wanted to perform the operations during chemo. The risk of infection from being paralyzed causing my skin to heal extremely slow conspired against my wishes. So no doctor was willing to perform the operations.

In one of my last meetings with Dr. Franciose I put my arms around his neck and told him that if he would not do the operations I was going to take my own life. I could not live with incontinence any longer. One week later at Vail Valley Hospital Dr. Franciose conducted both procedures simultaneously, a rarity having both at the same time, but he felt it necessary in my case. I woke up in the recovery room. Dr.Franciose and the team of doctors pulled the breathing tube out of my mouth. Although still pretty much out of it, I will never forget hearing Dr. Franciose say, "Tred we did it! It was a success!" As part of this deal, I agreed to try one more chemo called Retuxin that Dr. Urquhart suggested.

Something new had recently been discovered about Retuxin, though I have no clue what. As with all chemo, for two or three days after receiving it one became so nauseous and sick that it took every bit of strength to get through it. In the privacy of my own bedroom I cried.

During this time, we hired my dear young friend and assistant, Daniel Montoya. I quickly grew to love that man! Daniel sat with me during the worst of times. He helped me turn myself from side to side every couple of hours during the night. Daniel helped me shower and do just about everything.

Three months into the chemo, Dr. Franciose came charging up the Longbow Ranch driveway with his horn blaring. My bedroom door flew open and he ran in holding a handful of papers that showed my blood counts had improved due to the chemo. A complicated graph showed my disease improving! Over the next four months my colostomy and such worked perfectly and the Retuxin continued to beat the crap out of the cancer. At six months my blood looked even better. A year after initial paralysis, the cancer had been arrested.

I got stronger and stronger. One day as Daniel and I finished my weight and bungee workout, I looked at him and asked if he would stay with me for the entire ride. He always had a snappy answer. I remember him saying, "From the beginning to the end boss. What's on your mind?" I grabbed his arm and said in a loud voice, "It's time to shoot my bow again. Time to ride my horse again. It's time to ski again and it is time to do my TV show again!" With that he gave me a high five!

Chapter Twenty-Three
THE NEXT CHAPTER – RETURNING TO THE LONGBOW

ALIVE AND FULL of hope! I desperately wanted to return to all the activities I had engaged in prior to getting sick.

And truly a miracle had happened. People often tell me they do not believe in God or fate. I am telling you, or rather asking you, what gave Dr. Franciose the insight, wisdom, and energy to make me independent again? What gave my oncologist the drive to push the *Retuxin* that became the perfect bullet against my cancer? What brought Daniel Montoya, a ranch hand and now personal assistant into my life? How did Anni muster up almost super-human resolve to keep me pointed in the right direction?

You know what I believe, but no matter what you may think, many things certainly had to align. For the first time in later life, I felt truly driven. Thankfully (and amazingly), through all of what happened to me, I didn't lose much upper body strength. The biggest problem was I had no torso strength, no control of my stomach muscles whatsoever due to being paralyzed just below my chest.

Anni had devised a strap system similar to a Formula One safety harness. The straps wrapped around the back of my wheelchair and crisscrossed over my chest, allowing me to pull the longbow back to my anchor point. Then I could get the proper 45-degree angle with my front hand, my back anchor point hand, and my head all positioned at the same time. The adjustable harness allowed me to lean forward to a perfect distance and to release the arrow.

Historically, the longbow arguably represents one of the hardest weapons to master. Very few people shoot it because of the tremendous time investment to become proficient. Even prior to being in a wheelchair, my maximum proficient distance limited out at 30 yards. In my career, I killed well over 100 game animals within this distance. I took many animals — such as my bull moose in the Yukon and the grizzly bear in British Columbia — within ten yards.

Adjacent to my renovated bedroom, I had a small, man cave where I made my own cedar arrows. Any paraphernalia that revolved around my outdoor sports ended up in this room. In that room, my life seemed OK. Daniel set up targets outside my bedroom patio: 10 deer, a couple of turkey, a full-size buffalo, and some coyote and fox. These Styrofoam archery targets let me practice shooting at distances from 10 to 40 yards. I got back to where I really shot well. I couldn't retrieve my arrows, but I definitely made the shots.

As a result of this, I felt ready to resume my TV show "Best and Worst of Tred Barta." My first show took place on a private ranch in Texas. Our normal film crew, Danny Kirsic and David Abbott, manned the cameras, my very dear friend and longtime hunting guide, Dan Harrison, came to lead me to a white tail deer and my always indispensable personal assistant, Daniel Montoya, came along to help me with any personal needs.

Prior to my cancer the film crew and I made a tightly knit team. Now the team had to adjust, to reinvent every aspect of making a TV show around my wheelchair. The camera crew constantly discussed new camera angles and how to reposition themselves to get the best shots. Remember, during filming I sit down the entire time.

Shooting a TV show in a wheelchair proved no easy task. Even just traveling on a commercial airline from Colorado to Texas became more difficult when paralyzed. But as each part of the journey unfolded, the normalcy of my life came back very quickly. I just opened one door at a time and walked – or wheeled through it. In my own mind, it became crystal clear that life offered very little that I could not accomplish with a little help from my friends and family. Along the drive from the San Antonio Texas International Airport to the ranch, we passed through oil fields in a very arid wilderness of cactus and thorny buckbrush — an unforgiving land that time had forgotten. If only some of the abandoned, weathered houses and cabins could talk. Some three hours later, Dan and I drove down a winding red clay road to the ranch house where we would be staying.

Hunters in wheelchairs have precious few options. Places where I could hunt had to have wheelchair access so Daniel and Dan could somehow wheel me into a blind from which I could actually shoot — no easy task! Not only did we have to rethink how to make TV around my wheelchair, now we had to figure out where they could take me to hunt. Adding to the frustration level, I had communicated with Dan that wherever I sat in the blind had to be level. With no core muscles to keep me upright I could not lean against my supporting straps for a very long time. And the final kicker, I could only aim and release my arrow in a very narrow window to the left and right of where I positioned the wheelchair. If an animal came in from my left but did not cross the exact shooting lane I could get my arrow to, then I couldn't accurately shoot the animal! The task of hunting with a longbow just got harder and harder due to my paralysis.

In a desolate area of the ranch, we found a great location where a natural spring fed a small pool of water. Obviously in a parched countryside, every animal at some point had to drink. During this hunt, I attempted to shoot several feral hogs when they came to drink. My arrows flew over their backs or struck the dirt before them. As the days passed by, we started running out of time and the film crew out of patience. This frustrating effort wasn't working. On our last day before we headed back home, a flock of 50 turkeys went airborne onto a ridge before us right at dusk. They roosted on a huge dead oak positioned some 70 yards in front of my blind. What a spectacular sight to see these monstrous birds fly over our heads and then almost crash onto their perches for their evening roost! These great birds reminded me of B52 bombers overhead. You could hear their cackles and feel the air off of their wings — an incredible experience.

Now, with 50 sets of telescopic turkey eyes looking down into my blind, and with all of 15 minutes hunting time left, I thought to myself, "If a deer does come in, the turkeys will give away any movement that I make." Some discussion arose about trying to blow the turkeys off their roosts to get them away from the watering hole, but Dan wanted none of it. Suddenly, walking across the pasture toward the small pool of water came — what seemed to me — the biggest white tail in Texas. I believe it had a small basket rack consisting of four points, two small main beams, and two brow points.

The deer cautiously made its way to the pool, put its head down and started drinking, completely unaware of me or the team's presence. You could cut the tension with a knife. The film crew were running out of light. Dan Harrison was about to club me over the head for not shooting and I could see his eyes saying, "What the heck are you doing? Why aren't you shooting?" Another new reality set in. I couldn't shoot because I couldn't swivel my body to get the shot. Any movement I made would be noticed by the small buck and the game would be over. Everyone had forgotten my capabilities except me. After taking a drink, the buck exited the stage to the left and guess what? He crossed exactly where I could loose my arrow. He stopped and looked away from my blind. I drew, leaning forward against my restraining straps and sent the arrow on its way. The shot — low and a touch back from ideal — hit the deer. Dan, always very professional, but in an uncommon fashion muttered, "Yes!" just a little too loudly. The deer spun around in its own tracks and charged up a small hill which led down to the watering hole. As the deer almost crested the top, he fell over backwards, slowly put his head down, and expired.

Dan stood up absolutely jubilant! The film crew were ecstatic. The turkeys busted off their roosts and flew in all directions. Hey everybody, we're back in the game! I had just harvested a white tail buck as a T4, Asia A paraplegic.

I made a choice while recovering at Longbow Ranch. I planned to hurry up living or hurry up dying. My decision was now made. By golly, I would live larger and longer than ever. The wheels underneath me would now be my legs. I no longer considered myself impaired, no longer a paraplegic. I counted myself as merely inconvenienced by the wheels and no legs.

During all of the time I had known Dan Harrison, I had never seen him tear up. When he picked up the deer's head and put it in my lap, Dan couldn't hide his emotions. A wonderful moment among men… Tred Barta — back in the game!

Chapter Twenty-Four
MY OLD FRIEND BADGER

MOVING TO LONGBOW Ranch in 2007 gave me the opportunity to ride horses again. Initially, I looked worldwide for a great horse but ultimately found what I wanted much closer to home. My dear friend, Dan Harrison, located my horse, Badger, an arena show horse qualified in ranch and roping skills. Badger's owner, a woman in Montana who was fighting cancer, had easily spent a couple of hundred thousand dollars training the horse who won several ranch and roping medals. Badger could stop on a dime, spin right or left in an incredibly tight circle, and side step an entire arena. This horse could sort and cut cattle and you could shoot or rope off him. With the proper rider, Badger could win any ranch competition around. Badger measured 1,500 pounds of solid muscle. He took a light touch on the reins and an even lighter touch on the spurs. I considered him a "Cadillac ranch horse" times ten, and the price I paid for him reflected that.

Before my paralysis, Badger and I saddled up for a two-hour ride before work at least three days a week. I wasn't a great rider by riding competition standards, but for a businessman and ranch owner, I was top of my class.

I owned a 30-30 caliber Winchester lever-action rifle, purchased because Winchester manufactured it in 1952, my birth year. That old 30-30, two ranch ropes, and a yellow cowboy slicker were always strapped to Badger's saddle. Everyone who worked on the ranch knew to give this horse special attention. Badger got the best stall, trailer space, pasture or whatever. The boss's horse deserved nothing but the best of everything. I rode with a lot of local cowboys who would always put Badger through his paces. I consistently learned something new each time I rode him.

When I got sick and my future seemed hopeless, I arranged for Badger to be trained by a top western trainer, Caden "Blue" Allen, from Blue Allen Training Stables and other trainers. Blue and his wife lived in Alamosa, Colorado. Blue was a quintessential trainer's trainer. Badger needed to be comfortable near a wheelchair. Badger had to be trained to stand still and accept chaos around him while a crane lifted me onto his back.

I had a special saddle made to accommodate being paralyzed from my chest down. The saddle had a series of Velcro straps and a canted back support.

Strapped into the saddle, my torso would be supported. Of course if the horse tripped, fell, or stumbled to the ground I had an excellent chance of dying! But any life worth living involves risk. Nobody endorsed my riding Badger again except Dan Harrison, my trainer, and finally (but reluctantly) Anni.

The trainers built a 200-pound human dummy with a cowboy hat to train Badger. During his training sessions, they raised and lowered the dummy onto Badger's back with a Caterpillar tractor using a winch. Badger could not move an inch during the process or I could be hurt.

One very chilly, dreary, overcast day, three local cowboys, Anni, Daniel Montoya, and Dan Harrison met me at the barn. It had been too long since I had ridden Badger and I was anxious to get into the saddle again. Anchors with a winch bolted to them had been driven into the barn floor. Above, a pulley and cable system attached to the barn rafters. The setup included a Hoyer strap. The strap slid under my legs and behind my back while I sat in my wheelchair. The Hoyer straps attached to the cable and I winched myself out of the wheelchair by a remote control. There I hung freely above Badger.

Badger, already saddled and bridled, walked underneath me and I lowered myself onto his back, a tricky and potentially dangerous process. Somehow, Badger knew I was injured. It is amazing how horses and dogs can sense your fear and pain. He knew I needed his help and I think Badger knew he was being trained for this very day. With Ahi and the other ranch dogs running underneath his legs and up and down the barn, the winch making its grinding noise, and throughout all of the distractions of those trying to help me, Badger never flinched.

As the trainers led the operation I slowly winched myself down onto the saddle. Badger did not move even a fraction of an inch. Quick hands strapped me in. They placed my feet in the stirrups as I held the pommel. I let all the tension off the lifting Hoya straps and I sat — for the first time since being paralyzed — on Badger's back.

All of a sudden everyone was clapping. People were happy I had achieved my goal of getting on Badger again. As Badger and I were led out of the barn and down to the stable, I pulled back on Badger and took the lead rope, wrapping it around the horn. Badger and I rode ahead of everyone. We side-stepped to the gate. I unlatched the gate with my left hand and Badger pushed it open with his chest.

From the get-go, riding proved very uncomfortable for me. Riding on flat land was OK but going up and down hills was extremely jarring. And just about all the land around the ranch was hills. After all, I lived in the mountains! One major problem I encountered was my catheter pinching between my leg and the saddle. It was also very difficult to shift my weight when I started to slide off to one side of the horse because I had no control over my torso muscles. Being strapped into the saddle basically immobilized the upper part of my body. Since my paralyzed legs kept me from pushing down on either of the stirrups to even out my weight, I always needed someone next to me to slide me back upright. Although I hated to admit it, I knew from the very onset that my desire to ride Badger was full of insurmountable problems.

We had spent a small fortune on saddles, trainers, and special equipment to make it possible for me to ride again. How could I now complain about how uncomfortable it was to ride? It took five or six people just to participate in the thought of me riding. When I went on a trail ride, my local cowboy friends rode on each side of me and when I started to slide off the saddle they would grab the back of the saddle and literally pull me back onto the center of Badger's back. It became critically apparent that I needed three trained horsemen to ride with me at all times and they had to be completely dialed in. One false move and I'd be in major trouble.

The first time I rode Badger I tried to trot and lope — completely out of the question producing jolting and terrible pain rather than pleasure. The belly strap which held me into the back of the saddle brace often pushed against my colostomy bag, breaking it open onto my stomach: Extremely demeaning as you can imagine and the cleanup very awkward for everyone.

Honestly, the best part of the rides soon became picking Badger's hooves clean and washing him down with the barn hose. I could sit for hours — unsupervised — with my friend, Badger. He'd place his head in my lap and allow me to hold and caress him. People who are around horses for a long time talk about how a horse often looks right through to your soul. I felt Badger could see everything that was good in me and ignored the bad things.

To show off in front of people, I used to wheel myself underneath Badger and scratch his belly. People were impressed and though this could be incredibly dangerous, it wasn't with Badger. He accepted me no matter where I was. He always responded so gently when we were together.

As time passed, riding seemed to be more risk and trouble than it was worth. Often when cowboys came up to ride Badger and give him a workout, they would lead him from the lower pasture to the main barn. As soon as Badger saw me in my wheelchair up on the back porch of the house, he'd break free of the halter and come galloping up to the house, stopping at my wheelchair. He'd lower his head into my lap and would not move. It was so sad. Both Badger and I knew that I wouldn't – and shouldn't ever ride him again. This was perhaps one of the saddest things I have ever gone through.

On one of my last outings with Badger, I asked my next-door neighbor and a dear friend, Nate Pitman, a cowboy's cowboy, to witness my last ride with Badger. We had to time it so nobody would be around, including Anni. I wanted to spin Badger one last time in the indoor arena. My friends stood on each side of Badger acting as my safety net. I needed to feel Badger go into a hard right-hand spin one last time. I added just the proper touch of rein and nudged him with my riding crop. Badger put his head down and off we went into a very tight circle. We all knew I would come flying off the horse. I made it through five tight revolutions before I flew off the saddle into Nate's arms. We both hit the soft arena sand. As I lay there in Nate's arms, looking at Badger, I sadly knew in my heart it was my last ride. Badger walked up to me and put his head down to my face making sure I was OK. I reached out and felt his soft nose and mouth for the last time. Nate helped me back into my wheelchair and we unsaddled and unbridled Badger together. I wheeled Badger to his stall.

I agonized over not being able to ride Badger the way he deserved to be ridden. Three weeks later I sold him to a very kind cowboy in Montana. Today, Badger tends cows and relaxes in a summer pasture with other horses, right where he should be.

I miss riding Badger through the spring and summer pastures where the blue and white bell flowers and blue bonnets bloom. I miss the coolness I felt entering a stand of aspens, their beautiful leaves fluttering in the wind. Seeing the birches rise so majestically above all of the undergrowth — I'll miss it all. On our rides, Badger used to carefully lift his legs high to walk over a timber short fall so as to not jar me on the saddle.

Most of all, I will miss Badger getting a well-deserved drink from a pure mountain stream. When he drank, I often lost hold of the reins, but when Badger finished drinking he stood still so I could grab them. I miss my horse, and so much of what I used to be able to do. The key to my life is self-evident. I can only do what I am capable of doing and must maximize my efforts at those things.

I would love to see Badger again before I die. I think it would be good for the soul.

As a tribute to Badger and my friendship with all of the local cowboys, I was asked to give the Pledge of Allegiance and prayer at the big Eagle Rodeo. Local cowboys carried me up to the stage microphone. I gave the prayer and received a standing ovation. I did it more for Badger than for myself.

Tred Barta on Badger at Longbow Ranch

Chapter Twenty-Five
Piñas Bay, Panama – Tropic Star Lodge

DURING MY ULTRALIGHT tackle career, I traveled to Piñas Bay, Panama over a dozen times from the mid-1970s with some fishing trips lasting for three weeks. I set new world records at the lodge both on conventional and fly rods. During the many years that I went there, I got to know the Kittredge family who purchased the lodge in 1976. Conway D. Kittredge and I did three aircraft deals, and my last transaction with him was the sale of a 25-passenger FH-227 produced by Fairchild. When I lived in Southampton, New York, Hank and Mickey Altenkirch used to put together trips to Tropic Star Lodge through Larry and Scott Furhman, two superb light-tackle anglers.

Conway's daughter, Terri Kittredge, and I dated for a short period of time when I was young and single. I always had an absolutely fantastic time at the lodge. Today, Terri Kittredge Andrews and her husband, Mike, run the world famous sport-fishing mecca.

Panama's 480 rivers run down to its Caribbean and Pacific coastlines, where you can choose from 1,518 islands to visit or start counting the 936 species of birds in the country's 78,046 square kilometers. Tropic Star Lodge — located 150 miles south of the capitol, Panama City — is cut out of the mountain on the fringe of the Darien Jungle. You can only get there by boat or plane since no roads come within 100 miles. Charter flights for guests fly into a remote village on the Jaque River and transport to the lodge which means a 30-minute boat ride along the rugged Pacific coastline.

Originally, back in 1961, an oil tycoon named Ray Smith, built the Pacific Ocean Lodge, opening it as a fishing lodge in 1963. Ray caught the first IGFA world record marlin on 12-pound test there. There have been over 300 world records and numerous Junior Angler world records set at Tropic Star since then, arguably more than in any one single place on the planet!

This secluded lodge ranks as one of the top five billfish lodges in the world. Every fisherman has it on a bucket list. Zane Grey Reef, or as some call it today Piñas Reef, sits approximately 20 minutes from the lodge. This reef supports an underwater mountain sloping from 120 to 350 feet, creating a feeding spot along the natural migration route for all the big marlin in this area. The famous author, Zane Grey, discovered reef fishing here back in the late 1920's, but like so many fishermen, kept it a secret for decades. Anyway, Tropic Star is a magical place with five-star jungle service. It takes a great deal of effort to keep the lodge up to its five-star standing: Yes, it's carved out of a jungle, but if not maintained the tropical flora surrounding the lodge would completely reclaim it within months.

While at the lodge, I went on several hunting excursions and had the opportunity to spend quite a few days back in the Darien Jungle with local guides. I have never in my entire life seen a more desolate, wild, and unfriendly environment than this Panamanian jungle. I hunted with my longbow and a rusty old .22 single-shot rifle they lent me. Finally, after several attempts, I harvested a thirty-pound animal which looked like a rat. I never learned what kind of animal it was. I brought it back to the lodge where we cooked it in palm leaves. I judged it as one of the most disgusting things I've ever eaten. The old-timers still talk about it.

The Tropic Star fleet is comprised of twelve 31-foot diesel Bertrams. The engines are loud and the electronics crude, but after all, when fishing in a world-class tropical paradise, fancy doesn't necessarily mean success.

Standard operating procedure at Tropic Star consists of catching live bonito or yellowfin tuna along the rocky shoreline and placing them nose down into tuna tubes. I've had days at Tropic Star where I've caught six black marlins in one day! On my best sailfish day, I tallied 32 releases!

One of my greatest Tropic Star battles — a 226-pound black marlin caught on 12-pound test — garnered an IGFA world record, but only for a short period of time. I hooked the great fish on a live bonita and the epic fight lasted nine and a half hours. A gifted photographer and friend named Larry Lambrecht accompanied me from Southampton, and took some fantastic aerial shots of this battle. I also caught a 34-pound dolphin on 6-pound tippet on the fly rod December 23, 1980. That IGFA world record still holds today and can be seen in the 2015 IGFA World Record Book.

Over the years, I developed a loving and loyal relationship with the lodge and the people. It is here that many of my light tackle angling and boat handling techniques were born. They have been ingrained in the fabric of who I am as a fisherman. After I successfully shot a wooden arrow into a grizzly bear at eight yards for *The Best and Worst of Tred Barta* on NBC Sports, in 2012 the top executives pushed the heck out of me to come up with a classic and impossible Barta Special for TV — while in my wheelchair. Mr. Impossible himself decided to try catching a black marlin at Tropic Star Lodge in his wheelchair, with the help of one of our sport's great innovators, Mr. Dennis Braid.

Dennis pioneered the standup harness industry, having caught giant bluefin tunas with his many different harness systems. Dennis, formerly a mechanical engineer I believe, spent hours with me brainstorming how to accomplish my goal. One day he called, announcing with all the confidence in the world, "Tred, I know exactly how we are going to do this and it will work!"

After reviewing several diagrams and knowing Dennis had helped other paraplegics fish before, the trip started shaping up to become a reality. We booked our flights from Colorado. The film crew, Danny Kirsic and David Abbott converged in Miami and the next day Dennis arrived from California. Then we all flew to Panama City together. Flying in a wheelchair is never easy, but this flight went off without incident.

We landed in Panama, whereupon six burly men set upon me, picked me up out of my wheelchair like a rag doll and placed me in a twin-engine DeHavilland Otter. I've always found the flight down the Panamanian coastline truly sobering. No roads. No airports. No marinas. Just pure tropical jungle. What a wild ride. The aircraft made a low swinging turn and suddenly, there in front of me, a postage stamp-size runway appeared. My immediate reaction to the runway was, "Please,

please Lord, don't let this be our runway." Despite prayers that apparently go to no one, we lined up with what looked like it could, might, possibly be a runway. Of course, the landing went fine and friendly people greeted me. In the olden days, guests really did take their lives in their hands, riding panga boats out a tiny and treacherous inlet to reach the lodge some 30 minutes away. My most recent trip took a short, 15-minute boat ride directly to the lodge.

My arrival at Tropic Star proved bittersweet. I knew everyone and most everyone knew me. But nobody had been prepared to see me in a wheelchair. Jungle people in general are a very simple, honest, and naïve. The remoteness insulates them from the outside world. Many of the boat captains and staff knelt down next to me and started crying. It was most unsettling.

Customarily, Tropic Star clients spend a day doing tourist things like viewing the Panama Canal. An Indian Village nearby sells handicrafts, and whale watching peaks in July through September. But we had more important things to do to make this trip successful. After spending time with Terri Kittredge, Dennis Braid went about making the harness system which would hopefully enable me to catch a black marlin. The system had two main lines going from the fighting chair arms to the reel rings. When the rod butt rested in the chair gimbal, these two lines ensured the rod stayed fixed at a 45-degree angle, whether I was in the chair or not. A second set of lines led from just above the rod's hand grip down to a set of pulleys on the chair arms. These lines wrapped around the back of the fighting chair and both attached to wooden handles.

Since my spinal cord infarction, I have no control of the muscles in the lower half of my body. I commonly say I have no stomach muscles but what I really mean is I have no control or feeling in my stomach, but can operate my arms, shoulders, and hands, Braid's concept to hook the fish called for me to freespool on the bite. Then place the reel in gear and reel like heck on the strike. If we hooked up, Dennis could pull the rod back using the two lines attached to the two sets of pulleys, and when he let the rod come back down again, I'd reel like crazy again taking up the slack. The rod stopped at a predetermined location from the two initial safety lines.

With six missed fish in the next four days of hard fishing, we remained optimistic about getting the system to work.

On the second to the last day, we hit the standard area around the point for bait. In spite of trolling blue and white feathers for an hour, we found nary a small tuna. Several other boats in the area also came up empty in the bait department. We finally hooked up with four small yellowfin tuna. The baits seemed pretty big compared to what we normally used. The yellowfins probably weighed about 25 pounds each and we couldn't fit them into the tuna tubes. Tunas don't last long without a ton of water to breath. Tuna tubes are large, vertical PVC pipes with a pipe attached at the bottom pumping sea water up into the tube where it overflows the top. When you place a small live bait nose down in the tube, sea water flows through its mouth and gills, allowing you to keep the tuna alive and useful as bait during the day. Usually four to six tubes connect to each other on the transom. This tool has become very popular on all boats using live tuna for bait. We resolved our problem – sort of — by tying the yellowfin tuna to the hand rail on the side of the boat. We ended up towing the bait out to the fishing grounds.

For those of you who have been to the tropics — such as Islamorada, Florida — but never have been to a real bona fide jungle, prepare for a huge difference. One of the biggest is the beauty of the jungle. It kind of shouts at you in a primeval sort of way. The Panamanian jungle grows right down to jet-black, rocky cliffs on the shoreline where we collect our bait every day. The waves crash along the coastline pushing huge plumes of white water upward. It is absolutely breathtaking. As the water recedes and flows back to the ocean – logs, twigs, coconuts, and all types of jungle debris float back with it. Monkeys can be seen all along the shoreline eating plantains and other tropical fruits.

Tropic Star has some of the best roosterfish and cubera snapper fishing. When I first started going to Panama, plug casting for shoreline fish wasn't much of a sport. Today, some people go to Tropic Star strictly for this type of fishing.

Upon arriving at Grey Reef, we trolled two yellowfins in the outriggers. The outrigger clips consisted of a large spring between two pieces of teak which were kept together with a rubber band — a method still used today. They actually wrap the line several times with white paper towels to protect it from chaffing. Unfortunately, in the jungle, air conditioning on the boats is not an available option and under the hot Panamanian sun, two large umbrellas provided the only place I could hide.

At 11:30 AM, while laying on a mattress on the deck, I heard a sound like a shotgun. "Marlena! Marlena! Marlena Negro!" Suddenly four people lifted me up and put me into the fighting chair with a special soft pad under my butt. Strapped into the bucket harness, the right rigger rod placed into the fighting chair gimbal and secured as I sat ready. The right rigger line kept trolling. However, I could see the yellowfin bait had drifted way out of position and was acting very nervous. With both cameras recording, I got my first glimpse of an honest 500+ pound black marlin launching itself like a Cape Canaveral rocket. With the 25-pound yellowfin sideways in the great fish's mouth, the marlin came tight on the line on its first jump and that line came out of the rigger clothespin. Both cameras rolled, one on me and the other on my right hand on the lever drag, letting line fly off the reel in freespool. Both the captain and mates kept yelling frantically, "Set the hook! Set the hook!"

I did nothing but wait and feed the fish. After a 15-second drop back (which frustrated everyone), I motioned with my hand for the captain to roar forward. I put line on the reel as fast as I could and as the slack came taught, the fifty-pound rod bowed over. We were hooked up! Man alive were we hooked up! Our black marlin grey-hounded from left to right, ending that run with a spectacular jump — white water exploding everywhere; one of those jumps that takes your breath away. I knew both Danny and David filmed the bite and first series of jumps. I knew it because I could hear them exchanging many four-letter words which said only one thing. Great TV! The billfish sounded and moved away from the boat, digging for deeper depths. I don't recall ever being so uncomfortable fishing as Dennis pulled the rod up and back so I could get ready to gain line. Some of the parachute straps cut the air passage across my throat and neck. When Dennis released the tension on the rod, it slammed forward so quickly that it almost shook the rod butt out of the gimbal.

No doubt about it — we had a timing problem and no idea how to solve it. After 45 minutes, it became evident we had to modify — on the fly — almost everything Dennis designed. Now the mate let the rod lean over his shoulder while facing me and he pushed the rod up while Dennis pulled the rod and we had a slow count to three. As the mate walked forward and with Dennis pulling to the rear, a slow count of "One, Two, Three," was said out loud. Then the word "Pause" and then "Release." At the end of the word "Pause" I started turning the handle as fast as I could. As the rod was released, I took as much line as I possibly could. The system started working — quite well in fact. After an hour and fifteen minutes fighting time, we had three quarters of the line back on the reel. I was having a hard time breathing and regulating my core temperature since we were near the equator and the temperature always hovers between 80 and 90 very humid degrees. Plus, I had a 500-pound black marlin on the end of the line. Though in fact, five grown men helped me at the same time, it didn't matter one bit to anyone.

The day began partly sunny with broken clouds. Now intermittent drizzle fell from the overcast sky. Somehow the stark reality struck me that this great marlin had no idea about someone in a wheelchair playing at fishing. The fish fought for its very life. We suddenly got another show with the marlin tail walking across the ocean's surface, a little to the left and straight away, its entire body up out of the water! The water looked black and the fish looked even blacker. The silver lateral line ran the length of its body and right into its eye.

I rarely admit to myself, "I can't do this" half way into a challenge. But I honestly didn't believe I could get it done. We got six or seven more jumps out of the fish before the show ended in a spectacular series of what I call "rodeo bucks." The fish, too, did not have quite enough energy to get its body completely out of the water. The marlin realized it half way up and landed on its side with a huge explosion of water. As the water flew into the air, it looked like the silver spray just hung there. It is hard to explain but I detected a meanness to it. I sensed a raw display of irreverence that seemed to say, "Tred Barta, I don't care if you have cancer. I don't care if you are paralyzed. We are in the jungle and not in Palm Beach. I will not make this easy for you."

After 2 hours and 20 minutes the spectacular boat handling gave us our first shot at the leader. I was so tired, that the only way we could do this was for everyone to count out loud to five. At five, the boat backed down hard and I wound as fast as I could. My recovery time between onslaughts got progressively longer. I knew one thing for certain; when the mate got hold of the 300-pound monofilament leader, he wouldn't let go under any conditions. We knew that if this fish sounded one more time, I wouldn't have enough gas left in my tank to get the job done. Every once in a while when a large marlin fights, it seems to stop and almost assess what the situation might be. This marlin laid almost motionless on top of the water, then suddenly the rod bowed right over again. The fish moved forward — immediately countered by the captain. I could feel the tension building. I could feel the mate starting to prepare himself. The mate turned my fighting chair sideways. I thought this strange since the line now pulled off the side of the guide. Then the screaming began, "Reel! Tred reel!"

Unburned grayish-black fumes filled the cockpit. The captain pushed the throttles forward. We ran the fish down; the leader mere feet from the rod tip. The great marlin jumped straight up into the air as if to come down in the cockpit. As I prepared myself for this very possible disaster, I saw the mate take double wraps on the mono. The great fish jumped twice on the leader, each time the boat captain stuck to it like glue. The next time I looked up both mates had the leader. The fish floated sideways with a large circle hook in its jaw. Everyone jumped up and down, clapping, yelling and screaming. Five other boats had been watching us fight the fish and when they heard the news they all circled us. On this day, I bit off much more than I could chew. In my opinion, I wasn't meant to win this battle, but somehow I did.

Amazing Side Story to the Day's Adventure

During this trip with Dennis Braid, I have another story that sounds unbelievable but it's true. At the end of the day, trolling back to the lodge, an extremely large dolphin sucked down one of the lures. I lay on the deck resting at the time, but noticed how long Dennis took to fight the fish on an 80-pound outfit! He put an immense amount of pressure on the fish without gaining much line.

Finally, the entire crew started talking about this being one of the largest dolphin they had ever seen. I didn't think much of it at the time as I expected to see maybe a 60-pounder come over the gunwale. Eventually they gaffed the dolphin and threw it into the cockpit next to me. In my entire career, I had never seen a dolphin that big. When we arrived at the dock, I noticed Dennis couldn't lift the fish for pictures. The dolphin was bigger than Dennis!

The film crew was all over me as we burned daylight. They had an interview to do boat side. The dolphin was quickly weighed and not made part of the day's story.

When weighed, I heard someone say during the interview the fish weighed 54.4. I remember saying to Dennis, "Well that scale is off." After the interview, Dennis came running down the dock in a panic. The scale was in kilograms and not pounds. Our dolphin was 120 pounds!

Dennis ran after the dolphin which the guide had dragged toward the kitchen. By the time Dennis got to the fish, it had been filleted. Dennis Braid caught a 120-pound dolphin and I was his witness, which would have made it the largest dolphin ever caught by a sport angler. It should have been both an IGFA all-tackle and 80-pound world record.

I don't tell this story very often because people refuse to believe me. On my living room wall, I have a 64-pound dolphin mount. The largest dolphin I ever caught touched 74 pounds. Braid's fish dwarfed both of these. To make matters worse, everyone complained at dinner about the dolphin being very tough and over-cooked. I guess we know the real reason why.

This story has been refuted by many and it really doesn't make any difference to me. I can tell you what I saw: Braid's dolphin was gigantic, thick, wide, and colossal. In my entire life, I have never seen any dolphin this big. Let me finish by saying, "I, Captain Tred Barta, who has fished all over the world, has never seen a dolphin this big."

So let's leave it at that.

Pinas Bay, Panama – Tropic Star Lodge
World record dolphin @ 34 pounds caught on 12/23/1980 on 6lb tippet.
This dolphin took one month to catch. This record still stands today.

Pinas Bay, Panama – Tropic Star Lodge
Terri Kittredge with Tred and a very big, black marlin

Chapter Twenty-Six
A Slippery Slope

IN THE WINTER of 2010 as I gain strength and confidence, I make lists of what makes me happy. I ask myself why I moved from Southampton, New York, to the Vail Valley in Colorado. From a place of my childhood where I loved to fish in the canyons, to the mountains so far from saltwater. Colorado, where my wife wanted to live, offered me world class fly fishing, spectacular big game hunting, and the ability to ski again – all good.

If you live in Islamorada, Florida, you fish. If you live in Nebraska, you hunt pheasant. The net is, certain places are known for their opportunities and their assets. If I did not love skiing, then I probably would not have moved to Colorado. It was as simple as that.

At the time, I found myself shooting the longbow and filming episodes of the "Best and Worst of Tred Barta." As winter approached, everyone in Vail Valley who knew me, including my medical team and trainers, all had the same message "Be happy and stay off the slopes." Their consensus was I would probably never ski again and any attempt at it was not highly recommended. As a T4, Asia A, paralyzed from my chest down and having no upper abdominal function and struggling with sitting balance, everyone thought skiing would be a disaster for me. Well, that was all I had to hear!

The sport of skiing for the disabled dates back to World War II when many wounded soldiers came back from the wars. In the beginning, it was restricted to amputees, but in 1969 Jean Eymere, a former ski instructor, lost his eyesight and established a skiing program for the blind in Aspen, Colorado.

My research guided me to the best and brightest in the handicapped ski world, Chris Werhane. Chris sported a six-foot-plus frame and a never-give-up personality as big as Wyoming. He was simply a mountain of a man and so was his beard. Chris possessed mind-blowing credentials. He taught and certified instructors worldwide on how to deal with people like me. Simply put, he was the teacher's teacher, the best of the best! In the world of paraplegic skiing, Chris Werhane wrote the book and in that vein, represented the Hemingway of handicap skiing.

Our first meeting took place at Longbow Ranch. Chris picked me up out of my wheelchair and carefully placed me into a sled with two skis. He controlled the sled by a tether. By leaning to the left or right I could help turn. I got into the contraption which look more suited for a ten-year-old than myself. Chris pushed me ten feet, pulled me out of the sled and gently placed me back into my wheelchair. I looked up and said, "Chris, what was that all about?" To which he replied, "You just skied ten feet. You can ski!" As we sat in the ranch house, I told Chris that his little toy did not represent what I considered skiing. I had no desire to be led down a mountain on a tether. I wanted to discuss other options. Suddenly the room came vividly alive. Chris Werhane knew all about pressure sores and different challenges of paraplegics. He knew all about getting people back into the game since he was one of the top ski instructors for Wounded Warriors.

I'll never forget what happened next. Chris knelt in front of me, grabbed both of my forearms, and asked me how much I wanted to ski. However, I answered his question, it must have been enough to satisfy him. Two weeks later I was in Denver, Colorado getting fitted for a shell that encased my legs from my knees to my upper back in a form-fitting material. This fitting process by Ride Designs in Denver took about four hours. The shell — a custom ski racing insert – was made by the same company as my wheelchair seat cushion. They fitted me into the molded poly shell and with sheets of foam padding, customized the fit to be secure. This shell design primarily protected my body from pressure sores. Any arms, chest, and head movement transmitted quickly down through my torso allowing me to control my mono ski — also specially designed for me. The end product, made from a flexible material, transitioned into hard black plastic. Several buckles and Velcro straps held the shell to my body. Essentially the shell resembled a ski boot covering my body from my knees to just below my chest.

If you take me out of my wheelchair and put me on a hard surface, or have me sit on a hard object like a small rock, I can develop a pressure sore in a matter of minutes that could take months to heal *and* possibly kill me. A paraplegic's body does not heal like that of a healthy person. The lack of muscle tone combined with diminished blood circulation inhibits the healing process by a ridiculous amount of time. Hence, the critical need to have the main parts of my body extremely protected when skiing.

Now let's talk about cold weather. If I was not watching and you thrust a knife into either one of my legs, I would have no idea it happened. Similarly, my entire torso and my extremities are extremely susceptible to the cold and frostbite, the latter a possible death sentence to a paraplegic. All clothing including boots, gloves, and pants had to be fitted specially.

My first two weeks of training with Chris I spent on a foam mat, learning how to stay upright without falling by using two outriggers to stabilize myself on the slopes. Then came another two weeks of practicing batting a tennis ball. I wore the special outriggers, adjusted for length. Then I had to be schooled on the releasing and locking mechanism to move the outrigger ski from a poling position to a flat skiing position. The outriggers resemble forearm crutch supports atop a short cane, with a short ski on the bottom. Chris rolled tennis balls in my direction and by turning the outrigger sideways like a hockey stick I batted them back to him. After mastering that I was ready for the chairlift.

In 1967, Josef Shrall built the first "sit-ski" specifically for people in wheelchairs. My mono-ski or sit-ski — a specially padded, molded bucket seat that is mounted onto a metal frame with a shock absorber under the seat. The shock absorber made it a softer ride and helped me to turn the mono-ski due to maximizing the ski to snow contact. Chris quickly lifted me up out of my wheelchair and into the mono-ski chair, attached me to it with a safety restraining strap. I picked up my outriggers and was ready to hit the slopes!

One of the hardest parts of skiing for a paraplegic, especially for a person with such a high level of injury, was how to get onto the ski lift. What a monumental learning curve I had there! Just getting on the lift more often than not becomes the deal breaker for many, who end up just giving up on ever skiing again. On a Sunday morning, Chris and I jumped onto the chair lift ascending the mountain.

I remember thinking that one of the best parts about skiing was the ride to the top of Vail Mountain. On a clear day I could see over the entire mountain range surrounding Vail Valley. As we ascended, the town of Vail became smaller and smaller until it matched the size of a postage stamp. It was one of those days when the Colorado Rockies just light up and glow with the early morning sun. Large piñon and ponderosa pines along with clusters of aspens defined the different ski slopes. What an absolutely glorious day!

I also appreciated the often windy nature of the chair lift ride as I enjoyed seeing the morning snow blow off the top of the conifers as we rose up the mountain. The snow — like a mystical mist — formed a tail which sparkled with colors of blue and yellow against Colorado's famous deep blue sky.

As a hunter, I loved looking down at the fresh bobcat, mountain lion or any big game animal tracks crossing the slopes. It fascinated me to follow the tracks and visualize what the animal was doing and where it might have gone. I quickly learned that the unseen parts of everyday life really were the most important. No doubt I was becoming a better, stronger, and more understanding person than I was before being paralyzed.

All through prep school I had skied downhill. No matter what mountain I was on, I was always one of the best skiers, showing no fear and skiing aggressively. Not being afraid to fall was one of my greatest skiing strengths. Skiing was second nature to me and no matter how steep the slope, it would always be my friend.

My mono-ski had a removable handlebar in the back. I skied and my instructor, Chris Werhane held onto me from the back of the mono-ski with his two skis straddling my one. I wore the outriggers to help me balance and make the necessary turns back and forth down the ski trail. The small ski pole had a high camber towards the back where a jaw-like brake attached. By pointing the outrigger at a certain angle you could engage the back of the ski as a brake.

I won't enumerate the many times I fell boarding and exiting the ski lift. But every time I kept a smile on my face and laughed at myself because even the best skiers fall loading and unloading the ski lift at times.

I soon transitioned to a new technology – called bi-ski or dual-ski. By having two skis below me, both fully articulated, I became more stable and secure. I could feel the snow much better. Please shut your eyes while you become me — and we are skiing. I have no feeling from my toes to my chest. By learning how to manipulate my upper body, weighting and unweighting my shoulders by moving my head, the rest of my body followed these cues.

I lowered my left shoulder, articulated my left outrigger into the hill, and pushed down, then reached forward with my right ski, lowered my head and twisted my upper torso into the hill. My hips, butt, and knees pressed into the hill even though I have no active muscles to do it naturally. The dynamics of my body and the way it attaches to my skeleton allows me to feel, see, and initiate that turn. I can "feel" the process, I can anticipate it in my brain.

Okay, I understand. I have a darned hard time explaining it to someone who is not paralyzed.

After three weeks of skiing on Vail Mountain, the only instructor who'd ski with me was my friend, Chris. I skied aggressively and extremely fast since I felt confident on the slopes.

A great thing about skiing deep powder like we do in the West is it slows down the tremendous mass created by my 190 pounds combined with Chris's 250 pounds. That is a lot of weight falling down a hill. As a result, we accelerated extremely quickly on a normal slope, but on powder days we could almost ski straight down the fall line with the deep snow slowing us down.

In deep powder my ski completely disappeared from view. The powder rolled up onto my knees like a bale of hay, over my lap, and finally curled over my shoulders making visibility very difficult. I sometimes put a skin diving snorkel in my mouth so I could breathe without inhaling the snow. Sometimes snow blew over my head giving a sense of diving in the snow. It provided such an outrageous experience that I usually hooted and hollered with sheer joy when we stopped!!

Admittedly, paraplegics rarely get to enjoy such adventures. Very few instructors have the skills to take them into the powder. Chris never held me back. Since neither of us feared falling, our great success made life as sweet as it could get. The feeling? Like floating on air — absolutely marvelous!

In general, I skied intermediate blue and some black trails with Chris. Obviously moguls and I didn't get along, making my ride uncomfortable and painful. They jarred me to death! I had no fear of extremely steep inclines, speed, or black diamond super-steep walls. But if moguls entered the equation, I drew the no-go line.

In any sport, a man develops a unique trust and comradery in the most dangerous times. For example, as a couple thousand pounds of charging buffalo is coming at you, the backup gunner saves your life, dropping the buffalo at your feet. However, this in no way resembles the bond that forms with someone who goes to the movies with you. Charging down the Vail mountain with Chris — literally placing my life in his hands — created a trust which only a few get to experience in their life time.

For a skier, life does not get any better. On any given day I could be seen skiing under the lifts making beautiful carved turns. People cheered as I skied by and when waiting in the chair lift line, Chris and I often received words of encouragement from other skiers. This definitely made it worthwhile and I called on those moments of positive reinforcement when I struggled with other areas of my life.

I felt grateful that I could verbalize my feelings to Chris. It made me extremely teachable. When I occasionally complimented him, Chris used to say, "It's not hard to teach a great skier how to ski." At last, I was skiing, and skiing well. I loved the speed. I loved the mountain and being one with nature. I loved the snow, the wind in my face, and the noise I heard when going really fast. I just loved it! It gave me another reason to fight to live and to move forward into a new normal.

Skiing and all it encompassed was part of my DNA. Although more difficult than I originally imagined it would be, took more time than I expected, and carried horrendous risk, I touched upon my old life again — just a little differently. After a morning of skiing, it usually took me two days to fully recover.

As I look back to those times of life and death, and at life on the edge, I realize that the bonds from the experiences carried much more significance than the actual accomplishment. Chris Werhan became a lifetime friend and it has been a privilege to ski with him. We developed a bond of trust that will last throughout my life and will continuously extend thousands of miles from any ski slope. I am eternally grateful for the fun and exhilarating experiences all made possible by Chris Werhan.

> *"Tred always attacked life as if he was on a double diamond slope. You're only safe when you're driving by leaning forward; down the steepest slopes. That's just Tred. We lived on the edge without going over."*
>
> *Quote by Chris Werhan*

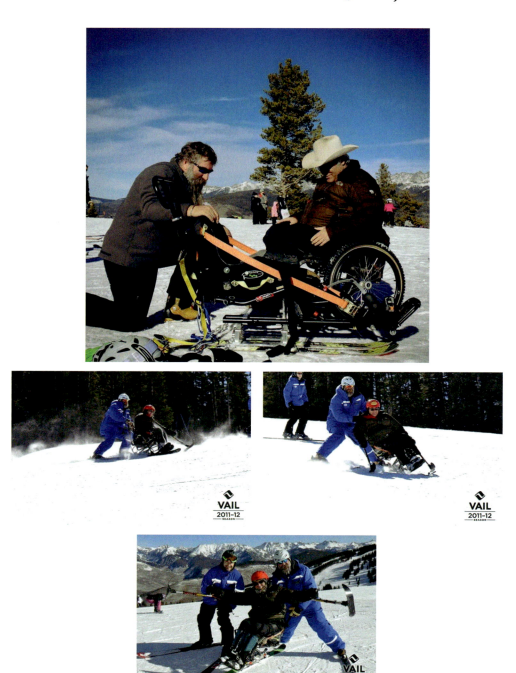

Tred skiing with Chris Werhan

Chapter Twenty-Seven
WEIGHTLESS

IN 2010 AFTER being paralyzed about a year, it became self-evident my new mission in life should be to inspire others. For some reason, I have been blessed with incredible energy, stamina and guts. Even when I had both my legs, that was my trademark. I vowed to myself I'd re-accomplish all the things I was passionate about before I was in a wheelchair. During most of my life I constantly heard, "You can't do that; It won't work; It will never happen" and "That's impossible." Whether an IGFA world record on light tackle or starting a fishing tournament with no Calcutta that supposedly nobody would fish, if I had passion for it and believed in it, not only could I attempt it, but I would be successful at it.

My entire life, I've been fueled by a burning passion directed at accomplishing my dreams. "You cannot win if you are worried about losing" stands as one of the great themes I preached before and after my physical tragedy. When I returned to my passion for diving, all of my doctors and everyone who knew my medical circumstance said, "Out of the question!" And for most people, that would end the discussion — but *we* are talking about Tred Barta!

I wanted to scuba dive again and so I simply had to work through the stumbling blocks methodically, as I always have. To start: I have a colostomy and a suprapubic catheter; so how can I protect these areas from water? Secondly, having no use of my body from my chest down, how can I stay upright and control myself underwater?

In my past life, I certified as a master diver, having dived all over the world. I did a tremendous amount of night diving and developed a love of spear fishing. I had friends at Beaver Divers, a small dive shop located in the Vail Valley. They hold the dubious notoriety of being the highest dive shop in the world at 8,000 feet. The owner and founder, Casey Zwaan, has taught diving for 37 years and logged more than 5,000 dives. His wife, Emily, also an experienced instructor co-owns the shop. After long discussions and many meetings about my goal, we met in the community pool.

Welcome to perhaps the most denigrating initial experience I've ever had. While laying nude on a chaise lounge cushion, *we* attempted to don *my* wet suit.

I swear putting a wet suit on a walrus sprang to mind! There I lay, flipping from one side to the other while four grown men – all virtually strangers — pulled my wetsuit up inch-by-inch, obviously threading my urine tube down my right leg. We designed a large blue stretchy band out of fabric similar to a balloon that would hopefully keep my colostomy bag dry.

Of course, that problem might be moot as another ugly fact rose to the surface. Since I'm paralyzed, I can't control my bowels. Excrement no longer travels to a controllable colon and sphincter. It comes out my abdomen, and I don't know exactly when I am going to have a bowel movement. It is just part of the paralysis ugliness.

To safely SCUBA dive, I had to remove the ostomy seal and attach a special pouch to hold my waste inside until a later time when I could relieve it. I continue to paint this picture so you can see it took a lot of preparation and thought for me to get safely in the water. Most people in my condition would be so embarrassed, so degraded, so dehumanized, they'd never even attempt what I planned to accomplish. There comes a point in all of these activities when I, a T4, ASIA A victim, can only get through them or attack them via shock and awe. In front of everybody, I changed my colostomy flange, cleaned up with baby wipes, and got my wetsuit top on.

Remember, paraplegics can get a pressure sore from hitting or scraping any hard object. A bruise on the hip, leg, or feet might take months to heal, due to compromised circulation and muscle tone. Returning to my wheelchair, they hooked me to a device which would lower me into the swimming pool. The transition to the lift was ugly, but it worked. Again, it took four people to get me into the device and accomplish the transfer to the water, but these kind people made the impossible possible.

As I lowered into the pool with my BC (buoyancy compensator) vest partially inflated, I floated in water for the first time. A million words can't adequately express that fabulous feeling. I was weightless — it felt as if a thousand hands massaged me simultaneously. It felt wonderful and soothing. From everything I have read and much of what I believe, this approximates heaven.

I realized one major problem as soon as we started to advance: I had difficulty keeping my head above water. I had to relearn the "treading water" technique using only my arms. If I ended up face down, turning my body around to get air would be very difficult since I couldn't control ¾ of my torso. An anguishing sense of horror "harshed my mellow." I thought, "Here's yet another endeavor requiring lots of specially-trained people to accomplish." I remember feeling the anger. Isn't there anything I can do by myself again?

I had one major advantage, however. As a trained and certified diver already with many hours spent under the water, I enjoyed a comfort level there even with the equipment, so I didn't panic during my learning curve. Before long, I laid on the bottom of the pool with my tank and regulator feeling incredibly comfortable.

Soon I was taking my mask off, sharing my regulator with other people, taking my tank off and putting it back on – fulfilling all the dive certification requirements every diver must. My renewed comfort qualified as nothing short of spectacular. Training progressed and I started using a self-propelled sea scooter, a "James Bond" device allowing me to move around the pool and control my depth without assistance. The scooter became a real life saver because now I could propel myself along the bottom without the use of fins.

But this learning adventure merely struck the match. I focused all my training on being able to dive in the ocean again. My success in the pool convinced me that day was coming. Soon thereafter, I sat on a flight to Miami where I'd have my first practice dive in John Pennekamp Coral Reef State Park in Key Largo, Florida.

As usual, when we arrived in the Keys, it blew a gale. Our dive had very low visibility, but it did show me how I should conduct myself on future dive boats. Casey and Emily from Beaver Divers came with me on my first dive. Our hard work together had built an impenetrable trust between my dive instructors and me.

Both extremely kind and patient, Casey and Emily exuded confidence, which gratefully spilled over to their student. By this time, we had developed a wet suit with several zippers to help in putting it on. You wouldn't think a simple zipper up the legs or arms would make a life-changing difference, but it certainly did! The band protected my colostomy, and donning my wetsuit went quickly. But another scary problem surfaced in route to the dive site. I started overheating — a common problem accompanying paralysis. The brain has difficulty regulating temperature because of the massive nerve damage caused by the paralysis. To solve the problem, the crew poured buckets of cool, salty seawater over me. Unfortunately, every silver lining still has a cloud: within a short period of time my $5,000 wheelchair started to show serious rust and corrosion. No surprise, I guess, as the manufacturer never designed my wheelchair for immersion in saltwater.

As we neared the dive site, the crew placed me on my back on a chaise lounge cushion. They dragged the cushion to the boat's dive entry area where two people helped me sit up and don my tank and BC. The dive masters slowly carried me down two steps and finally to the water's edge of the swim platform. Next thing I knew, I was in the water, both Casey and Emily by my side. I kept close eye contact with Casey. The doctors had warned me against any depth greater than 12 feet as they feared the possibility a blood embolism. And how the water pressure would affect my lung capacity while underwater remained an unknown. I descended to 12 feet below the surface and felt no problems whatsoever. I continued to descend to determine my *real* limits. Ultimately, I reached the ocean floor at a depth of 25 feet. Clearing the pressure in my ears proved easy and normal.

Wow! Maybe the best part turned out to be my self-propelled sea scooter moving me through the water with ease. Casey swam with me, holding the valve stem on my SCUBA tank while Emily swam below continuously making eye contact, the only real method to determine a problem early on. Casey's spare emergency regulator on his tank hung over his left shoulder where I could always see it as we swam along. If I had an equipment failure, I was confident my safety was assured.

Sigh! I was diving! I witnessed the beautiful tropical fish, coral outcroppings, and the underwater world which I knew so well and loved so deeply. It's so totally heartening for a paralyzed person to accomplish the things he/she hears can't be done! Momentarily you actually forget your paralysis. You feel 100% normal again. In fact, you feel exactly the way you felt before your particular tragedy struck you.

The day after my Pennekamp diving success, we boarded a Cessna Caravan headed for Belize. I had never visited the Blue Hole off the Belize coast, but I was about to experience it. I had read about it and seen pictures. As one of the world's top-ten dive locations, most divers have it on their bucket list. I had a two-pronged goal in Belize: catch a bonefish on a bamboo fly rod and dive the Blue Hole. Oh, and making one of my best TV shows ever in the process!

The Blue Hole — a collapsed oceanic sinkhole filled with ridiculously clear blue water that lies near the center of Lighthouse Reef — sits 62 miles from Belize City. Some 984 feet across, it has a depth of 410 feet and is part of the Barrier Reef Reserve System, a UNESCO World Heritage Site.

In the mid-1970s, Jacques Cousteau's boat *Calypso* and his crew conducted its famous investigation of the Blue Hole and the Belize atolls on their TV show. The show brought the beauty of the underwater world to many and probably not coincidentally, corresponds with the explosion of dive travel to Belize.

We landed the Caravan on a private airstrip at Blackbird Cay on Turneffe Island, where I settled into a quaint bungalow right at the pristine water's edge. What an absolutely gorgeous place, owned by a Belizean gentleman named Michael Feinstein, a good friend with whom I had done aviation deals. The resort built several access ramps around the property and truly went out of their way to make filming and my stay nothing short of perfect. The run to the Blue Hole was about 20 miles, and after entering the water, I descended to a world that can only be described as like the movie *Avatar*. The water's crystal clarity defied imagination.

Its coral rim teemed with wildlife. At 30 feet, I started to feel uncomfortable pressure on my lungs, so I mentally established 30 feet as my biological ceiling, not the 12 feet doctors originally suggested.

As I held onto the cliff wall of the Blue Hole, I felt totally relaxed and enjoyed the wonderful, magical experience of being completely weightless and more importantly, devoid of my everyday life pressures. What a mind-boggling experience. In fact, way beyond what I am capable of describing in words. Large schools of crevalle jack patrolled the reef. Everywhere I looked, small communities of abundant varieties of tropical fish of every color imaginable popped out. The scenery included large tube and giant basket sponges, large purple sea fans, and giant schools of jewfish, snappers and permits. I witnessed a large moray eel come out of the coral, its brilliant bluish-green colors and beady eyes making him look like a sinister reef robber.

This underwater paradise provided me with one of those wonderful moments… the ones which you earn and pack away in the back of your mind to cherish forever. These special moments keep me going and give me strength. They'll remain special till my last breath. As my dive came to its completion, I knew with certainty that I would commit the rest of my life to doing all the things everyone said I couldn't do. I hope when my number comes up and it's my time to die, that I pass on while mounting one of these quests rather than withering away in a hospital bed in some dark hallway.

Though it took a huge effort and lots of work by quite a few people, I once again could call myself an ocean diver. I received my paraplegic PADI card (which they call a scubAbility card). I carry it proudly in my wallet. Many people viewed this adventure on my TV show. Disabled or not, it proved to them that if they wanted to scuba dive, they could.

The Blue Hole by no means represents my only dive adventure. My passions aren't once-and-move-on affairs. Since moving to Islamorada in 2013, I've dived extensively with Key Dives in the Florida Keys. They have been patient and helpful in making my dives successful and exciting. Friends invited me to visit the Cayman Islands where Donna De Weil and I dove with Epic Divers. Interestingly, this particular company has lots of experience with disabled divers as they frequently run dives for Wounded Warriors. They know the game and know it well. They pulled off our dive at Stingray Alley to perfection.

Grand Cayman's world-class diving includes many colorful species of tropical fish including varieties of angelfish, blue tang, soldier fish, flounder, fairy basslet, parrot fish, trigger fish, and large moray eels. The beautiful underwater landscape includes fire coral, black coral, and tube sponges. Whether visiting magnificent restaurants; the turtle farm; walking the paths at the Queen Elizabeth II Botanical Park; visiting the National Museum with historical, natural and scientific objects of interest; or touring the natural scenery of the island in a handicap van, we found the people to be very friendly. We also fished with *Slackem Charters* on their boat *Keepin' It Reel*. We hoped for a marlin but it wasn't in the cards. We did have a fabulous time with Captain Jon and his mate catching some good size dolphin however.

I want to prove to every person in need that life as you knew it, is still possible. The things you used to do, you can still do. In addition, you can share these treasured experiences with friends and family. Life cannot exist without hope. Life cannot exist without passion. It is not worth living without dreams. My name is Tred Barta. I can do almost everything I used to do – with a little help. My life is rich, rewarding, and has a punctuation mark after the word hope. Probably the only difference between me and you — in the simplest terms — is I have traded my legs for wheels, and I probably use more WD40 maintaining those wheels than any man alive.

Donna De Weil and Tred with Epic Dive team in Grand Cayman

Tred with Epic Dive in Grand Cayman

Chapter Twenty-Eight
I CAN DO IT!

AS I LAY in my bed at Longbow Ranch, I contemplated how the profound ugliness between me and my wife, Anni was becoming visible to everyone. I had finished two TV shows in my wheelchair, one of them hunting elk with a bow, in which my friend, Juan, stood in as the archer. Juan had also been a stand-in on a deer show. It resulted in decent TV — but not great.

In both shows, I trained Juan how to make wooden arrows. Then we'd shoot them at elk and deer targets set up thirty feet away in my backyard. It made for interesting TV, and we got good ratings. But everyone knew the sad reality. If I couldn't make *great* TV hunting or fishing in my wheelchair, NBC certainly wouldn't continue supporting the show. It represented an unspoken fact that our producer Mark Freedman, the director, the cameramen, and I all knew.

For weeks I pondered on what the next show should be and how I would shoot it. If we didn't hit the next show out of the park, they'd pull our show. Big business doesn't survive on compassion for the handicapped. Welcome to "All or Nothing!"

We had shot little vignettes around the ranch with me getting on and off Badger. We filmed me throwing a rope around a bale of hay and doing general farm chores. We even accented the show by having me and Anni witness the foaling of the ranch's brood mare. But as cute and wonderful as this was, it still lacked the drive and pizzazz of the former "Best and Worst of Tred Barta" episodes where I always tried to do the impossible. Despite all the positive reinforcement, no matter how hard everyone tried to fake it for me, I needed personal proof that I could sustain myself in quests such as I had done over the last eight years of shows.

I regularly worked with weights and could once again pull a 60-pound bow with ease. But I didn't have the stamina to fight a big fish due to chemo knocking the crap out of me. The problem arose when we needed a fishing show.

And so I went to sleep that evening searching for strength from the very nemesis that has driven me my whole life. Welcome everyone! Let's join an evening with my father, Joe Barta.

Historically, when I've needed strength, I've always drawn it from two places: First, the woman in my life who inspires me. When I cannot find that support and that drive anywhere else, I still go to my second resource, my father. I remember that evening specifically. Even in my thoughts he was sarcastic, mean, and right to the point. He spoke as if sitting at my bedside, saying, "Son, what is the hardest thing you could possibly do but nobody thinks you can do? What is the adventure that would bring you back to the top of the ladder without question?"

I have never understood dreams, but often when I face hard questions, I wake up in the morning with answers. Somewhere, walking in my dream, I kept begging my father to see my disabilities, to accept the incredibly hard time I was experiencing, and to understand that it took every bit of guts I had to accomplish what I have done so far. What seemed to me so unfair (a very common theme in my dreams involving my father), is he just didn't give a damn. I don't know to this day whether to translate it as meanness or a perverted type of love. Maybe I will never know. In my dreams, my father was always well dressed as he was in life. He wore a Brooks Brothers blue suit with a white starched shirt and red tie. As he walked out, he offered a helpful parting comment: "Do it right or don't do it at all," said without a hint of compassion in his voice.

Absent the love I wanted and needed at the time, I woke up feeling quite alone. I had only five days left to announce the TV show's location and subject. I had already been to Casa Vieja Lodge in Guatemala several times, literally becoming part of the family down there, or perhaps I should say they treated me like family. But that didn't qualify as new, stunning, or a ratings grabber!

In my adventures, I have talked about some of the skill sets required to catch big fish on light tackle. My 215-pound bigeye tuna, caught in 5 hours and 17 minutes on 20-pound test line, still holds the IGFA world record today. My 65-pound yellowfin tuna on 6-pound another of those mind-boggling accomplishments. In fact, to my amazement my father even said, "good job" on one of those world records.

I called my agent and show producer, Mark Freedman. In our short and to the point conversation, it could just as easily have been my father talking. I said, "I am going to catch a sailfish on 2-pound test. There will be no other tackle allowed on the boat. I will only bring my 2-pound rods with me and it is all or nothing." Mark became extremely defensive. Our budget ran about $120,000 per show and got eaten up very quickly with salaries and all the ancillary costs involved to get to a final product. Mark said in a loud clear voice, "Tred when you gamble a very important show like this one, and you know what I am talking about, you are also gambling with the jobs of many people." This included the film crew and Bob Wheeler and his son, who actually did all the post-production work like editing the raw film, adding music, voiceover, graphics, and the rest of the final touches. These guys, based in Atlanta, turned our rough video into a story. I felt quite taken aback by Mark's comments. I felt like telling him "to take a flying leap." I came back in a stern voice, "Well Mark, I bet the farm on the grizzly show. I bet the farm on the moose show. I bet the farm on trying to kill a mountain goat, of course with wooden arrows with stone points. Why is this any different?" Mark replied, "We're coming from behind. We've already made two mediocre shows and we need to deliver an incredible one!" Again I aggressively came back with, "The Best and Worst of Tred Barta is based on the 'Bartaism' that you cannot win if you are afraid of losing, and that one should never give up and never say never." I don't remember what Mark said after that but I recall it being something stupid like, "Those sayings are for the TV show and not for real life." For the first time in my life I really took a stand and said, "it is two-pound or it is nothing"! Mark reluctantly agreed. The truth be known there are only a few people in the world who can legitimately catch a sailfish on two-pound test. On any given Sunday I would say at most 10 people.

Mark Freedman is a friend, and without Mark, "The Best and Worst of Tred Barta" show on NBC Sports wouldn't exist. Freedman and his company Surge Licensing also developed and brought to market the Ninja Turtles. If you think he might be a multi-millionaire, you might be underestimating his achievements. I had never stood up to Mark Freedman before. Quite frankly, I never had to. He had always listened to me and understood the risks on any show. A brilliant man who in any given confrontation was probably right, but in this situation I felt I knew the stakes better than he did.

I had to produce the miraculous. If I could have done something before I was paralyzed, why couldn't I do it now? The feat in question required not strength, but finesse and a light touch. I still had those qualities in spades! I packed three 2-pound rods designed by me and custom made by The Rod Shop in Islamorada, Florida. I brought five Avet reels specially modified by the factory to give me an extremely light-weight cam. I easily found freespool to within 1/4 pound of drag every time. These one-of-a-kind reels served but one purpose: To catch a Pacific sailfish on 2-pound test at Casa Vieja Lodge. The fishing line manufacturer I use sent me four gigantic spools of certified 2-pound IGFA line. I checked each spool on an Instron line tester. Three spools failed, but the last spool tested absolutely perfect. That spool I packed. My next few days came filled with negativity. From my cameramen to the lodge to Mark Freedman to Bob Wheeler — all telling me to reconsider my proposal. I wasn't listening.

We prepared to board the airplane to Guatemala. When confined to a wheelchair and you have special needs, protocol dictates that you board first and disembark last. While I waited to be wheeled aboard, gate agents scrambled to get the proper airplane-aisle chair –considerably more narrow than a regular wheelchair so it can fit down the plane aisle. Normally, I have to be transferred and strapped into the airline aisle chair. Then they roll me down the aisle of the aircraft and lift me into my seat. I overheard discussion of me not being able to go on the flight. Apparently, *I* was the one holding everybody up because *they* could not find the aisle chair. Being very grateful for my freedom and always going out of my way to thank servicemen for their sacrifice, I could not help notice about six of America's finest in uniform. They, too, awaited this flight. I explained my dilemma to them and how I had to fly from Eagle, Colorado to Denver, then Denver to Georgia and now I was about to miss my flight because they could not find the special chair to take me to my seat.

I remember quite a lot of commotion at the front desk, followed by six strong American servicemen picking me up, with my urine bag flapping in the breeze. I literally boarded the airplane with these servicemen cradling me, probably no different than how they have been trained to take an American hero off a battlefield. Anyway it was really cool. I sat in my seat and am very appreciative of these guys. I had hopefully passed my last hurdle on my way to Guatemala to catch a sailfish on 2-pound test! The aircraft captain got on the sound system and thanked the servicemen. Everyone on board clapped! When I departed the aircraft in Guatemala, I was, as always, taken aback by the wall of humidity that hits you. It's like taking a bite of fresh-baked German brown pumpernickel bread. You just say, "Whoa!" The driver had removed the back two seats of the van and put a mattress in its place allowing me to sleep for the hour and a half drive from the airport to the lodge. Just one more thing the wonderful staff did to accommodate me.

This marked the first time everyone at Casa Vieja Lodge saw me in a wheelchair. I had been to the lodge quite a few times in prior years and became close to the owner and staff. When you arrive at the lodge, custom dictates that all employees not out fishing greet the van in their beautifully colored shirts when it enters the compound. They have trays with different cocktails, ornate with flowers and little umbrella things. My drink of course had always been chocolate milk so an icy cold glass of chocolate milk awaited me. Many of the employees couldn't wait to see me. The van door opened and TA-DA! Captain Tred Barta, lying half naked and paralyzed... not exactly the entrance I had dreamed about. After getting my pants back up, everything arranged, and me back into my wheelchair, we all shared an extremely emotional moment that I hadn't anticipated. One by one, my dear friends knelt on the cobblestones putting their arms around me. Some burst into tears when they saw me. It was just too much to take. Sure, everyone was happy to see me alive, yet were horrified at what was left of me. Not exactly what

I needed right then to maintain my resolve. As usual when I'm uncomfortable, I made a couple off-hand, inappropriate jokes and suddenly the mood lightened.

Like everything in life that gets thrown at me, I needed to discover the realities of how I could move around the Casa Vieja compound first. Several areas I couldn't reach solo. I found I could go almost everywhere except the short distance to the pool and bar area, thanks to a steep ramp. My room had a single step up to enter and another to access the shower — speed bumps I needed help with. The lodge graciously built wooden platforms in three places so I could move around the lodge freely! Those who know me well will appreciate that if areas exist where guests are not permitted — those rules certainly don't include me. So into the kitchen I went to visit the chefs. I had always hung out with all of the cooks and wait staff, getting to know them quite well over the years.

I always liked carefully going through my tackle in the dining room before each trip. Everybody knew it and without asking, all of my tackle sat on a table for me to put together. The reels felt silky smooth and we tied Bimini twists connected to loop-to-loop wind-on 50-pound test leaders. The end of the wind-on leader attached to a ball-bearing Sampo swivel which then attached to the actual ballyhoo bait rigged to a circle hook.

Due to the great lobbying efforts of my dear friend, Captain Ronnie Hamlin, Guatemala made it illegal to use J hooks. He also pushed to make it illegal to bring a dead billfish back to the marina. If you do, you get fined $5,000 and it's strictly enforced.

On this trip I had the pleasure of fishing with Captain Chris Sheeder. I had done several TV shows with Chris with phenomenal success, including releasing a blue marlin on fly on film and releasing two blues in a day on 12-pound. We also enjoyed a successful overnight trip for tuna some 100 miles offshore. That made a great TV show. Another great show saw me catch one sail on 12-pound, then one on 8, then down to 6-pound, another on 4-pound and I almost caught one on 2-pound. Again, great, exciting TV.

As of March, 2016, Captain Chris Sheeder's billfish releases total 29,186, with 1,176 of them blue marlin. His career billfish total on fly tallies 6,693 released with 42 of them blue marlin. Absolutely staggering numbers! The global fishing community considers Chris Sheeder and his crew one of the best at light-tackle in the World, with a capital W! Chris and I have now caught enough fish together that we've developed a technique we thought would work for releasing a Pacific sail on 2-pound test.

We planned to troll two hook-less lures or teasers on the left and right long riggers and two more teasers on the left and right shorts. Additionally, Chris would control two daisy chains loaded with hook-less squid on the teaser reels that he works from the fly bridge. The two mates in the cockpit control everything else. A billfish that found our teasers attractive naturally chased after them. Like a child's bullying game of keep-away, the teaser in question kept being pulled away as the fish tried to eat it, each time getting closer to our transom. When it came close enough, I dropped my hooked bait in right next to the teaser and the teaser exited the water — the technique that inspired the term" bait-and-switch." Then I'd bait the fish on a 2-pound rod and reel. As the fish engulfed the ballyhoo, I immediately went to freespool. Captain Chris timed the maneuver so he could back up over and almost sit on the fish out of gear. I gently reeled in the slack using no more than one pound of drag. When the sailfish felt like something was wrong, it would jump and try to free the hook from its mouth. Now, by going down to ¼ pound of drag, the weight of the ballyhoo either being flung out of the fish's mouth or gullet drove the super sharp and extra thin circle hook into the jaw somewhere and we would be hooked up. Of course this was only theory because we hadn't gotten the job done yet. After all, "There can be many a slip 'tween the glass and the lip!" When it works as planned, the fight begins.

Casa Vieja Lodge is my favorite place to fish in the entire world. I love the owners, David and Kristen Salazar. I have the greatest respect for what I consider some of the world's best billfish captains. Most of Casa Vieja's guests don't rig their own baits. I always help the crew rig baits each day as I really enjoy it.

Casa Vieja Lodge has 5-star service so phenomenal that they *deserve* 10 stars! They've decorated the deluxe rooms exquisitely with local art. They always greet guests with big smiles, and nothing is ever a problem, meaning the resort staff will always accommodate your every need with a smile. They deliver coffee to your room each morning before you go to Café Pez Vela for an American or Guatemalan breakfast. The freshly squeezed orange juice makes for a special treat. After fishing all day, most guests sit around the pool and snack on chicken, fish, or freshly made guacamole and chips. Then comes the four-course dinner. Oh my, what incredible food! The chef will always change the menu if you want something special, like fresh ceviche or sashimi from the tuna you just caught.

To this day, it amazes me as a cripple in a wheelchair, that everything I did so easily before is now so difficult to do. Things you might never even consider, like the fine sand in the parking lot at the marina, and the slope of the ramp heading to the docks at low tide. Life throws me challenges on a minute-to-minute basis! But as with most things, we figure it out and go with it. The van drove up to the gangway and they brought me down the ramp backwards (so I wouldn't fall out of my wheelchair). It's really not a problem, just another of the little hurdles I constantly face. You just need people to help you — and you know what? People are *always* willing to lend a hand. All you have to do is ask.

No matter where you are in the world, successful fishing destinations always maintain a blur of activity at the marina each morning. This trip proved no different.

Every boat in the fleet was booked; both the fishing and the weather was nothing short of spectacular. It felt like the whole marina had taken steroids. As the crew lifted me aboard, I immediately noticed that all the tackle normally on the boat for other customers had not been taken off. I knew exactly why. I had requested the tackle be removed, but producer Mark Freedman had communicated to the lodge countermanding that order. I'm sure his reasoning was simple. If I couldn't catch a sailfish on 2-pound, we could bail the show out on 8- or 12-pound test. But, here we were in Guatemala and Mark Freedman's voice went silent. I again requested the tackle to be taken off the boat. Reluctantly, Chris removed every single rod and reel including spinning and fly rods. The only rods and reels aboard were my three 2-pound outfits. The film crew became very uneasy, and I know for a fact emails flew back and forth to NBC, creating quite a stir on the dock, especially as all of Chris's tackle paraded down the dock to the lodge van, where it would remain.

We headed out on a flat calm ocean; nary a ripple on the water ahead of us. You could actually see the reflection of the boat in the water. Our strategy called for us to head out about 16 miles offshore where most boats had been averaging between 10 and 50 bites a day. Nobody questioned the fact that I was rolling the dice. We successfully baited 10 fish in a row resulting in 10 break-offs in a row. But with each successive fish, we got closer on our learning curve and maybe (and I say again maybe), catching one on 2-pound test.

One of my biggest problems was our inability to move the wheelchair around the cockpit fast enough to get the leader for a release. When fishing 2-pound test, the boat captain critically orchestrates the cockpit activities of the crew and angler, though all three facets carry equal importance. But on 2-pound, the margin of error almost can't be measured without a micrometer.

The film crew began to panic. Obviously, a TV show can't bear fruit based on 10 break-offs in a row. As for me, catching *any* fish requires that 1) I don't fall out of my wheelchair, 2) I move around in the cockpit extremely quick, and 3) I survive being strapped into the chair using a special harness and a green bungee strap that wrapped around the back of the wheelchair and around my chest with Velcro for extra support.

As if that was not hard enough already, by 3:32 in the afternoon, we had raised 25 fish for the day. Fifteen of them failed to commit to the teaser or be drawn to the last teaser in order to be able to put the fish 10 feet or less behind the transom. We could have brought the bait to just 15 feet back, but that wasn't close enough. When using 2-pound test a short hookup becomes absolutely mandatory. Chris and I had failed so many times on 2-pound, we knew this to be a fact.

Oh, about the other 10? We hooked, broke off, or the hook pulled. I even fell out of my chair. Bottom line, they all escaped. No wonder my film crew had the jitters! In fact, I cannot tell you how frustrated this made the crew. They were just not used to raising 25 solid eaters, and having their catch score be "zero." Unheard of! After every lost fish, I brought everyone together and chanted, "We can do this! We can do this!"

At 3:45 PM, already 15 minutes after the fleet normally heads back to the marina, here comes a sailfish on the right-long rigger — lit up like a Christmas tree; like somebody plugged it into 220 amps — its pecs a brilliant royal blue. All of us who have fished for billfish know exactly what I'm talking about. This fish came in hot. We lured him into the position on the short, hookless teasers when the son of a gun disappeared. The camera crew and everyone knew this was our last fish for the day. Chris bellowed from the bridge, "He's gone. I can't see him." All of a sudden it showed close in, right behind a short-left bait. Chris usually speaks in a very soft voice. I explained to him that when I'm facing away from him, half the time I can't hear him. So in a loud voice Chris yelled, "That's your fish! That's your fish!" Both mates quickly got everything else out of the water. I always fish on the right side. I feel more secure there as I can hold the gunwale with my right hand. I also grab the rod and drop back rightie. One of the mates grabbed my chair while I undid the locks on my wheels. He desperately tried to get me to the left side of the boat, around the fighting chair, but by the time I got there the fish had disappeared! Chris had pulled the teaser out of the water and now we had no fish to be seen and no baits in the water.

Chris muttered in disgust, "Get him back on the right side with one ballyhoo." I put the ballyhoo 15 feet behind the boat and we trolled for 30 seconds with nothing and then loud enough for all of Wyoming to hear, Chris yelled, "It's on your bait!" I lifted the rod above my head with the wind-on leader literally still on the rod. The fish came in hot, missing the bait on the first pass. It settled below my bait, about five feet down. I could hear the anger and frustration in Chris's voice as he yelled at the fish, "Eat the bait, you bas….d." As if following orders, here it came straight at my bait, this time lunging at it with mouth open. No more playing with this bait. Time for dinner!

Danny Kirsic stuck a damn camera right in my face making it twice as hard for me to see the fish. I gently pushed Danny to the side and to my amazement he quickly moved left. David is on the bridge filming down on the bite itself. The fish opens its mouth and swallows the bait. In freespool I dropped it right down its gullet. Chris gently reversed the boat as I drop back, ending up with the fish

10 feet down and 10 feet back. Chris said, "Set up!" I yelled back, "Not yet!" We sat over that fish for what seemed like an eternity, but in reality probably only took a minute. The Universe proceeds in slow motion at moments like these. I put the lever all the way up to one pound of drag, slowly reeled in the slack and felt it come tight. The little noodle of a rod bent over and our sailfish went airborne, proceeding to go berserk behind the boat.

One of the mates moved my wheelchair to the left side of the boat. I am now down to ¼ pound of drag as the fish tail walked in almost a complete circle. Chris, of course, does a masterful job of keeping the transom to the fish. As we complete this maneuver, black smoke and carbon from the exhaust lay on the surface of the water like a dirty film. We ended up with the sailfish diving just below the surface and starting to swim away.

The roar of the engines is very disturbing. Both Danny and David wipe their lenses off with special camera cloths. I kept yelling to Danny, who was in the cockpit with me, asking if he got the shots to which he replied, "Tred I'm on you. Dave is on the fish." As I sat quietly at the transom holding the rod slightly bent over, Chris asked, "Do you still have it on?" When I replied, "Yes!" Chris belted out, "We're in business!"

The great fish slowly swam away from the boat only about a foot down. The movement of its tail and dorsal fin creating a whirlpool disturbance on the water's surface making it easy to follow. The fish started to slow down and cut to the left. Then the fish demonstrated some of the finest acrobatics I have ever seen. It was magnificent. It jumped towards the sky, tail violently slashing back and forth, sail fully extended and almost flapping in the breeze. No sooner did it slam back into the water than it went airborne again.

To be perfectly honest I stayed calm as a cucumber. I knew exactly what had to be done. To catch a fish on 2-pound requires everyone to do their job and then you need to add a 90 percent mixture of luck. I could only go to freespool and add a whisper of thumb pressure. Amazingly, the fish didn't want to leave the boat. It must have been a Guatemala Department of Tourism fish.

After six magnificent airborne salutes, the fish cut violently to the left side of the boat, sending white water everywhere, adding to that created by Chris's maneuvering. It charged straight back away from the boat, executing several airborne antics and finished off with a gigantic belly flop. I still had the fish on when Chris yelled to me, "Tred are you ready?" The cameramen, mates, and I all knew what Chris meant. Time to try to get a legal release.

Reversing at full throttle, the engines' turbos screaming and the entire boat shuddering as if begging for relief, I reeled like tomorrow didn't exist! I bumped up to as much as 1-1/2 pounds of drag pressure. Any contrary movement from the fish would break the line instantly. Water rolled up almost to the top of the transom as we flew backwards. Fifty feet. Forty feet. Thirty feet. Again the fish cut a little to the left but Chris never fell for the feint. He led with the starboard engine overbalancing the port in reverse, gently causing the boat to shear slightly left. The fish took another magnificent jump at the boat, almost landing in the cockpit, forcing me back into freespool. Six feet from the mate grabbing the leader! Chris shouted, "Ready Tred?" and then yelled, "Now!" We came tearing backwards with me reeling like a banshee. The mate reached out and grabbed, taking a wrap on the light 50-pound leader and by some miracle both mates grabbed the bill before the leader broke.

I screamed with joy! The cameramen kept rolling. Chris came off the bridge and gave me an old fashioned bear hug. I happily yelled, "Congratulations everybody, we did it!"

They placed this great sailfish across my lap for a picture. I held up my rod. Both cameras kept rolling. As we released the fish to fight another day, both cameramen came into the cockpit and said, "We need a close." I looked both lenses in the eye, threw up my fist and said through my clenched teeth, as much at my naysayers as the viewing audience, "Never Ever Say Never!" Then I shouted to the crew, "Another day, another adventure" and both cameras swung off me.

Now came time for celebration. As the news of the historic catch — a release on 2-pound test, — went out on the VHF-radio, many of the captains congratulated Chris. Back at the lodge that evening everyone celebrated our catch. What a glorious time we had. Both David and Danny admitted that we certainly had a TV show but needed to fill in some blanks. NBC Sports and Mark Freedman got the news of our success, making both teams very happy. The next morning, I slept until 10 am. Later, my crew and I filled in the "B roll" — ancillary footage that every TV show needs. I talked to the parrots, ate lunch, and toured around the lodge complex. Most importantly though, despite everyone's misgivings, this show went on to become one of the most popular we ever produced — a huge success.

Donna De Weil and Tred with Sailfish caught on a 2 lb. test

Chapter Twenty-Nine
BAMBOO BARTA

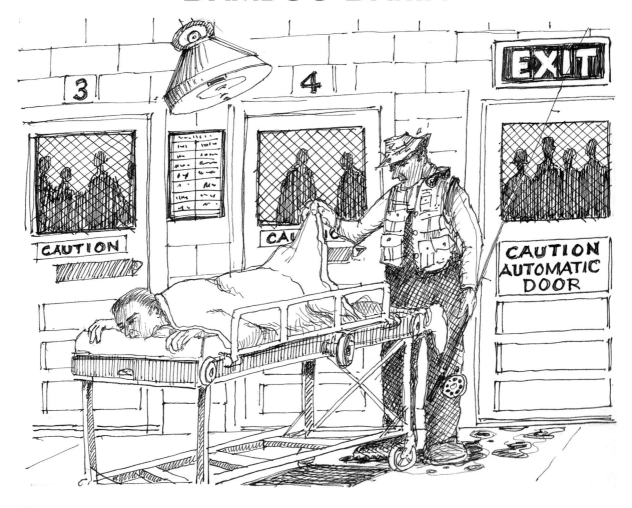

ONE OF MY philosophies that I often discuss with people at charity events or travels around the world regards the excitement you can find in your own backyard. If done properly, nearby adventures can be just as exciting and important as the most expensive African safari.

For example, if you live in an area with gray squirrels, walk in the hard woods with your grandfather or other family members and take a scoped .22 rifle or a .410 shotgun. Bingo, real Brunswick stew. What about snowshoe rabbits in the dead of winter or setting up a blind on a beaver pond? Great Hassenpfeffer! The excitement of any hunt done well qualifies as a backyard safari.

If you think about it, your local bass pond, trout stream, or really any body of water can often offer an enthusiast the opportunity to indulge his or her passion. Florida is riddled with canals that almost always offer peacock bass, largemouth bass, brim or catfish.

You'll find some of the best trout fishing in the world within a 10-mile radius of Longbow Ranch in Colorado. Before I lost my legs, I fished with a great group of guys who are absolute fly-fishing fanatics. As a result, I tried to get them all to go down to 2-pound tippets and fish dry flies as well as small nymphs. It's all about the challenge and trying it the hard way.

So, let's talk about a backyard safari. One might ask how a man like me, who has fished almost every corner of the globe for the biggest fish that roam our oceans, can get completely enthralled over fishing for cutthroat, brown, and rainbow trout just down the road? We come to my point exactly. Whenever you fish in a stream, river, or pond, and you attack what is available to you, making it as absolutely difficult and sporting as can be, you suddenly have a real challenging game.

In Colorado, I fished nothing but split bamboo rods in zero weight to a maximum three weight. Something breathtaking happens when you cast a Royal Coachman fly perfectly. Having the fly float just so — very lightly in the wind — and then settle on still water like the gentlest kiss… It's absolutely fabulous.

I've always hated snobs — especially in our sport. People who put other people down or make fun of them because they don't have the money to travel to exotic places or afford the absolute best, most expensive equipment. I absolutely despise that type of person.

I have always said, "Make the most of what God gave you." If you know anything about western fly fishing, you know every guide and angler has a fly box in which they take great pride. One of my dearest friends and fishing guide, Mike Salomone (www.MichaelSalomone.com), came and got me at least three times a week after he finished work. He's responsible for a very large part of my mental recovery. I had purchased a number of Zebra nymphs in a brilliant lime green color with black and silver wrapping that worked very well in a local pond.

One spring evening in 2010, sitting in bed, I took all of my wooden handmade fly boxes out and arranged the flies like little soldiers by color, size and type. As I was arranging them, Ahi, my ranch dog hopped in bed and the flies I was working with bounced all over the bed. After putting the flies away, I fell asleep, eagerly awaiting my fishing expedition the next day,

Come morning, wild turkeys woke me as they visited our flower garden. I got up and turned on the news. Daniel, our ranch hand and my assistant, was picking up hay in Leadville so I was home alone.

Each morning, I always do an inspection of my privates as well as the tube which drains my bladder, just to make sure everything is OK. You have to remember I have no feeling below my chest. To my horror, I felt several bumps on my left testicle. I remember asking myself, "What the heck is this?" I quickly grabbed a mirror to investigate. After I rolled around a bit, I noticed some blood on the sheets. That got me really worried. You will never guess what was in my left testicle. I solved my mystery. Five zebra nymphs embedded themselves fairly deeply into my skin. I got dressed and called the emergency room in Vail. By this time, I knew every single doctor at the Vail Cancer Center and most of the people who worked in the ER. Trying to reach my doctors, the head nurse finally said, "Mr. Barta. Tell me what's wrong. You don't want to talk about it?" When I told her what happened, she burst out laughing on the phone. Just about everybody in Vail, Colorado either fishes or lives with someone who fishes. That's just the way it is.

The drive to the hospital seemed like it took forever. Thanks to my TV show on NBC Sports, it seemed that every time I even farted, it ended up in the local newspaper. It came with the territory.

As I rolled into the emergency room, I had quite a bit of blood on the crotch of my khaki pants. And there — to my horror — stood "Head Nurse Ratchet." She said, "Well Mr. Barta, it looks like you had quite an evening." I did my best to lay low out in the hallway, but apparently by the time I got to the ER, everyone on the floor had heard I was on my way. Each had a comment like, "the newspapers are going to like this" or "world record holder catches his left nut on two-pound test." I finally got into an ER exam room. One of the hooks got caught on my khakis. Two female nurses and a male intern with a flashlight and a big pair of scissors labored at cutting off my pants. Of course while all of this was happening, my pulse and blood pressure were taken as doctors had some thought of me going to another room for actual surgery.

I kept wondering, "How in the heck will I ever live this down?" I noticed a crowd building outside my room, accompanied by a lot of laughing and giggling — so much for privacy. And just when I thought things could get no worse, here comes the head ER doctor — wearing full waders, a fly vest, his fishing hat, and carrying his fly rod. As he walked in, everyone roared, including me. Now that's funny! Anyway, with all of the surgical lights shining brightly and all of the people outside, I figured having a good time and laughing about this crazy situation was my only recourse. One by one, the doctor extracted the zebra nymphs, placing them on a silver-colored metal tray so everyone could get a good look at them. Thankfully, I couldn't feel anything as the flies came out, but at least I'd get to reuse them for their intended purpose when this adventure ran its course. I don't know how you can possibly bandage a testicle. To this day I remember the doctor trying to tape gauze on that area, to no avail. So much for an early morning start.

It was now afternoon and off to the local pond Mike and I went. My first cast laid out to absolute perfection. The bamboo rod bent over and I caught a beautiful 14-inch brown trout with the Zebra nymph which just a couple hours earlier had been embedded in my package.

Yes, I took lots of ribbing for a couple of weeks. While certainly a horror-show in the beginning, it all turned out just fine. Truth be told, sometimes you just have to make fun of yourself. To this day I have a box that says Left Testicle Nymphs. Oh well — another day, another adventure.

Chapter Thirty
REBIRTH OF MAKAIRA

I SAT ON the porch at Longbow Ranch, the sense of it being paradise now greatly tarnished. My marriage to Anni no longer represented that idyllic happiness. I had sold my beloved horse, Badger, and again I yearned for the ocean, in a way that I can only describe as a constant calling.

I had lived on or by the ocean most my life. It becomes a part of you that never goes away. Prior to being in a wheelchair, I traveled the world, to the best fishing destinations one could imagine. I still yearned for the smell of low tide and the sea birds. I often wondered if they contained the souls of sailors passed.

Lawyers drafted the separation agreement and divorce papers. In my mind, I searched where on the East Coast I should live next. I needed a place where I could fish in my wheelchair as captain in command – both in my own boat and of my destiny. Although all evidence pointed to the fact that I could neither medically nor physically be a captain again, I totally disagreed. My place-to-live requirements included short runs offshore for big gamefish, not the 75 nautical mile runs of my youth off Shinnecock, Long Island.

Previously, I had looked at homes and condos from Beaufort, North Carolina to Key West. Everything kept pointing me to Islamorada in the Florida Keys. Islamorada drew me in like a magnet because of its spectacular fishing. No matter how hard the wind blows, Islamorada always has a place to find a lee from the wind to fish. It is known as the fishing capital of the world for one reason. It's what they do there.

Islamorada offered me the opportunity to fish the fabulous Everglades and Florida Bay, punctuated with thousands of named and unnamed islands. At the same time, within five miles of the marina, I could troll for blue marlin, sailfish, wahoo, dolphin, and blackfin tuna. No place in the world has comparable fishing diversity such a short distance from the marina. Here I could literally be fishing three and a half miles from the marina and the longest run of nineteen miles would allow me to fish the Islamorada Hump and the 409. Every restaurant and early morning café fills with fishermen and charter captains discussing topics on blue water or flats fishing for bonefish, permit, and tarpon. The ebb and flow of everyday life surrounds itself with some aspect of the sport.

In 2013, I purchased a condo at Beacon Reef on the ocean, right across from the restaurant *Mad Dog Ziggy's*. My bedroom slider and balcony overlooks the ocean with a clear view of the docks and pool area. Alligator Reef Light is nearby and can be seen when on the condo dock.

Islamorada has become my home and the center of my fishing universe. I planned to dock my next boat, *Makaira*, at World Wide Sportsman, a Bass Pro shop and marina. I secured a slip. I knew many there and they knew me from my TV show and because I had given fishing presentations at World Wide Sportsman, they welcomed me with open arms and told me, "Tred, you are welcome here and we will make it work." The process of building a new home started.

Throughout my travels around the world I knew the panga-style boat design. The design makes it extremely seaworthy. A 22- to 30-foot vessel can be pushed easily without a lot of power. It's designed to carry a lot of weight and on top of all of this, it has a shallow draft. It seemed the perfect design for me to fish in Islamorada. With good reason, the Panga (or Pirogue) stands as the single most popular boat design in the world.

Next I searched boat companies in the U.S. for what could very well be my last boat. It took months to thoroughly research the latest and greatest. When word got out that I was back in the saltwater game, no fewer than ten boat companies offered me a boat, either for free or at a token price. Not one of them, however, was equipped nor willing to provide necessary modifications to accommodate fishing in my wheelchair. It created one very frustrating time. They all wanted me to take the boat as they sold it and modify it afterwards – on my own.

While researching I came across an amazing family owned and operated company called Andros Boatworks located in Sarasota, Florida. They are known internationally as custom-built boats of quality and excellence. I immediately befriended the Eggebrecht family. Andy, Don, and Danny Eggebrecht as well as their team of experts put out about 70 beautiful, fuel-efficient boats a year. At that time, most of their boats bore the unique panga hull design I desired, with sizes ranging from 18 up to 26 feet. Andros boats run comfortably, dry, in deep or shallow water and can be used offshore or inshore. They also build an offshore 32-footer with a modern deep-V hull design.

At the end of my first meeting with Andros Boatworks I reached out to Don Eggebrecht and gave him a hug. Tears streamed out of both of our eyes. I was so grateful to Don and the Andros team to be willing to build a boat so I could be on the sea again. Don believed in me and gave me his word that we could accomplish this very unusual custom boat build. Throughout this book I talk about tears streaming out of my eyes or I cried. When you spent five decades walking, climbing, and scratching yourself all over the world and now find yourself confined to a wheelchair, when people offer you kindness it is often overwhelming. When I had my legs I helped people all the time simply because that is what a good man does. When you learn what that kindness feels like when you are the recipient I can tell you from my point of view it is overwhelming.

The Eggebrechts and I had many meetings to completely redesign a 26-footer. The boat's helm not only had to accommodate my wheelchair, but the floor plan needed to provide wheelchair ingress and egress from the bow to the stern, too. Some of our design concept we thought would work, failed after further research. This design process provided quite a learning curve for us all since such a vessel had never before been built. But the more we failed, the more determined we became to succeed.

At Andros, first they wax the boat mold. Then the selected color of gelcoat sprays into the mold, covering it completely. Besides giving the hull your choice of color of which I chose San Mateo Wheat, the gelcoat acts as a waterproofing barrier and a bonding surface to which the fiberglass and resin adhere. A thin layer of special fiberglass lays on gelcoat to prevent "print-through" the ability to see the weave of the fiberglass fabric through the gelcoat. Once this layer is cured, high-quality, biaxial structural fiberglass gets laid in the mold by hand. For the hull, deck, and usually the console (but not on my boat) a composite core material, usually high-density, closed-cell foam, adds strength to the laminate without adding significant weight. Additional layers of fiberglass sandwich the coring between stiff fiberglass layers resulting in a strong, watertight hull.

Stringers (the boat's skeleton) set into the hull bottom and bond to the hull with space-age adhesive putty. Two inch holes are drilled into the tops of the stringer grid allowing structural foam to be injected into the stringers for flotation and additional strength. Finally, they pull the hull from the mold and the rigging process begins. Rigging the boat includes installing wiring, plumbing, electronics, fuel system, T-tops, towers, engines and all other options. Rigging in the hull and decks happens separately before the two parts bond together.

Next, in the pre-decking phase, the console mates to the tower or top (if you selected one), and those parts mount to the deck. Once all those pieces fit where they belong, the hull and deck go together. Andros uses both chemical and mechanical bonding processes to permanently bond the deck and the hull together. Lastly, the final stage of the rigging process where everything is connected, electronics, the rub rail, and upholstery are installed, and engines programmed. Of course they water test every boat!

For the next two years Donna De Weil, a dear friend, would be at my side. Everything with Donna was exciting and wonderful. She joined the boat design team and always carried a tape measure. At this time no one knew me better. Donna understood the wheelchair and how my life unfortunately revolved around it.

Standard center console designs would have barred me access to the bow area. I'd be confined to a very small cockpit area by the transom. While designing the hard top for *Makaira*, the Andros team came up with a fairly complicated system where I would reach up and pull down the retractable console to my wheelchair with a lever using hydraulics!

We were far along the planning stages and we were still trying to iron out the console issues. Andy, Don, Donna, Andros team experts, and I met at the Andros Boatworks shop. I remember the meeting well. Donna belted out, "Hey! This is not going to work." That's Donna; not afraid to be heard and unafraid to bring forward the facts as she saw them. This woman buys houses, renovates them, and sells them. She does most of the construction work herself! She knows what works and what doesn't. Her opinion? The complicated pull-down electronics box and steering console just made no sense. The amount of electronics and the joystick needed to maneuver the boat would have been too heavy and more importantly, I couldn't lock my wheelchair to the console.

I had been lobbying a long time for a side console, which Andros had previously never designed or built. A side console allowed me full access in the boat, and it could be custom designed around my wheelchair needs.

The meetings dragged on and everyone on the Andros team started being very challenged by the task at hand. And now Don, the patriarch of the company, brought up a few salient items. Where is all the wiring going to go? Where are the batteries going to go? In other models, all that lived in the center console. The standard console not only stored all the ship's systems, but with enough room left over for a walk-in head! Now we had to take 50 pounds of stuff and put it in a bag meant for five pounds. So it looked like my 26-foot Tarpon model suddenly became a *very* custom design.

Once we finalized everything and put it to paper, guess what? Everybody liked it — including me. And now people describe it as sexy, good-looking, and practical. And Andros incorporated it into their model choices for other clients.

Despite adopting many of Donna's suggestions, the project became a boat builder's nightmare. The helm console had to be custom designed and built from scratch to accommodate my wheelchair. The Andros craftsmen built it out of aluminum and finished it off in Awlgrip white. The end design allowed my feet, legs and thighs to fit comfortably under the console. An Andros pro welded two metal eyes onto my wheelchair. When I'm at the helm, two cables snap onto the welded eyes, not only securing me to the console but preventing me from flipping over in a heavy seaway. Due to not having any control of my torso muscles, my reach to operate the electronics, control levers, and Optimus joystick had to be precise. The exact angle of the steering wheel was critical. After three meetings, the carefully calculated measurements allowed me to reach everything and comfortably control the boat. It may not sound like a big deal, but it evolved into a truly arduous task that took numerous hours and multiple meetings.

I decided to go with a 16-inch Edson steering wheel with a Sure-grip rubber insert that doesn't slip, as my right hand often spasms and if that single disability was not enough I had ripped my bicep off my right arm the year before which further exacerbated the pain and spasming of my right hand and also contributed to a loss of strength and soreness throughout my right arm. The net was if the position of my chair to the console and the position of the steering wheel and controls were not absolutely perfect there was a good chance I would not be able to run the boat which then made the whole project a huge waste of time since the boat was being designed around one single purpose – the ability for me to run my own boat.

On top of the console sits a blue-faced Ritchie magnetic compass. Many people no longer have a compass on their boat since the latest electronics give them the same information. Call me old school but I can always get back to the marina with one.

I was fortunate to be able to choose the electronics I wanted for *Makaira*. I chose a Simrad NSE12 multifunction display with chart, echo sounder, radar, navigation, and fuel counter. It had to be installed in the correct location and height so I could see over everything to navigate while in my wheelchair. I laughed to myself one day at all of the electronics. *Makaira* had more advanced electronics than the first corporate aircraft I flew to Europe as pilot in command.

I know this sounds a touch boring but let me tell you something, the artistic design of my sculpted console qualifies as a masterpiece. It's a work of art. So many moving parts to contend with in the design. My wheelchair had to be secure, I needed visibility over everything so I could navigate the boat. I needed an ergonomic joystick, throttles, and steering wheel. The steering wheel had to be precisely placed with an exact angle and distance from my chair so I could use it. After hundreds of man hours, the console debuted as a thing of beauty. To the untrained eye it is just a boat console. But to me it represented an exciting and new way to be independent.

Donna pointed out to the design team that my worst enemy was the blazing tropic sun. It caused me to overheat and as well as to suffer hypothermia easily in the cold, factors that definitely needed consideration in the boat design. To Donna's credit, she also pointed out the size shortcomings of the standard hard top, and after everyone reluctantly listened, drew up an old-style Grandpa's version.

The aft section of the hard top hinges with an extended canvas top attached, so you can flip the canvas up and secure it. The Andros team was fabulous at always resolving problems and this top was just one of many items throughout the boat design and build.

The transom features a flip-down bench seat so I could lay down if I was tired. The team originally designed it at the same level as the transom caprail, so I could stretch out, but Donna feared that I'd fall asleep and roll off the boat. Therefore, they lowered the seat a couple of inches below the caprail. Another custom feature finds a folding passenger seat with a removable backrest to port.

During *Makaira's* build, we traveled the four hours to Andros Boatworks many times to insure the boat physically worked right for me. In the beginning, four of the Andros team physically lifted me into the boat hull, but at one point they raised the hull onto a wooden dolly, so from then on, they lifted me with a forklift and lowered me into the boat. It was quite hilarious being lifted by a forklift and they made sure I stayed absolutely safe during the lifting process.

With all the measurements taken and space allocations assigned, then came the fun stuff. As I waited for my boat's delivery, I worked on some of the details.

With the help of Seastar Solutions' Optimus joystick, the Evinrude controls allowed me to switch over to the Optimus joystick at a moment's notice. This system lets me maneuver the boat effortlessly even with my disabilities. I can change the "lock to lock" rotation making the motors turn quicker than the wheel at slow speed. It can move the boat sideways, diagonally, spin it, back up, go forward… in truth, I have never been able to maneuver a boat so comprehensively in my life! What incredible technology! I can even push a button, and the steering system, combined with the GPS, holds the boat within a few feet of where I want it, on the heading I was on when I pushed the button! That dynamic positioning used to cost oil-drilling ships millions and now I have the same thing on my 26-foot Andros!

I chose Evinrude E-tec outboards, counter-rotating 150s. The E-tec platform offered a two-stroke design in its last year of production. My 150s had the best power out of the hole and weighed cumulatively some 800 pounds less than Mercury, Yamaha, or Suzuki – all four-strokes. The facts that Evinrude builds its engines in the United States at their Sturtevant, Wisconsin plant and that its two-stroke technology had never been better led me to this choice. The Icon fly-by-wire control system gave me "Troll Control" so speed could be added or slowed by increments of 50 rpm with a touch of a button. Evinrude's Icon also allowed me to switch to the Optimus joystick. The resulting helm station ended up as the perfect paraplegic console tied into the perfect power plants for *Makaira*.

One other feature I added — a 10-foot Power Pole installed on the transom — allowed me to anchor almost anywhere in shallow water up to eight feet deep at the touch of a button. A deep, wide live bait well holds all the bait needed for fishing in Islamorada. Located in the center of my transom, the livewell is flanked by a combination second livewell/storage compartment to starboard and a freshwater washdown/storage compartment to port.

I mounted rod holders everywhere. I ordered the outriggers and rod holders from my dear friends at Rupp Marine. I've used their Top Gun model outriggers for years and by use of a small PVC pipe and some custom welding, I can adjust the outrigger halyards myself from my wheelchair and that means I can put out my own lines. A remarkably big deal.

Here's a bottom line quote straight from Donna that guided every design dilemma: "If Tred can't get to it, it's of no use."

Though I'll always use my Power Pole to anchor in shallow water, we also installed a Lewmar electric anchor windlass on the foredeck. With the proper anchor chain and line, I can anchor up to 200 feet of water just by pushing a button on the helm console.

I have never wanted an "ordinary" boat and truthfully, every boat I've ever owned has been totally unique. I've always loved the look of teak on my boats but my fiberglass Andros made that slightly more problematic. A new product called Flexiteek shows the burrs and imperfections of real teak but with 1/100 of the maintenance. Flexiteek installed on *Makaira's* decks give it a beautiful and classy look while remaining super easy to clean.

I can trim my boat's running angle in three ways – by the trimming in and out on the Evinrude engines (raising and lowering the bow); by trimming the Porta Bracket jack plate which raises both engines almost completely out of the water vertically together or independently (for shallow water); and with Lenco electric trim tabs (bow up/down and lean left/right) that respond quickly and sensitively to the touch when needed. Think about it, as a professional captain of big boats with but one way to trim a boat, I can trim *Makaira* three ways! Pretty impressive!

I run stainless steel 14-3/8" Cyclone four-bladed props with 17 degrees of pitch. At 3,800 rpm and proper trim, *Makaira* cruises at 27 knots. Keep in mind the E-tecs can turn 5,800 rpm in the corner, making top end about 35 knots.

Makaira holds 100 gallons of fuel in a custom tank. We added a cool ladder – deployable from the water — so guests could take the occasional swim and I went completely nuts by adding three 1,100 gpm bilge pumps.

Building a custom boat inspires much more anguish, angst, and tension than buying a production boat. Not because of all the decisions that must be made, but with waiting time. You can go and buy any production boat and pretty much have it delivered tomorrow. Custom boats combat instant gratification by taking a longer time to deliver. In September 2014 that great day finally came when I took delivery of *Makaira* after 17 months of planning, design modifications, and the final build. A fabulous day! It soon became evident that my Andros represented everything I had hoped and prayed for. Honestly, there was nothing I couldn't do with my new Andros.

You can tell by now that I am a staunch traditionalist. But I added one more feature that has probably never been seen on a sport fishing boat before: When attached to the console, I can't see anything behind me due to my paralysis. I added a cool professional waterskiing mirror to the hardtop legs and now have a 360-degree view around the entire vessel.

During the initial sea trial, the entire vessel leaned to starboard thanks to the weight of the side console, battery position, etc. Everybody ran around in panic mode except me. I suggested they just cut the deck floor on the opposite side and add ballast — no big deal at all. So that is exactly what we did, adding about 200 pounds of sand encased in plastic to the left side under deck. Kapang! Problem solved!

Makaira now resides at World Wide Sportsman in a perfect slip right next to the restaurant. We have successfully taken the boat around the gulf-side back country for mangrove snapper, tarpon, and snook and fished offshore for blue marlin, dolphin, sailfish, and swordfish. We have also fished all of the inner reefs for grouper, yellowtail snapper, mutton snapper, and one of the most overlooked fish which are delicious, porgies.

My Andros has been an absolute success! The marina became my social center, hanging out with the captains after work and enjoying my many new friendships. The boat, marina, and the marina environment constitute a huge part of my life. I love fishing in Islamorada and my new boat makes it even sweeter. I consider it yet another example of the greatness of mankind. "Never Say Never." Despite overwhelming adversity *Makaira* sails again.

So here's the bottom line: When I am piloting *Makaira*, all the adversities and struggles I go through all day and everyday fall away from me. Aboard *Makaira* I am no longer a cripple, but am the captain in command, as I always have been. In many ways when one discusses the rebirth of *Makaira*, it would more accurately read the rebirth of Tred. I say to everyone at Andros Boatworks, to all of the vendors, sponsors, Donna, and supporters, kudos to you and many thanks for believing in me.

Andros putting the two sections together for Makaira.

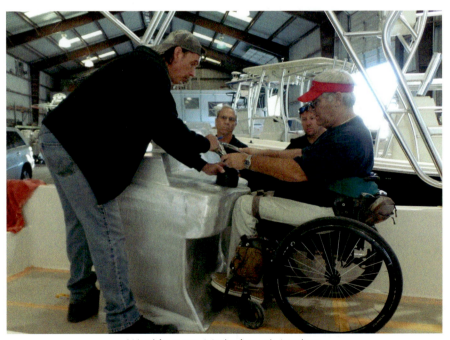
Working on Makaira at Andros

Tred being lifted by the fork lift.

Work on Makaira at Andros

Tred on the forklift

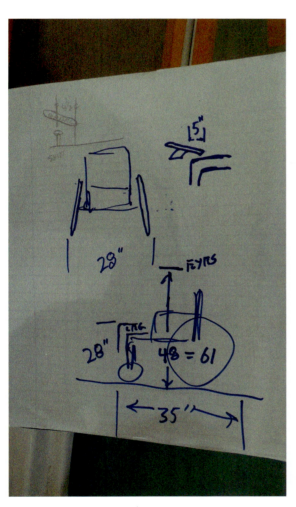

Notes on the Makaira dimensions.

Tred with Andy, Don and Dan Eggebrecht

Chapter Thirty-One
FOUR TWELVE

ONE OF THE bad things about trying to fish with world-class captains is the fact they're often busy. They're busy because they excel at their jobs and their bookings fill up months in advance.

On August 8, 2015, Billy Chapman, one of the Florida Keys' best captains, called me to let me know he had a fishing charter cancellation the following day. He asked me if I'd like him to join me and go fishing on my boat, *Makaira*, instead of his charter boat in Islamorada, Florida. I excitedly called my dear friend Doc Bennett, one of my regular fishing buddies and another friend, Richard Logan.

For the past 25 years, Doc has lived in Islamorada. His parents lived in Marathon, Florida, in the 1960s, so Doc has spent decades fishing the Florida Keys. A gentle, soft-spoken man who has caught big game fish across the globe, Doc retired after 35 years as a gynecologist specializing in oncology.

Richard — a retired Canon salesman — has lived in different parts of the country and now resides aboard his 1966, 45-foot Hatteras docked at the World Wide Sportsman marina. Richard usually helps in getting gear together for a fishing trip.

We'd have a crew of four including myself, plus I invited a young lad named Evan Goins, whom I nicknamed "Maggot." Maggot is the 19-year-old son of a marina tenant. I nicknamed him "Maggot" since he was the youngest man on the totem pole, with plans of going into the Coast Guard after high school. Anyway, I remembered a movie I saw once where they called the new recruits "maggots."

Makaira, my customized 26-foot Andros, docks at World Wide Sportsman's marina in Islamorada Florida, on the bayside at Mile Marker (MM) 81.5.

For most of my life, I chose to hang out at a marina after my work day. Now I hang out at the World Wide Sportsman marina each day until dark. The full-service marina which is now a part of Bass Pro Shops, has 40 slips and comes alive after 3 PM when all the marina residents and charter captains return from a day of fishing with stories of their day's catch.

The Islamorada Fish Company next door, and part of World Wide Sportsman, has a restaurant and bar next to the marina serving lunch and dinner. Along the walkways, visitors feed numerous hundred-pound tarpon daily and love seeing them swimming in a cove and around the docks.

World Wide Sportsman's back-country fishermen run their businesses out of this marina. Some extremely solid blue water captains work out of there as well.

Since I am not in the charter business and am confined to my wheelchair, I pose no threat to anyone in the marina. Everyone there has always been helpful, kind, and generous towards me. I feel lucky because they feel like family to me.

I frequently amaze outsiders. They can't believe how a private boater such as myself, and confined to a wheelchair, consistently produces the fishing results I turn in weekend after weekend. Truth be told, every charter captain in the marina willingly shares their hot spots with me or tells me exactly where to go on any given day. You might say, if anybody knows what is going on in the Florida Keys on any given day, I do. But with that said I also share *my* hot spots and results with those very same captains.

With this trust goes tremendous responsibility. These captains make a living fishing and insuring their clients have a great day of fishing. They give me their best locations right down to the exact GPS numbers.

When I am asked where I caught my fish or where someone should go to catch the same fish I am unloading from *Makaira*, I turn to them and say "Sorry, but I can't tell you. I gave my word to that charter captain over there that I wouldn't share his numbers. Often those who ask totally understand. Sometimes they don't…

August 9, 2015 turned out to be a magnificent day with light and variable winds and the temperature in the mid-80s. If any of you have been to Colorado on a perfect, cloudless day, you can attest to how brilliantly blue the sky can be. On this particular day, the sky in Islamorada shone the same brilliant blue.

I consider Islamorada one of the world's most beautiful places and I can attest to that since I have truly traveled all over the world. As we left the head pins on Indian Key Channel, the water changed from a light green to pastel green and then lit up with the sun to an aqua color. If this sight doesn't take your breath away, you must be dead or color blind. The combination of these unforgettable inshore colors just pop as you leave the verdant green and brown of the palm trees accenting the Keys' coastline. At the hundred-foot edge just outside the reef, the sea becomes cobalt blue. Another mile offshore finds pure gulf stream water.

As *Makaira* sped offshore, frigate birds accompanied us to conduct their daily life of eating, flying, and just plain living. The ocean laid out flat like it had been scraped with a level. It gave us the illusion of not even moving. I often experience this very weird sensation when the ocean goes flat calm. We also passed several man-of-war jellyfish with their multiple shades of blue and pink.

The night before our fishing trip, Captain Billy had attached alligator clips to the Daiwa MP3000 deep-drop reel on a curved butt 80. We modified the electrical cord so the reel could get power directly from *Makaira's* batteries. Billy brought onboard a harpoon, deep-drop weights, and a small yellow bag with all of the tackle necessary to rig the bait and leader sections. We brought two bonitos caught the day before and planned to catch a small dolphin on the way to the grounds. If we had no luck with that, then we'd use the bonitos as bait. We absolutely preferred fresh dolphin belly though.

We finished our final check list, which included picking up our usual order of 21 pieces of Dion's fried chicken from the local Mobil station on the way to the marina, my large green Stanley thermos full of Chock Full o' Nuts coffee, plenty of water, and apples. The delicious smells of the freshly fried chicken rolling out the white bag makes it very difficult not to grab a chicken leg and nibble on it immediately. With everything set, we pulled out of World Wide Sportsman's Marina at 8 AM.

On the way out, making a very easy 28 knots, Doc and I chatted about the day to come. Doc always sits on the seat to my left. We've come up with our own sign language as he directs me, preventing me from running over lobster buoys and debris underway. Truth be known, with *Makaira* trimmed perfectly, I can always use another set of eyes as I pilot the boat. I often miss the multiple rows of lobster and stone crab pot buoys that litter the waterway all the way out to about 60 feet. Doc usually stands as he directs me for the first five miles of the trip.

Doc is my navigator and second set of eyes — not a bad thing when you're in a wheelchair. Jeff Bennett, who everyone affectionately calls Doc, has caught more than 400 swordfish in his career and that stands as his absolute favorite fish to catch. In case you thought that might be a misprint, it's not. He's also caught more than 500 giant bluefin tunas in his day. Doc knows more about swordfishing than any of us can imagine. We share a tremendous respect for one another as we have both paid our dues all over the North Atlantic. Captain Billy Chapman, a Hollywood-good-looks type of fellow, is in his 30s and has already accomplished a tremendous amount in his lifetime. Billy has worked for some of the top captains on the East Coast and has learned his craft well.

The departure leg turned out pretty much uneventful and as we cleared quite a distance south of the 409 we crossed into 1,500 feet of water. It is here where the pedal and the metal would meet. We hadn't seen any dolphin on our way out so Billy quickly rigged a bonito belly as our bait. Billy likes a fairly small bait. He rigged the bait onto a seven-foot leader of 175-pound mono crimped onto a barrel swivel, then attached to a 200-foot-long, 300-pound wind-on mono leader which eventually tied to a full spool of 60-pound braid. Using a long line clip, Billy attached 10 pounds of lead weight leader and we were ready to drop.

Although I'm new to daytime deep-drop swordfishing, I'm no novice to surface swordfishing in the northeast. I have caught 16 swords on top and close to 100 while fishing at night in the northeast canyons. I trained under the venerable Carl Darenberg, Jr. of Montauk Marine Basin. But when it came to deep dropping during the day, call me an absolute greenhorn. The first two drops constituted absolute disasters! Billy started to lose patience as I kept screwing up the boat handling. A huge part of daytime swordfishing lies with the captain's ability to position the boat exactly in relationship to the angle at which your line enters the water.

The boat drifted east at approximately 5 to 6 knots with the gulf stream current. Ten pounds of weight wanted to be positioned about 20 feet off the bottom, in more than a thousand feet of water. If the captain doesn't keep the boat in the correct position, thousands of feet of additional line dump into the ocean making a huge curved bow on the line. Straight down makes a better presentation.

So this exact science of positioning the boat, retrieving and freespooling line, and reading the current and the wind all at one time takes a touch that some captains just do not have. Or didn't at first, but fortunately, I quickly learned this discipline and by the third drift Billy was doling out small compliments here and there about how quickly I learned how to run my boat.

At the end of our third drift a barely perceivable tap displaced the rod tip one quarter of an inch. Billy and Doc jumped to their feet simultaneously. Immediately Billy put the electric reel in gear and retrieved about 70 feet of line. The rod tip again deflected half an inch. I remember thinking "You have got to be kidding. This looks like a goldfish bite. It couldn't possibly be a swordfish." Then Billy and Doc discussed what should be done next. Before I knew it they freespooled the line and weight back to the bottom, then raised the weight by 15 feet and waited. A few minutes later the rod tip deflected an entire inch. I remember thinking to myself "Whoopee isn't this exciting!" All of a sudden the rod bent over and everyone shared high-fives. We had it on! What an incredibly light bite! I would never have believed that anything could have taken the bait let alone a swordfish. At about an hour and twenty minutes fighting time we had the great fish within sight. As the beautiful, 250-pound swordfish came closer, Billy took a shot with the harpoon, but unfortunately he missed terribly… a pathetic shot. Ten minutes later with the fish nicely settled down, it came right to the boat. With the harpoon and two gaffs waiting for him, the hook suddenly pulled. Dejection reigned supreme at losing the swordie.

Billy and Doc explained that pulling the hook boat-side often happens in daytime swordfishing due to two reasons: 1) their soft mouths and 2) fighting the fish from such depths while pulling a ten-pound weight at the same time, can often make quite a large hole where the hook entered the jaw.

We repositioned for our last drift. Believe it or not the bait held up fine throughout the fight with the first lost fish so we used it again. As I inspected the bonito belly with a blue and silver skirt, I set up for the last drift. If this was not successful we would be on our way home empty-handed.

It had been a long day and I started to overheat from being in the sun all day. It had been a very long day for me to start with and fighting this last fish took the starch out of me. I wanted to go home. I had been recovering from a bicep pull on my right arm. Surgery exacerbated a chronic and excruciating pain in the pinky area of my right hand. Pain so excruciating that I took methadone when necessary. Nonetheless, we set up the fourth drift to simulate what we had done on the lost fish.

We started our drop at 1,558 feet. I nailed the drift with the boat. Billy sensed me starting to lose it and putting his arm around my shoulders, said "See how the fishing line is 90 degrees with the boat?" I nodded and Billy said, "It can't be done any better. Good job!" Maggot had no experience offshore so we relegated him to keeping the boat clean and tidy; gaff, harpoon, and tackle in their places ready for action. Richard —a capable yachtsman — had quite a bit of experience on the ocean but not much in bluewater fishing. There comes a time on unproductive trips that everyone aboard resigns themselves to the fact: Getting skunked happens! Perhaps my crew didn't want to believe it, but our time grew short. Doc tended the rod when the tip gave a good 4-inch bow. Doc bellowed, "That was a bite!" Quickly he freespooled the weight to the bottom. While he let line out, for some reason which I couldn't tell by looking at the rod and reel, Doc put the Daiwa electric reel in gear. Line curled onto the reel with the rod bent over. Hooked up!

Over the next hour of what seemed like hundreds of gear changes, the fish wouldn't budge. We'd work it up to about 700 feet off the bottom, then it seemed to rest before taking hundreds of feet off the reel. During a fight like this, everyone takes on their own particular job or I might say the job finds that person. Richard's job? To keep me in the game. As a paraplegic I am susceptible to overheating, dehydration, and muscle spasms — just part of being paralyzed.

Doc insisted I take a methadone pill to help me ease the pain in my arm. Doc, Maggot, and Billy fought the swordfish from time to time but Doc put in a solid 90 percent. Richard faithfully brought me cold towels for my neck and head, and dipped my straw hat in seawater. It became quite apparent the sun and this battle were taking its toll on the captain and unfortunately I was that captain. As we fought the great fish, thick weed lines started forming on the water's surface, a very bad thing. Weed could get caught on the line and work its way down. Small peanut dolphin kept showering small ballyhoo intently seeking the protection of the weed line. At one point I announced "Hey everybody! Look around! We are fishing in the finest oil painting ever made." Three frigates pinwheeled above us, circling the weed line. A small pod of porpoises worked their way to the east. During the fight, we saw a six-foot sunfish and several Kemp's ridley sea turtles floating lazily in the current. What beautiful creatures!

It seemed the fish was uncatchable using our techniques. Tired, I started getting rude and snappy. Billy tried to keep the swordfish on the line. Doc and I felt frustrated and thought we needed more drag. While Billy, Doc, and Richard were all captains, I was the captain in command. On my boat, even though I'm paralyzed, I still rated the respect of my crew on any particular day. Billy's philosophy called for light drag, and not adding more unless absolutely necessary. Doc and I felt very differently. Both coming from the northeast, fighting hundreds of giant tuna each, we like to hammer a big fish with maximum drag, either pulling the hook or busting him off, but testing the waters very early on. I often use the quote "Let's do everything we can do to lose the fish in the beginning and if the hooks don't pull then hammer the drag with maximum pressure and be very aggressive in the fight." At about an hour and a half into our second epic battle, I could take no more. I gave Doc a hand signal. He added more drag and the rod literally buckled over with about 40 pounds. I thought Billy would have a heart attack. Luckily, the hook didn't pull. It seemed we just injected the fish with nitrous and our swordfish went absolutely berserk.

Now we actually fought the fish! Hundreds of feet of line disappeared off the reel, and then we gained back major line— like a seesaw – line off-line on. Meanwhile, I made hundreds of gear and throttle changes, maneuvering *Makaira* in quick response towards and away from the fish, always trying to break its plane. After two hours of fighting, Doc and I shook hands. Doc whispered in my ear, "That hook is not going to pull." My response, "I agree." Finally, the line slowed and we began taking line as fast as the reel would put it on. Billy yelled, "We lost him!" My heart sank. The line came up and up and up.

Richard thought he saw color but he didn't. Some ten minutes later we saw our fish on its side. The wind-on touched the reel. Billy readied the harpoon but the fish was nowhere close enough. Line from the end of the harpoon attached to a buoy and the buoy attached to a rod and reel on the opposite side of the boat, allowing us to reel in a harpooned fish.

The main rod bowed over with maximum drag on the reel. Though completely exhausted, I was on top of my game with all of the excitement. No one had to tell me what to do. I had spent my whole life doing it. This swordfish looked big in the water, but just how big we couldn't tell. At this point Billy said, "We've got him. It is on its side — almost dead." Everyone was pumped.

I reviewed the gaffing procedure with Richard again and again. My homemade wooden gaff, made out of a highly varnished closet pole and a work of art, became his responsibility. At the right time, Richard needed to sink the gaff into the swordfish's gill plate. Billy stood ready with the harpoon and Maggot held a large metal holding gaff. No doubt about it, inch by inch the fish came closer.

Richard whispered something to Billy. I don't know what they talked about but I guessed it concerned my health. I was starting to hyperventilate and was really overheated. During this entire battle, all of which took place on the starboard side (the same side as my helm), I constantly leaned over the gunwale to monitor what the fish did. When I bend over at my waist, having no diaphragm muscles, I cut the air to my lungs in half. Billy came over to me after their talk and asked me several times if I was okay. I told him the truth. No, I wasn't okay, but I could make it. Doc forced me to take a second methadone pill for the pain.

We came within 20 feet of Billy throwing the harpoon. The swordfish turned towards the bottom and despite 40 pounds of drag, took 1,600 feet of line off the reel in one shot. In all of my fishing career, I have never seen such a reserve of power. None of us could believe it. We were in absolute awe but totally disappointed.

I figured there must be a cold thermocline somewhere around 400 feet down. In this thermocline, colder, denser water, holds more oxygen. Our great swordfish rested there, regaining strength. For 10 minutes, we couldn't gain one foot of line. The rod bent over, showing no movement whatsoever. All of a sudden, the rod tip came up — normally indicating you no longer have a fish on the line. Yet, every once in a while, we saw a tiny little bump. At maximum speed, line flew onto the electric reel laying perfectly evenly on the spool thanks to the level wind. Billy shouted, "Get the gaffs! Give me the harpoon! It's coming up dead! It's coming up dead!"

Billy told us the first thing we'd spy is the bill coming straight out of the water. Billy yelled, "As soon as the bill breaks the surface I want everybody to do their job!" We stood ready. Up and up the great fish came. The electric reel started to overheat and Billy told Maggot to fill a t-shirt with ice and place it against the gear motor to cool it off. Richard saw the fish first. Now on its side, it had stopped its upward motion. Suddenly, the rod buckled over again. The great fish took another run and dumped over half the spool! Poor Billy took serious abuse from everybody. We kept yelling, "Oh, yeah… that fish is dead. Billy, that fish is dead." In reality, the fish was nowhere near dead! We now hit upon three hours of fighting time. It became very apparent to the crew that if we didn't catch this fish very soon, we'd have to cut it off. No fish was worth me ending up in the hospital emergency room. Although Billy wouldn't normally challenge my position as captain, he was coming very close to it.

I didn't think I could make it. I was panting. My right hand spasmed uncontrollably. I asked Doc if I could take a third methadone. The methadone are only 10 mg tablets, but three was more than I had ever taken in a short period of time. Doc authorized it and Richard stuck to me like glue. He covered me in wet towels, trying to bring my body temperature down. At three hours and 15 minutes, we reeled the fish back into sight. When the 10-pound weight reached the rod tip, Billy unhooked and removed it.

The swordie got aggressive on top. Swordfish represent one of the most aggressive fish in the sea. It's not uncommon for one to physically attack your boat during the end game. Ours kept changing directions now, making me spin the boat with maximum power and gear shifts. I kept *Makaira* going in a tight circle.

I don't want to pat myself on my back, but I did a great job. For a change, I didn't feel crippled or even that I sat in my wheelchair. I used my lifetime of skills and didn't miss a trick. I knew Doc and Billy recognized I was doing everything right.

At 3 hours and 20 minutes, Billy had a shot with the harpoon. While I thought it an easy shot, Billy missed again. None of the crew were happy, but said nothing. One thing we knew without a doubt, we were going to get a shot at this fish.

Finally, the fish and the boat synchronized, moving in the same direction and at the same speed. The rod bent over and inch by inch, line returned going onto the reel. The wind-on again rolled onto the spool. The swordfish surfaced on its side and it was huge! Its eye seemed as big as a volleyball and its bill stretched over four feet long. The entire purple and black back highlighted its lateral line running straight down its middle. Its tail also looked extremely wide. It got closer and closer.

I knew Billy wouldn't miss with the harpoon this time. I told Richard to lean over me and put my wooden gaff into the gill plate when I said, "Go!" as we had rehearsed. The fish rose right beside me as I peered over the gunwale, laid out before me at 20 feet, 15 feet, 10 feet. Billy raised his voice and said, "Wait!" The fish laid just below the surface, five feet down. Billy put the harpoon right through the front of the fish. Maggot with his hand on the metal gaff slammed it down into the gill plate and Richard worked right behind him with my wooden gaff and into the shoulder it went. Billy came tight on the harpoon lead. Doc got off the reel and tied on a tail rope. I collapsed on the steering wheel. I yelled as loud as I could, "We did it! We did it! We did it!"

The great fish was ours, but I was in trouble. I had no more left in me. I asked Doc to kneel by my side and just be there. We just fought a fish for 3 hours and 32 minutes. We had fought hard and won. The day was ours. Now a bigger problem all settled in on us. Everyone seemed to reach the stark reality at the same time. How are we going to get that huge swordfish into the boat? I became somewhat delirious for the next 30 minutes because I don't remember anything. I don't remember the fish coming aboard. Richard must have put something on the steering wheel because I may have fallen asleep.

They tell me that they tied a line around Maggot's waist so he could lean over the side. Doc, Billy, and Richard set up two separate pulley systems with a line that ran over my panga's hardtop. With all of our weight on the opposite side of the boat, they somehow managed to get the great fish into the cockpit.

The discussion blurred, but they considered taking me out of my wheelchair and laying me on the deck. Doc stopped them because I could get pressure sores. The fact remains that my body heals from injuries 200 times slower than the average person.

I know this may sound ridiculous to anyone reading this adventure: I don't remember driving back to the marina or docking the boat. I remember lying back in my wheelchair with someone draped over my shoulders on the way back to the marina. After arriving at the marina, I remember four men lifting my wheelchair out of the boat onto the dock and looking over at the fish hanging beyond the rails on both sides. I vaguely remember wondering how they ever got it in the boat? I don't talk much about my diabetes, but the only likely explanation for my wooziness was a low blood-sugar level.

Billy swore the fish weighed 350 to 375 pounds. Doc and I estimated the fish to be over 400, though I honestly thought it closer to 450. When we called the marina on the radio prior to our arrival, we gave a lower estimate of the weight just in case, but requested a scale be available to weigh it.

As we arrived at the dock we could see people everywhere. Our return sparked a monstrous fanfare. A World Wide Sportsman marina employee drove a forklift with a certified electronic scale dockside. As they raised the fish and it swung completely uninhibited, Miles, the dockmaster, quickly flipped the scale switch. He yelled out, "Four hundred and twelve pounds!" The crowd went wild. There were hugs and kisses, high-fives, and copious cocktails.

Billy started to butcher the swordfish, which by the way, would only be consumed by our marina friends, not sold. The dockmaster informed me that this represented the largest billfish ever brought into World Wide Sportsman in its history. It also stood as the largest swordfish Captain Billy had ever caught. That swordfish bill, now on my wall, stretches 49-1/2 inches long!

Yes, it was a big swordfish, but in 1980 Doc caught a 680-pound swordfish *dressed*, meaning gutted and with its head and tail cut off. That would have made it an 850- to 900-pound swordfish! As Billy cut up the fish, Miles came up to me and said, "Tred, you look terrible." Doc and Richard were all over me. I had nothing left. Someone helped drive me home and left me safely inside my condo. When I tried to make the transfer from my wheelchair to my bed, I couldn't do it. Something I do every day I no longer had the energy to accomplish. On my third try, I fell to the floor and couldn't get up.

Luckily, I have the Islamorada Department of Fire Rescue, station #20 on Upper Matecumbe Key on speed dial. The chief, Terry Abel, recognized my voice and four men from the fire department showed up in my bedroom. One of the firemen stayed with me for about ten minutes. When I saw him later in the week, he told me I was sound asleep moments after I hit the bed. The day following our fishing trip, I couldn't even get out of bed. This often happens after a long day of fishing or exercise.

Our great fish created a transition in my new wheelchair career. Facts talk with a loud clear voice. When I had my legs and I was firing on all cylinders I caught big fish and broke many local records all over the world. Now in a wheelchair by goodness I have done it again. I may be paralyzed but I am not a cripple. I don't know why I have waited to the end of this story to mention a couple of facts on this great battle but this fish required exact and perfect boat handling. It required exact throttle control with many complicated maneuvers. I still have it and I am proud as a peacock.

Of course, none of it would have been possible without the knowledge of Captain Billy and Doc. I know and admit that. But as Captain Billy put it "Remember one thing: We could not have caught the fish without you either." So I say "Never Give Up, Never Say Never." Another day, another adventure. Some men live their lives vicariously and some live their lives victoriously. The choice is yours.

Tred and Sam Gibbons with scrimshawed 412 swordfish bill

Tred Barta with the 412

Chapter Thirty-Two
A Truly Great Woman

It amazes me that I have never had what I might call a "Woman Friend." I find this fact very disturbing, but unfortunately true. I've always been a man's man doing manly things. But, I like women and have nothing against them. This sounds like a ridiculous statement in today's world, but the fact remains, everything I do is usually done with men. I haven't had that much interaction with women and I've been married most of my adult life. Many of my married friends have wives who aren't interested in fishing or hunting.

I want to write about an extraordinary woman — my first woman friend. I met Donna De Weil at a Barta Boys and Girls Club Billfish tournament in Beaufort, North Carolina. At first sight, she bubbled, full of life. Not only did I find her very beautiful, but she seemed extremely smart, educated, and caring. Donna volunteered at the tournament and helped kids fish on the "Captain Stacey" party boat and at the Weigh-In station that summer I met her.

Donna worked as an international project manager at IBM for 23 years, then at RTI International in international development as a water and environmental project manager for five years. She holds an MSA, with specialties in Business Management, Human Resources, and Non-profits. She never flaunts her education, but often helps non-profit and for profit organizations as well as people she meets.

As I got to know Donna, I discovered that besides all of her executive-work history and her accomplishments, she also qualified as a knowledgeable carpenter. As a child she used to ride her bike to her father's woodworking shop each day after school and he let her take a few pieces of wood for her latest project. She has built several houses from the ground up and totally renovated seventeen. Donna buys them cheaply and renovates them herself.

I say renovate, but I actually mean not only the design plans, she actually does much of the work herself, a trait you normally do not associate with an educated business woman. I am absolutely amazed at her skill level. I found out she was capable of making the drawings of things like structural changes and once she brought them to an architect for sign off, they'd approve them as if they were dealing with a fellow architect.

She loves to create, making something valuable and beautiful out of what others consider junk. Recently she built three tables and a miniature horse barn out of scrap wood for her granddaughter, Ella. Donna can look at a pile of scrap wood and come up with a phenomenal design.

I am not the only one to be amazed at her building skills. On her first day of building houses at Habitat for Humanity she didn't brag about her skills. The second day she volunteered, two men instructed her to reinforce walls that were already standing. The men planned to install other interior house walls. She watched and waited. Finally, she yelled, "Stop!" She walked over and showed the men that they were actually installing the closet wall upside down. After that they gave her newfound respect and often asked her how to do a particular task on the house.

This woman has traveled all over the world for work and for pleasure. She worked on a Grevy Zebra project in Kenya and at one point negotiations were underway for the project's tracker to buy Donna as one of his wives. Luckily she escaped before being sold, but she has been asked quite a few times, how many goats she is worth.

While working on a vegetation project in Zambia's Kafue National Park she heard a herd of elephants charging through the forest in the distance. The small group she was working with shouted, shot their guns into the air and the elephant herd parted, stampeding around their group. A close call but they survived.

She also worked with Medicine on the Move in Ghana, with friends who established the program. The organization provides medicine and health information to people in remote areas. Red Bull made a video of the organization called "*Spirit of Africa*" for an airline inflight movie, but you can also find it on the Red Bull channel.

Donna's next African volunteer project takes her to help conserve rhinos in South Africa. The price of rhino horn generates ever-higher levels of poaching. With the value of rhino horn worth more than gold due to the black markets in Southeast Asia, drastic measures need to be taken to guard against the rhino's extinction.

I particularly enjoy sharing two endeavors with Donna: Cleaning the fish at the end of the day and cooking our catch.

World Wide Sportsman built me a special fish-cleaning table to accommodate my wheelchair, as well as other people with disabilities. Over time Donna and I have come up with a fun procedure; just thinking about it puts a smile on my face. As I clean the catch, whether it be mangrove snapper, dolphin, or black fin tuna, Donna passes me the whole fish from the cooler so I can fillet it. As the fillets come free, Donna feeds the carcass to the pelicans and the tarpon.

I always enjoy watching Donna as she entertains visiting tourists and helps them get good photos and videos. The pelicans sometimes get onto the dock and perch inches from Donna's hand as she feeds them the scraps. Donna plays tour guide and doesn't even realize it. She often communicates with visitors from China, Brazil, or France who don't speak a word of English.

As I cut the skin from our fish fillets, cutting out bad pieces of meat such as the rib cage and blood line, we again have a procedure where Donna hands me a fillet, I work on it and she feeds these smaller scraps to the great egrets, ibis and snowy egrets perched on the bush near the table. I am paying attention so I don't cut my hand in the filleting process, but Donna, being a gifted multi-tasker, hands me the fillets to work on, takes away the finished ones, putting them into Zip-Locs, and feeds the birds and nearby fish — just a fun time! The tourists, egrets, pelicans, tarpon and I all enjoy it. Recently a three- foot brilliant green iguana was watching us work on the fillets. He actually came onto the cleaning table and stole one of the fillets. Donna convinced me to grab his tail where it jumped for the mangrove tree. All the leaves and branches of the mangrove were crashing back and forth which created quite a stir with all of the ibis that were on top. We were both laughing so hard that the whole operation ended for a few minutes.

The other activity which I enjoy sharing with Donna is preparing the fish for dinner. Though supposedly cooking the fish together, truth be known, Donna is a great cook and graciously allows me to pretend like I am helping. Often when we have excess fish, Donna vacuum packs the catch. In any event it's just fun to fish together, clean and take care of the catch and eat together. It always makes for a fun-filled day with a great lady.

When we met, Donna showed a tremendous interest in big-game fishing. Not only did she want to learn, but she had a driving passion for bluewater. Coincidentally, she, too, grew up in Southampton, New York where I spent more than 30 years of my life. During the entire time we both lived in the same town, incredibly we never met. After hours of discussion with her, it seems like many times we crossed paths at the same place and time, but simply never met.

As a kid in Southampton, Donna fished for puffer fish, sea trout, bass, and bluefish but no big game. She also did a little fly-fishing in Vermont and in England.

Ironically, I knew her father, Andrew De Weil, a successful builder in the Hamptons. Stranger than that, I even went goose hunting with him several times. We hunted with a respected arborist and goose guide, Duane Arnister.

As I got to know Donna better and my divorce finalized, we became good friends. I began to understand what I had been missing my entire life by not having women as close friends. Unfortunately, I never knew Donna when I had my legs, only while I've been wheelchair-bound.

So, I started teaching Donna about fishing and worked with her on the vernacular of our sport, the rigging of baits, the basic algebra of light-tackle fishing, and the practical end of the fishing rod. Before I knew it, she had more basic knowledge than people who had fished for 20 years.

We wrote articles together and she always asked questions throughout the process, gaining knowledge rapidly.

I sometimes found her reading many of the fishing and boating publications, and within one year, I heard her belt out in the of middle an article, "That's not true!" Then we'd have a lively discussion on the article and more times than not she was right.

I love Donna's company. We traveled to Casa Vieja Lodge in Guatemala together. Donna quickly discovered her favorite type of fishing – sail fishing. I tried introducing her to ultra-light tackle fishing in the 2, 4, and 6-pound categories, but she preferred medium-weight tackle. Even in my world, that means 8- and 12-pound test. Most clients of Casa Vieja use 20- and 30-pound.

Donna, like so many aficionados, loves the visual aspect of sailfishing: The very visible strikes, spectacular jumps, aerial spirals, and grey hounding runs these great fish make. Sailfishing in Guatemala has so many benefits, large numbers of fish being primary. Donna especially enjoys fighting multiple hookups.

While out fishing, we frequently saw super pods of Spinner dolphins and hundreds of Ridley sea turtles. Donna loves to photograph those "National Geographic scenes." I've learned to appreciate how at times, she becomes mesmerized by the wildlife around us and has a difficult time concentrating on fishing.

With Donna, I found myself fishing less and teaching more. I have enjoyed watching her grow as an angler on these trips. On one of her favorite days, she was dropping back to and hooking up all of her own fish using a common sailfishing technique known as bait and switch. By this time, Donna had caught and released over 100 sailfish. She no longer needed my coaching.

I am a great teacher to only a very few who have the right disposition. Most people I either offend with my impatience or they shut down due to my aggressive, direct, and rude teaching methods. I strive to make them be their best, but they often don't want to be.

Donna handled quite a bit of my teaching. She still wants me to teach her in new disciplines, but for those she's mastered, such as sailfishing, she prefers to fish without her teacher in her ear.

During the heat of the day, I start to fade. One day, fishing at Casa Vieja, the crew lifted me out of my wheelchair onto the salon couch where I quickly fell asleep. I awoke to a change in the pitch of the engines, either backing up, or something other than actual straight-line trolling.

I felt in pretty bad shape since we had fished for four days in a row. Thanks to my paralysis, sitting up on the small couch to look out the salon windows at the activity demanded more energy than I had. Later in the day just before lines out, I heard the riggers being put up when one of the mates came into the salon and informed me Donna had gone 15 for 15 on sails. The only fish missed or screwed up that day had been mine, when I worked the cockpit earlier.

It saddened me I wasn't able to watch and applaud Donna during her best hours of sailfishing accomplishment. Sometimes, life isn't fair. All excited, she told me about the fish she caught and released. The captain and mates took photos as she fought the fish so we shared those pictures together as we always do at the end of our day.

Donna had only been fishing for a year and here she went 15 for 15 on sailfish on 12-pound test! A small percentage of guests at Casa Vieja could do as well. Although she's not overly interested in the technical aspect of knots and rigging bait, she loves the sport and the people in it. Everyone at the lodge and everywhere we go, people love this woman. A fact that became even more evident when people kept saying, "What's a woman like that doing with a guy like you?" Yes, I've heard that a lot.

A new reality dawned upon me: Life seemed to go better when I was with Donna, whether going out to dinner or on a cruise, writing articles for publications, traveling, daily life, or giving motivational talks. It just seemed that when Donna entered a room — in my eyes — the place just lit up. She is intelligent, beautiful, and athletic in her own ways. She never cared what her hair looked like in a rain storm or when heading back to port from the fishing grounds as wave after wave blanketed *Makaira*.

As time went on, Donna saved my life several times. In May 2015, I had to be airlifted back to the U.S. from Guatemala. Donna handled all of the negotiations, medical details, and getting me back to U.S. soil safely.

All relationships between men and women are complicated. In some of the best ones, you don't realize the value of the distance which you have traveled together until you spend some time apart.

I am lucky to have my friend, Donna, in my life, and I hope to go on many of life's adventures with her to catch her first marlin, halibut, or salmon. I have opened the door to the fishing world for Donna and I look forward to fishing with her on a FAD (Fish Aggregating Device – permanent, semi-permanent or temporary structures that are in deep waters to attract pelagic fish), in some exotic fishing location, or hearing about one of her fishing adventures.

Donna De Weil, Tred and Captain John with Mahi in Grand Cayman

Donna De Weil and David Salazar with Tuna.

Chapter Thirty-Three
MY BUCKET LIST

I HAVE BEEN privileged to fish and hunt all over the globe with the most talented mates, captains and guides. I have also had the privilege of hunting and fishing in popular remote areas — always at the perfect time of year. One could say I've been there and done that.

I went to dinner with some friends and one brought an out-of-town guest. The guest had fished quite a bit, and as usual, wanted to tell me about his adventures. As he told of the first adventure, I mentioned that I had fished there too. On his second fishing adventure, I told the group I had also been fishing at that location. On his third fishing adventure, I said I had been fishing there as well. These were all very remote fishing locations that many people have not heard about. Many places I have been lucky enough to fish and hunt multiple times. By the third time, this guy no longer believed I had been to these locations. He asked what boat I fished on, who the captain was, where I stayed, what restaurants I went to, and even asked what I ate.

Since I had truly been to all three fishing locations, I described to the group my fishing experience at each location with great detail. I proceeded to name the fishing captains and mates I fished with as well as the charter boats I had fished on. I talked about the restaurants and the foods I enjoyed and about a particularly notable seafood buffet and the lodges in which I stayed.

He finally said, "I thought you were just telling me a story that you had been to all of these fishing locations. I see you really were there!" I was astounded. And here I thought he was just interested in the details of my trips. I had no idea he didn't believe I fished there.

My new reality of being paralyzed has opened many doors, but has also shut many. For now, I gain satisfaction and happiness watching my best friend, Donna De Weil, experience many things which I have already done.

My bucket list seems to continuously grow, as I love to travel and experience nature, fishing, hunting, and meeting new people. My list contains things I've never done as well as places I would like to relive again, sharing the experience.

When Donna renovated my condo to accommodate my wheelchair, she got discouraged by helpers either not showing up or providing poor workmanship. Interestingly, she'd come to me and ask me to tell her a funny story. Off I would go telling some wild hunting, fishing, or childhood tale. Donna found them entertaining and relaxing, and often she would ask me to repeat the stories to friends. Some of these stories and experiences are in this book or will be in upcoming books. We are currently working on a book of my hunting adventures, as well as a cookbook. Completing these are on my bucket list. The cookbook will be a combination of recipes from me and Donna. There will be stories within the cookbook about the "catch" in the recipes.

My bucket list also includes wanting to go 120 miles offshore of Costa Rica to fish the FADs for blue marlin. Anglers commonly have chances at catching 10 marlin in a day on these fads. It would be a fun experience to go with friends and see them all enjoy catching marlin.

I'd like to take Donna and friends to Reykjavic, Iceland to witness and partake in some of the greatest salmon fishing in the world. I have traveled to Iceland several times, but not for a while. I would like to cruise to Faxaflói Bay to view the Aurora Borealis or Northern Lights. The Northern Lights remind me of fireworks on the 4th of July — so spectacular to watch. It would be fun to cruise to Akurey Island's jagged shore to see the Puffins in their natural habitat.

I'd also like to return to King Salmon, Alaska near Katmai National Park and Preserve. I'd really enjoy teaching friends how to battle a king salmon and watch the great salmon run one more time. King Salmon only has 450 full-time residents, but 30,000 people visit the area to salmon fish, view brown bears catching the salmon, and to enjoy wilderness at its finest every year.

Not that you should worry, but Katmai National Park and Preserve includes an active volcano. In 1918, the government established Katmai National Monument (an area, not a statue) to protect people (who have lived there for 9,000 years) from the volcanic devastation experienced during the Novarupta volcano in 1912. That eruption formed the Valley of Ten Thousand Smokes. The area, with 14 active volcanos, currently qualifies as one of the most active volcanic areas in the world.

The Becharof National Wildlife Preserve and Alaska Peninsula Wildlife Reserve nearby offer awesome sportfishing and Alaska's beautiful nature. Established in 1980, the Preserve consists of 1,200,000 acres in the Aleutian Mountain Range of the Alaska Peninsula.

I am planning a fishing trip to Prince Edward Island, Canada for giant bluefin tuna. The season starts the end of July through the beginning of October. These same waters offered up the latest world record bluefin caught in 1979 weighing

1,496 pounds! The average size, however, shrinks to a mere 6-1/2 feet long and 550 pounds, though catching a 700- to 1,000-pound bluefin commonly happens! These spectacular tuna swim from the Gulf of Mexico and the Mediterranean to Nova Scotia and Prince Edward Island annually.

This summer we plan to do some swordfishing in the Florida Keys. It won't be the same without my fishing buddy, "Doc" Jeff Bennett but he will definitely be with us in our hearts. Hopefully Captain Billy will be available to join us and if all goes well, we'll catch another big swordfish.

I'd love to take a two-day overnight trip to my old familiar backyard, the Northeastern canyons, in search of bigeye tuna. How wonderful it would be to see the birds, smell the salt air, and fish in my old stomping grounds as well as see old friends.

I would love to take my son, Hunter, a canyon veteran, and watch him and my grandson, Skyler, battle a bigeye tuna. I also would like to be with Hunter aboard my 26-foot Andros in North Carolina to battle a giant bluefin. That would be a trip of all trips!

Traveling to Nantucket, Montauk, Cuttyhunk, Martha's Vineyard, and other fishing towns throughout the U.S. to see old friends, make new friends, and experience every aspect of these areas are all on my bucket list.

I want to see my beloved horse, Badger and give him some love and attention. I have dreamed of touching his silky nose again and feeding him some carrots.

So, I am a long, long way from being done. Truth be told, I could easily spend the rest of my life with my friend just searching for new wild places; to be offshore fishing for yellowfin tuna in Guatemala amidst a super-pod of Spinner dolphins; or just to experience the world of Nature.

I believe that if you have passion; if you have love for something; and you help other people along the way, you will find greatness. They say that in life, if you have five friends, you are a very wealthy person. That certainly applies to me and I wish them all following seas, hooks that don't pull, a fish box loaded to the top, and a heart as big as Wyoming. I love fishing; I love hunting; and I love my family and friends.

Looking back at all of the activities, conquests, and accomplishments since my personal tragedy, every one of them took me away from my life's daily reality. Shooting my bow; piloting my 26-foot Andros, *Makaira*; shooting a pistol or rifle; shooting skeet or trap; I used to love doing all of these things, and doing them now makes me feel normal again. Being normal… that's the message I have to communicate to the world — to help those in need. Suddenly it became apparent that perhaps God had a plan for me after all. I think He meant for me to inspire others through my actions.

I believe there is not one lesson about life that can not be learned in nature except one thing – the morality that humans have and animals do not. I believe I was put on Earth to bridge what Nature can teach us in a society that does everything in its power to disregard the very lessons I wish to teach. My life's slogan is "Never give up, never say never". I have always believed that every person must be and live to be the most they can be and not to do so is against and disrupts the very fabric of what God laid out for us.

My entire life has been based on an almost impossible deck of cards. What I have accomplished based on being cursed with ADD, ADHD, and dyslexia I believe has inspired many to live up to their greatest potential. I don't think I'm special but somehow I was gifted a tremendous talent for not giving up and just not quitting. As I close this chapter one might also say that it is the last chapter of my life. I pray that I don't die being run over by a bread truck. I would much prefer being gored by a cape buffalo or have a 500-pound blue marlin jump into the boat and take me out with its bill. A life lived well is a life that contains kindness, bravery, honor, code, and to help others. This is how I judge myself. I have a lot to give, share, and my glass is always half full and not half empty.

Tred and his son, Hunter, with Hunter's first bigeye tuna,
caught in 2 hours, 20 minutes on a 30-pound test in Hudson Canyon.

Tred with World Record rooster fish caught in Pinas Bay, Panama in 10 minutes 12/26/1980

Bigeye tunas, more tunas and more tunas at Indian Cove Marina. Caught on Makaira.

Bigeye tunas, more tunas and more tunas at Indian Cove Marina. Caught on Makaira.

Tred with 10 bigeye tuna and white marlin. (results of two 5x5s)

IGFA World Record bigeye tuna weighing 217 pounds caught by Tred in 5 hours and 17 minutes; establishing a new 20 pound class record.

892 pound mako shark caught in Block Canyon.
At the time, it was the largest mako ever caught.

892 pound mako shark caught in Block Canyon.
At the time, it was the largest mako ever caught.

892 pound mako shark caught in Block Canyon.
At the time, it was the largest mako ever caught.

Reprint of the "Barta Bigeye Bible"

as published in the
Big Game Fishing Journal

THE BARTA BIGEYE BIBLE

By Captain Tred Barta

To start with, as long as I live, Anni and I will never forget the kindness pointed our way from the Big Game Fishing Journal fund raiser led by Len Belcaro. It raised greatly needed funds as the cancer doctors said at the time I had two weeks to live. I will never forget and we will never ever stop saying thank you.

Today, I'm paralyzed from my chest down, a T4 (ASIA A) complete in medical terms. After two years of receiving a chemotherapy intravenously called Rituxan, I am now technically free of blood cancer, but I will never walk again, I only roll. I fish, hunt, have a TV show, sell corporate aircraft (I'm a 7500 hour jet and turbo prop pilot having over 22 ocean crossings as pilot in command), snow ski, scuba dive and am getting ready to jump out of an airplane, and believe you me, I appreciate every day and every minute on this earth.

Left to right: Skip Tollefson, Jimmy Ledderman, Captain Tred Barta. We caught 106 albacore, then as the sun went down, we did 5/5, 3/3, and a single bigeye, we never left the spot. Look at the color of the water, bigeyes and albacore in deep water like the same neighborhood.

I have lived an honorable life, a life of hard work, a life of honor and code. I believe in Jesus Christ our Savior and I feel good that I will meet other great fishermen in heaven when my time comes to an end. No boo-hoo for me. I've lived a privileged life. I've traveled the world four times over. I've hunted and fished in the best places at the best times with the best captains, mates and guides. I'm blessed to be married to the greatest woman in the entire world, my wife Anni. She is beautiful, sexy, smart, honorable and hard working, and she is my best friend. My partner of 45 years running in Barta Iso Aviation is my dear friend John Iso. John's mom wrote a poem that describes Anni to perfection. "When his white horse fell, she pretended not to see and helped him mount again." This describes Anni best of all.

I love this sport and the people in it, and from the Murray Brothers, Carl Darenberg, Willie and Gary Dickson, Charlie Hayden, Mike Forman, Jim and Jamie Hummel, Eddie Laurson, Skip Tollefsen, Hank and Micky Altenkerch, Ron Law, Jimmy Ledderman, and the list is endless, I've learned from the best.

BIGEYE TUNA — THUNNUS OBESUS

This article comes from my very soul and I intend to give you an insiders inside look at fishing for bigeye tuna—where to find them, how to fish for them, and many controversial subjects that I want to discuss with everyone before I pass on. On many of the topics I am brief because I'm not asking for an opinion. I'm telling you what I know to be true for me. I certainly am more vulnerable now then I have ever been before. You need to read what I say here and you need to realize that there are not many of us left that can teach us about the greatest of days gone before.

THE FACTS ARE THE FACTS

For over 12 years in a row, team MAKAIRA was hardly out-fished on bigeye tuna during the glory days of the mid-70's and early-80's. I was spending over $250,000 dollars a year, sometimes every penny I earned, on warm core eddy research. The funding of team

MAKAIRA, and the funding for flying up and down the 100 fathom line from Hudson to Oceanographers looking for life and water color changes literally broke the bank year after year. But by putting all the Barta techniques together, we ended up harvesting over 400 bigeye tuna including, I believe, the most bigeye ever caught in one trip—19 fish, and several trips with 8 to 15 fish. I will not discuss the thousands of yellowfin, bluefin, white and blue marlin and incredible catches of swordfish on the surface we had made. It was unprecedented.

There are some privileges associated with being 60 years old with four decades of bluewater experience under my belt. The bigeye tuna fishery will never be as good as it was then. Therefore, I have the privilege of defending and exploiting an era, perhaps gone by, be as it may, let me say what has never been said or written on bigeye fishing before. These words will survive me and are a legacy that I'll leave behind. You may judge for yourself the validity of what I say.

LETS GO TO WORK!!!
BIGEYE TUNA TROLLING SPEED

I've never been arrogant enough to tell people an exact speed to troll for bigeye tuna. There are so many variables from boat size, boat weight, hull design, shaft angle, etc., etc. Using the Barta method, let me say that it has always been between 6.4 and 6.7 knots, and sometimes much slower into a 4-to 6-foot head sea. The key to hooking up multiples is consistently having your spread close to the transom, trolling big lures at low speeds with a high rigger to lure angle. This high angle is achieved with center-riggers.

To make a big lure troll well at slow speeds, like the Sevenstrand Konahead above, (By the way, my log reveals this lure has caught over 127 bigeye tuna) we invented the Barta Porcupine System, get them in close, big lures, trolled at low speeds, high degree of angle from rigger to lure, big leaders, 300- to 500-pound mono, big hooks 12/0 to 16/0, Mustad 7731's or southern style close gap Martu single hooks. The Porcupine System used properly leaves hardly any leader material touching the water and this system

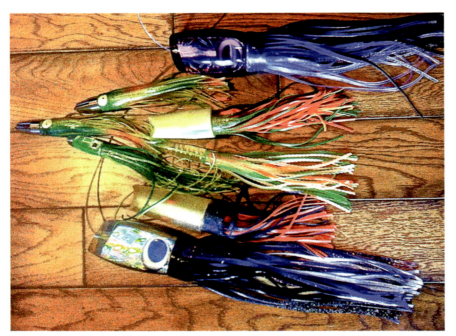

Lures were big, trolled at 6.7 knots. Large hooks, strong hooks, welded eyes. We drilled into the bottom of the lure to get a hook set deep inside the lure itself. Bigeyes attack the head of the lure 90-percent of the time, the closer the hook, the better the hookup.
God I miss the old days. I truly believe, give me a properly rigged boat, enough money and fuel and I can put 8 bigeyes on at one time, even today. We trolled 4 hookless teasers attached to a 1,000-pound cable covered with plastic or they would be ripped off the boat. I believe the teasers trolled closely helped us.

strike drag settings and using the "Barta Throttle Dance" upon a hookup is what made the MAKAIRA, MAKAIRA.

Today, lures are too small emitting too small of a signature. An average size bigeye tuna was 225 to 275 pounds dressed. (Dressed means gutted with the head off.) I remember catching our first bigeye tuna under 125 pounds. We never realized they were ever that small. So here is some great advice, troll big lures, use center riggers, slow it down, heavy terminal tackle, and get ready to dance.

NEVER OFF THE ROD TIP

Big lures trolled slowly at high angles close to the boat need very little throttle on and off centerline to accelerate and decelerate. Big lures also need no drop-back. We never troll any lure that isn't rubber-banded down with a #54 heavy industrial rubber band.

We always used a small spring clip. We found outrigger clips were always useless. You're not able to

is unequivocally responsible for putting the wolf pack in your lap.

Trim tabs should be all the way up, and the trolling wake must be made as clean as possible. The speed of the boat, the combination of large lures on heavy leaders and strong hooks, the proper trolling speed, the proper

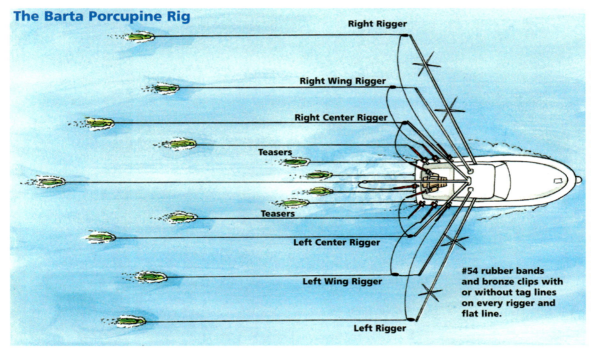

Nine single-hook lures and four teasers – this is the setup that took Captain Tred and crew six years to develop and prove. There is not a team around who will not testify that the Barta Porcupine rig is the killer rig on bigeye tuna.

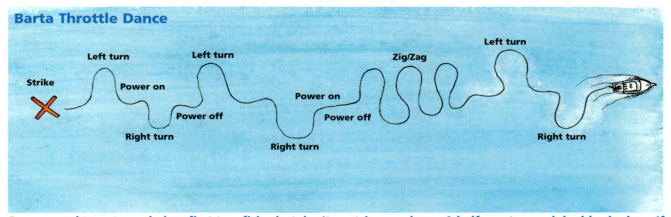

Barta Throttle Dance

Be prepared to get spooled on first two fish – but don't, watch your drags. A half empty spool doubles in drag. If you are afraid to lose 'em, you'll never catch the wolfpack. When Barta does the throttle dance by adding and shutting down power – acceleration and deceleration with hard turns to port and starboard, the lures look like a school of bait fish running for their lives. Watch out, here comes the wolfpack with multiple hookups from Mr. bigeye tuna.

tighten them up enough. When a bigeye takes a lure it will make the rubber band snap. It sounds like a .22 caliber pistol going off. Big lures close to the boat working properly do not get played with, they get eaten, and to catch multiple bigeyes, the hooks need to stay put. Back in the days, trolling lures off the rod tip was a no-no.

A built in drop-back was also taboo. When the bigeyes are in residence, you will never out fish a team which keeps their lures close with every lure put in a rigger, and flat lines attached to spring clips at the waterline level. The net results is simply this, bigeye tuna attack with a vengeance. If a bait is presented properly, their first bite will engulf the bait. The strong rubber band gives just a little bit of head drop and KABANG, he's hooked up.

BARTA THROTTLE DANCE

In my life and in my career, when discussing the proper techniques used for multiple hookup on bigeye, I still can't stress enough how important the "Barta Throttle Dance" is on hooking up multiples on all species of tuna.

For those of you who don't know what this is, let me take you through a hypothetical strike. KABOOM, there he is on the right short-rigger. The rubber band explodes and you are hooked up. at 6.7 knots. Count to three—1 Mississippi, 2 Mississippi, 3 Mississippi. Turn hard left then back to the center line, then troll straight. 1 Mississippi, 2 Mississippi, 3 Mississippi, turn hard right then back to center line. Back off on the throttles, push the throttles back up. Pull the throttles back down again then push them back up. Make a hard right turn at half throttle then power down and return to center line. Make a hard left turn and kick up the throttles. Now zig-zag with a hard left, a hard right, left, right, left, right, and back to the center line. The second or third maneuver will have given you additional hookups to eight fish on at one time. Ninety-percent of all canyon helmsmen do not use this technique. This is also extremely important in albacore fishing.

Back in the old days, especially early to mid 80's, there was between 400 and 500 boats fishing between the Hudson Canyon and the Fishtails. At night there was a sea of lights on the shelf. It was the heyday, the absolute apex of canyon fishing. Fuel was cheap, money flowed like water, and the fishery was spectacular.

People often ask how could MAKAIRA enter a fleet of 70 boats and out fish everyone almost every time? It's simple math—multiple hook ups. If I catch six and you catch one, if I catch eight and you catch three, and I catch five and you catch one, guess who caught more fish. MAKAIRA didn't raise anymore fish then anyone else. What we did was maximize the hookups by using the Barta Throttle Dance technique. By using center-riggers with the spread up close, using big lures, by adding throttle and taking it off, and by turning left and right, the lure spread looks like a school of bait which is under attack and trying to escape. When in a turn right at slow speeds, the port side spread speeds up, the right side slows down and drops lower in the water column.

The Barta Throttle Dance is supposed to emulate a bait ball under attack, if trolling the spread to far back, you will never see these subtleties. Trolling the spread to far back, there is too much leader in the water. If not using riggers, big lures get lazy and you will have to troll at higher speeds. if you have to troll at higher speeds, your spread must be further back. Does this make sense to anybody?

Let me tell a little story, and this story should drive my point home. There was a boat in Shinnecock Inlet, NY, a big Norseman, which was berth at Indian Cove Marina. They fished the same places at the same time as we did during the best bigeye tuna fishing in the world. As our numbers climbed over 250 and 300 fish, they had only caught six bigeye. They wouldn't listen when told the proper trolling speed for bigeye. They would not listen to any suggestions what-so-ever. One day in the Fishtails, I dove overboard carrying a satchel of big lures to the Norseman. I quickly threw out the spread on their boat and got one bite. By using the throttle dance, closing up the spread, using rubber bands, etc. etc., etc., when I dove off their boat to swim back to MAKAIRA, they had six-250-pound bigeyes hooked up at one time. Moral of the story is obvious.

WIRING AND KILLING

Most mates today haven't wired a lot of big fish. What they have done is wired a lot of small fish improperly. Wiring is only done one way. To kill a tuna on 300- to 500-pound mono, take a series of single and double wraps, get his head pointed at the boat, don't let go, then gaff him and kill him and put him in the boat.

Do you know how to wire? Do you know what to do when you get a tunas head? Do you know how to wrap double 19 din piano wire on a giant tuna? You need to learn, I personally had only let go of the leader to about 15 bigeye tuna in my career. We used welding gloves, if you can't break 200-500 pound mono attached to a cleat, go home and play golf. Wiring is an art form, it requires an athletic position, good strength, and it requires guts, stamina, and resources. If you want to play with big fish, learn how to properly wire. Jamie Hummel, Mike Forman and myself used to put a wire on the back of a pick up truck, and as the pick up truck moved off, we would either break the wire, or be dragged down the parking lot, believe me, we got good at it.

HOW DEEP?

Eighty percent of the 400 bigeye tuna in my career were caught between the 175 to 200 fathom curve. Today, bigeye anglers' fish too shallow. That's my opinion. There is nothing wrong with fishing on and off the 100 fathom line as long as a solid 80-percent is spending time between the 175 and 200 fathom curves. In my humble opinion this is, and will always be the ticket.

WATER TEMP

Best bigeye tuna water temperature is between 65-69 degrees Fahrenheit. The warmer the better in the spring, and the colder the better in the summer. Look for areas of cold water next to hot water. Bigeye tuna travel with albacore more then any other tuna. They both like the same type of water and are often found together in deep water. Find the albacore off the 100 fathom curve and the bigeye tuna will be there. It should be obvious to everyone that all the temps in the mid 70's hold almost all the fish, but when we find good water and good bait in the high 60-degree temps, watch out.

TEAM SPORT

Without Captain Mike Forman, Jim and Jamie Hummel, Captain George,

My dear friend Herby Lipke, circa early 80's Indian Cove Marina. Find the albacore, find the bigeye. The picture of the other seven are out of frame.

Eddie Laurson, Willy Dickson and a host of other mates, team MAKAIRA would not exist. It's that simple. Any crew is only as good as their captain and every captain is only as good as his crew, that's the way it is, that's the way it always will be. When I speak, I speak as one with all those who fish with me and not one of us is anymore important then the other.

THE BEST OF IT

The best place to find bigeye tuna is on the cold leading edge side of a warm core eddy working down and closest to the 100 fathom line. Okay, that's it! The preponderance of bait is always on the cold side closest to the 100 fathom line, by the way, closest doesn't mean on the 100 fathom line, closest could be at 500 fathoms. The eddy water is denser, its being stacked up and pushed by the warm eddy's clockwise rotation creating upwellings that push the bait towards the surface. Find the eddy, find the cold side, and find the bait—the wolf pack will show up. It takes patience and a belief in yourself. This is where it will happen!

DRAGS

When a spool is half gone, the drag doubles, I'll spare you the math. Using center-riggers, the Barta Porcupine Rig, the Barta Throttle Dance, Team MAKAIRA never used drags over six to seven pounds maximum initial strike drag. Let all the first bigeyes hooked up, take line and get out of the spread, over sized reels are mandatory for multiple hookups. When nine rods are trolled, don't be afraid to get spooled on the first fish, when it's time to actually fight one or two fish out of the eight hooked up, hammer them with drag to 35 to 50 pounds worth, and either pull the hook or break them off or catch them. Today, most people fish with too much initial strike drag and not enough fighting drag.

In the old days, a 800-pound bluefin tuna hooked on the troll off Nantucket was caught, gaffed, and in the boat in 15 minutes maximum. Any longer than that you were labeled a rank amateur.

MONO, DACRON, OR SUPER BRAIDS

Mono with reasonable stretch is the deal, Andi, Momoi, etc. Super braids and dacron have no use in the Barta techniques, you will pull to many hooks. Believe me I have been there.

TODAY'S MORALITY

Want to be like one of those jerks on Wicked Tuna? Go ahead, but if you're a captain or mate, act like it. Be courteous, kind, helpful and professional. Have pride in yourself and your crew, and don't use profanity on the VHF. I don't care how many fish you have caught, world records you have set or tournaments you've won, if you're not kind or a gentleman on the ocean you're nothing more than a jerk. Does everyone understand where I stand? The Northeast fisherman should call the Coast Guard on the Wicked Tuna crew for their conduct on the ocean. Northeast fishermen should put an end to the show, these guys are pikers at best, absolutely clueless and represent the worst in Northeast fishing today. By the way, these guys couldn't spend five minutes with the men of steel of the Deadliest Catch. Never ever pass up the opportunity to help another fisherman. This is where great fishermen come from.

IF YOU WANT HELP, GIVE HELP

Don't covet secret spots then ask for help on the VHF when you need it. This practice stinks and is of low moral character. There is nothing more important than moral code, integrity, and honor. You will do better in general by helping others, as they help you. There is one team out of Shinnecock Inlet, Long Island who is well funded, has a big boat, and when fishing is good, he won't answer the radio. When he goes 200 miles and catches nothing, then he becomes your bud looking for help and advice. This team, this captain, will never achieve any greatness. He is branded as a taker, not a giver, and I might add at the end of the day, he is a loser. Don't be this guy yourself.

THE BIGEYE WOLF PACK

Most bigeyes travel in a school of 8 to 20 fish. The first five years of my bigeye career I hooked up sets of three with a lot of singles. As MAKAIRA incorporated our style of fishing, five to six fish hookups was the norm. Nine times in my career I hooked up to eight and one time we had a nine fish hookup.

Today, the main reason why so many singles are hooked is a lack of technique as defined by me. I'm not trying to be rude or arrogant, I'm

My beloved dad Joe Barta and Captain Ron Law with a pair of nice bigeye tuna. I always addressed my father as sir, he was a World War II B-29 pilot and war hero. I feel his presence in heaven and always draw upon his strength.

telling you I'm right. The third, fourth, fifth, and sixth bite often doesn't come until the third left or right turn in the throttle dance. Bigeye tuna are right there behind your boat. They are shy and need to be teased. They are deep-feeders and don't like the surface as a general rule. If you're not 3/4 down on the spool after the first two hook ups, you are doing something wrong. Remember, keep your drags light. The Barta maneuvers have been documented so many times, it's time to get with the program and give it a try. If you hook up one fish, the wolf pack lurks behind your boat.

One of the biggest problems today is that after a bigeye bite has been realized, in a fishery that is being depleted, most captains are so afraid of losing the fish that they slow the boat down prior to the second or third bite. They won't risk losing the fish for the opportunity to fight six at one time. You know what everyone, I'm right on the money—no risk, no reward. The first time you get mugged with fish all over 250 pounds at one time, and land everyone of them, you will understand exactly what I'm taking about.

FIGHTING BIGEYE TUNA WITH HEAVY TACKLE

Hey everyone, it's a tuna! Mug em' with drag from 30 to 60 pounds. Show no mercy, don't be afraid to pull hooks. If you do, it wasn't meant to happen. This myth that bigeye need a smooth Orvis LLBEAN Treandoid fighting style is a bunch of horse pucky.

IF YOU FISH FOR BIGEYES, THEN DO IT

Want to chase bigeye tuna, stay at 100 to 200 fathoms. Troll high angles to your big lures, find the bait, find the edge of the oncoming eddy and put your time in. Don't chase radios, don't leave the spot, pay your dues and accept you might go home skunked. Bigeyes are not an accidental catch. It is

BARTA BULLET POINTS

1. Use the Barta Porcupine Rig system
2. Perfect the Barta Throttle Dance
3. Understand warm core eddies and fish the cold leading edge side.
4. Big lures, big hooks, big terminal tackle
5. Keep leaders out of the water
6. Watch your trolling speed
7. Watch your drag settings
8. Don't chase the radio, believe in yourself
9. Never miss the opportunity to help another fisherman
10. Most fishermen use to much strike drag and not enough fighting drag.
11. Most fishermen troll their lures too far back and to fast.

FIELD NOTES:

Spreader bars and bait did not come into the arsenal of team MAKAIRA during the glory days although we put a two-pound monster swimming mullet in the rig with a 16/ 0 hook and it did get eaten. It also caught every piece of grass from Hudson to Hydro. As the fishery got worse, the tackle got lighter, the emphasis on catch and release and lower expectations, small jets, multiple spreader bars have now become the norm as the use of ballyhoo and squid. Out of all the bigeye tuna we caught at night, we hardly ever chummed, we slept and trolled two hours into darkness. Man, how the world has changed.

the catch and perhaps the greatest of all.

BEST TIME TO FISH

The answer is simple,. When the reels are singing, but over the years, the first two hours and the last two hours of daylight are prime time.

FINBACK WHALES

Finback whales, in proper water temperature, with proper color and bait concentrations are signs of bigeye close by. We have taken at least 200 bigeyes on migrating finback pods between 100 and 500 fathoms. Bigeye tuna and finback whales go hand and hand especially in deep water. There are many a day I fished finbacks from sun up to sunset.

FISHING THE DEEP

While only about 15-percent of bigeye tuna aboard MAKAIRA have been caught in over 1500 fathoms of water, we have caught them there especially early mornings and in warm water filaments while heading towards the 100 fathom line. Don't be afraid to fish deep.

NIGHT TROLLING

We trolled six 16-ounce deep clones available at White Water Outfitters in Hampton Bays, NY. We fished them way back at 3 to 3.5 knots with a Cylume lightstick attached eight inches from the lure. They can be deadly on a full to 1/2 to full moon. This technique has worked well for us, especially traveling at nighttime in 300 to 500 fathoms running the Bigeye Highway, the 43300 line, to the east.

THE TERMS, LOCATIONS & THE FACTS

The Bigeye Highway named by the crew of the MAKAIRA is the 43300 line to the east. The name "wolf pack" for a school of bigeye was also coined by the crew of he MAKAIRA. "Sasquatch Alley" is the eastern ledge of Hydrographers Canyon named by Jamie Hummel. His nickname being "Sasquatch" while aboard MAKAIRA.

Bigeye Mountain was named by Mike Forman. We found it, we named it, and we caught over 109 fish on top of this mountain. That's something to think about. If MAKAIRA boated over 400 bigeye tuna, how many did we lose, break off, pull hooks on, and raise without a hook up? Hundreds of fish my friends, hundreds!

IN CLOSING

It is very obvious that over the years, I as many others have gone to lighter tackle. We have learned to release our billfish, use circle hooks on dead bait when billfishing and know the joy of just catching one nice tuna for dinner. It has satisfied the need and greed to fill the boat beyond our needs. I write this article on bigeye tuna so that the methods and techniques of an era can be shared. It's not for everyone, and I'm not even sure it's for anyone in today's environment, but by God it works! It's hard for me to admit that I've spent a lifetime perfecting much of what I've written about here. The truth be told—one yellowfin, one albacore, a medium sized blue or white marlin released is a great day.

I do hope that in your lifetime, you have the opportunity to fight six to eight bigeye tuna at one time as they explode on lures next to your boat. White water is often thrown in the cockpit. It literally looks like eight black Volkswagens coming out of the water at one time. It will hold you breathless. It will hold you speechless. And for a short moment, the blitz of the wolf pack is frozen in your mind forever.

The truth be told. It is my privilege to be in this wonderful sport. It is also a privilege to have you read my articles, and it is a privilege to teach you what I have learned in my lifetime. God bless everyone of you. Whether you're a supporter or a detractor, we are all bluewater fishermen. And if you are a Northeast canyon fisherman, we all are in the Brotherhood of the Bigeye Highway and all of us will one day look down upon it.

Till next Tide,
Capt. Tred Barta

ABOUT THE AUTHOR

CAPTAIN TRED BARTA

I have known Tred Barta since the bigeye heydays of the 80s. We have hunted the fierce snow shoe rabbits of the Maine wilderness and the tusked porkers of the Vermont hills together. The man has never cowed to public opinion, he has made plenty of mistakes, but he always admits them regardless of the consequences. I am proud to call him my friend.

He has raised one million for the IGFA during the Barta Blue Marlin Classics at Walkers Cay. He is also on his way to raising a second million for the Barta Boys and Girls Club Billfish Tournament in Beaufort, NC and is excitedly waiting for an announcement and getting started on raising a third million from another new tournament at Treasure Cay, Bahamas.

Captain Tred Barta's TV show "The Best and Worst of Tred Barta" has been on Versus/ NBC Sports for the last nine years. What a spectacular series.

Tred has inspired millions of people by his wheelchair adventures and his fighting slogans; "Never ever say never," "Never give up," "If I can do it, you can do it," and "There's nothing more important than the way we treat each other." To Tred these words are not just slogans, they are a way of life. Tred is, and continues to be, a legend of our sport and a pioneer of canyon fishing and warm eddy monitoring. That's right, Tred was chasing eddies long before I knew what they were. He wrote the book on the subject and it is as informative and useful today as it was back then. Come with me and enjoy the very best from the "love him or hate him," captain of captains, Tred Barta. This bigeye treatise was written by the man who has caught more bigeye tuna on rod and reel in the North Atlantic than anyone else in the world. Tred tells it all, much of which has never been told before.

Capt. Len Belcaro

Reprint of "Barta's Bluefin Bible"

as published in the
Big Game Fishing Journal

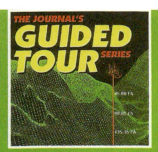

THE JOURNAL'S GUIDED TOUR SERIES

BARTA'S

Six professional captains share their secrets for fishing the great spring bluefin migration off Long Island, NY

There are a lot of people who feel this article should never be written. Many local fishermen feel the feature article I wrote in the Winter 1998/99 issue of *BIG GAME FISHING JOURNAL*, "A Guided Tour of the Bigeye Highway," was too revealing and gave away many secrets that should have remained as nothing more than local knowledge. From my perspective, however, the true reward of the sport is sharing not only the excitement of the bite, but also fishing knowledge to help other people enjoy the sport more. This in-depth "Guided Tour" of the local school bluefin migration across Long Island is directly taken from my logbook and those of five other charter captains who wish to remain anonymous.

Is this a bible? Well, every fisherman has his own set of numbers and his own philosophy on how the fish travel. But, the information you are reading is from six professional charter skippers who have spent their lifetime on the water. It is an unprecedented opportunity and perhaps the only opportunity many will ever get to see this in writing.

THE TWO BLUEFIN SPRING MIGRATION ROUTES

There are absolutely two specific routes of early spring bluefin migrations as they pass by Long Island on their way northward each spring: the inshore route and, secondly, the offshore route. Last year (meaning 2000), the bluefin followed what I have named Red Route 1 (RR1), the offshore route. This 2001 canyon season, the bluefin followed Blue Route 2 (BR2), the inshore route. To me, it's very obvious there are two routes. I base this on the reports from the Shinnecock and Montauk fleets, and more importantly, the early sightings and landings reported from Virginia, Maryland and New Jersey.

Simply put, when the bluefins are on the

BLUEFIN BIBLE

BY CAPT. TRED BARTA

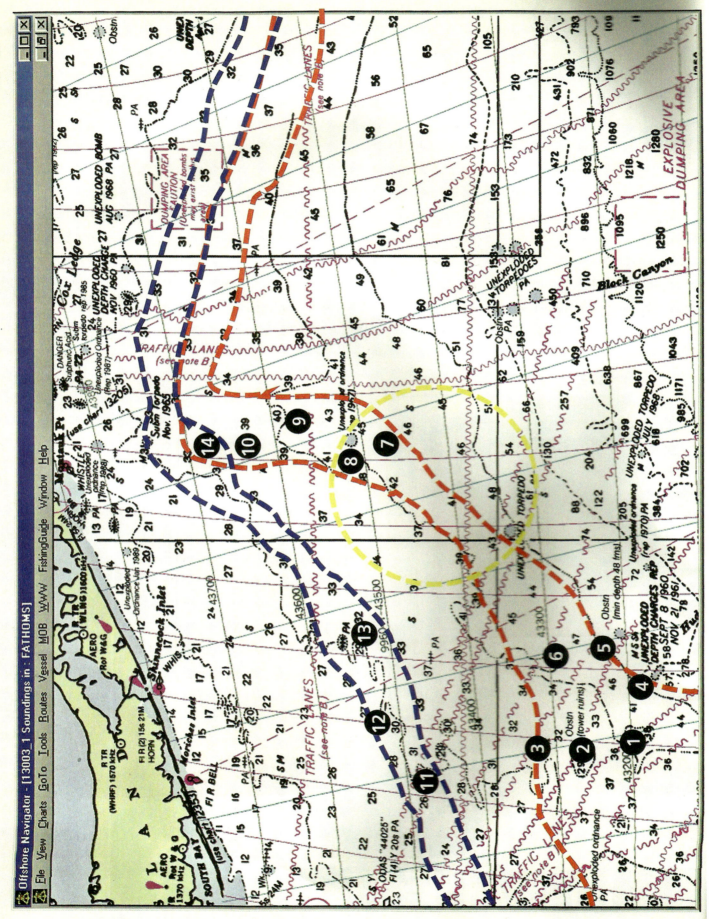

RED ROUTE 1, BLUE ROUTE 2 COORDINATES

1) RHINO HORN ON RR1
15110/43275

2) 29-FATHOM LAKE ON RR1
26340-26300/43275-43260

3) BACARDI AREA ON RR1
15113.2/43270.4, 15118.4/43265.7, 26250/43268.6

4) HUDSON CANYON TIP ON RR1
15050/43200, 15056.4/43202.7, 150559/43197.6, 15068/43202.7

5) THIN LAKE ON RR1
15040-14975/43214-43250

6) FIVE FINGERS AREA ON RR1
(Finger 1) 26265/43250-43330; (Finger 2) 26235/43270-43320; (Finger 3) 26210/43265.8-43338.7; (Finger 4) 26175-26189.4/43270.8-43339.7; (Finger 5) 26150-26138/43260.7-43323.6

7) HOT SPOTS TO EAST OF 41-FATHOM FINGERS ON RR1
14775.3/43450, 14725.6/43500, 14720.6/43482.6, 14712.7/43500, 14714/43490, 14713.4/43482.7

8) 41-FATHOM FINGERS AREA ON RR1
14850/43450 to 14800/43525 (The Riffle), 14775.9/43525 (Finger 1), 14765.3/43520 (Figner 2), 14812.8/43462.7 (Finger 3), 14760/ 43400-14725.2/43475.9 (Outer Finger)

9) THE PEAKS ON RR1
14675/43665, 14665.2/43672.4 14650/43675.

10) 31-FATHOM FINGERS AREA ON RR1
(Block 1), 14600/43712.7, 14600/43715.4, 14600/43721.7, 14610/43715.7, 14612/43718.7, 14615/43717.2, 14618/43719.6; (Block 2), 14650/43700, 14655.2/43710.4, 14658/43725, 14657.7/43732.6, 14650/43715.7, 14660.2/43712.4, 14662.6/43715, 14667/43717.8; (Block 3), 14600/43700, 14610/43705.4, 14608.7/43709.4

11) MORICHES HOT SPOT ON BR2
15100/43600, 15075/43600, 15078/43610.7, 15072/43612.7

12) NORTH/SOUTH EDGE ON BR2
14975/43600-14950/43650

13) 31-FATHOM HOT SPOT ON BR2
14875/43640, 14872/43642.7, 14871.4/43630.6, 14860/43612.7, 14862/43616.7, 14861/43618.2, 14850/43625.7, 14850/43650, 14852/43636.4.

14) RR1 AND BR2 OVERLAP
14675/43700, 14675/43750, 14575/43750, 14575/43700 (Spot 1), 14700/43700, 14701.5/43702.6, 14705.8/43705, 14712/43712, 14716/43713.2; (Spot 2), 14750/43725, 14752/43716.7, 14758/43718.2; (Spot 3). 14775/43725, 14778/43728.6, 14779.4/43730, 14752.6/43720.4; (Spot 4), 14800/43700, 14805.7/43702.6, 14802/43712.6, 14809/43716.2, 14807.6/43708.7

▬ ▬ ▬ RED ROUTE 1, OFFSHORE BLUEFIN MIGRATION ROUTE
▬ ▬ ▬ BLUE ROUTE 2, INSHORE BLUEFIN MIGRATION ROUTE
▬ ▬ ▬ 41-FATHOM HOT SPOT AREA ON RR1

---

move along Red Route 1, we are covered up with 40- to 80-pound bluefins during my early canyon trips to Atlantis and Veatch, and we often see thousands on each trip migrating east. When RR1 is prevalent, the 500-fathom curve is a bluefin highway. We enjoy this fishing from May 15 to June 30. Also, during a RR1 year, within a week of seeing the bluefin offshore, the entire RR1 "river" area on the chart is flooded with fish from about May 15 to July 10.

DETERMINING A RR1 FROM A BR2 YEAR

Why do they take Red Route 1 versus Blue Route 2, meaning the offshore route rather than the inshore? I have no idea, I really don't. Obviously, it has a lot to do with bait, temperature and water color, but I can't prove a thing except where they are.

I know that when there are huge concentrations of white bait, small mackerel, squid boats and anchovies present, and the bait starts out at the tip of Hudson, RR1 is usually in play. If in the early spring, Hudson is not filled with bait, and the conditions are not correct, the bluefin usually are 30 to 40 miles inshore on BR2—and it stays that way for the entire season. In the year 2000, RR1 was the path taken. This year in 2001, the bluefin decided to follow BR2.

The most significant indicators of RR1 offshore or BR2 inshore situations are the early showings of bluefin at the Bacardi, Chicken Canyon and the mouth of the Hudson. If this area is not flooded with school bluefins and mixed giants by May 10 to June 15, you can bet your bottom dollar they will be on the BR2 in 20 fathoms.

The action is close to home and on a good day you are often seeing thousands of fish on top. On a bad day, maybe you will see 20 to 30 schools on top. On several occasions, I have seen a school of bluefins which is 3 acres in depth.

Next, I want to share my best spots coming east-to-west on RR1, the offshore route, then venturing inshore to BR2. These spots have consistently played off for me and the five other captains who shared information from their logbooks. A survey of six aggressive offshore captains, in addition to the group which helped me write this article, from Montauk to Shinnecock prove to have an amazing amount of common ground on our numbers. The specific numbers mentioned below are all from specific logbook entries where bluefin have been caught. These are solid numbers that have consistently produced for six offshore captains. It is interesting to me that

SCHOOL BLUEFIN OBSERVATIONS

1) The best spring water temperature 59.7 to 64 degrees. Bluefins feed best in shore 62 to 64 degrees.
2) Water color doesn't mean squat. Find the bait, you'll find the bluefins.
3) Inshore on RR1 and BR2 bait, not water temperature, rules. However, a 56 to 62 or 58 to 61 degree edge always seems to be red hot on the migration routes.
4) In the spring, when you find 100s of gulls and turns sitting in the water offshore, the bluefins are home. If the birds are offshore in spring, even if they are not working, the bluefins are home.
5) Troll slowly with 6.2 to 6.6 knots being the maximum. The smaller the bait and the smaller the leader, the more stealthily you are, the better you will do.

all six of us had many numbers in common almost to the tenth place.

I'm sure you'll find it amazing to see what the bottom topography of each of these locations looks like on the Maptech charts. Is it bottom contour that makes this area productive? Or is it the combination of bottom contour and current that makes these hot spots consistently produce? Look at the 3-D charts and decide for yourself.

RED ROUTE 1: OFFSHORE MIGRATION ROUTE

Many of the place names you will see in this article are from my logbook and I have written down the names that I personally call them. Many other local fishermen call them other names. Please understand it was hard enough to write this article without having to go back to see what nickname was used in general.

Ok, before we begin our tour, let's review some general comments about Red Route 1. First, when RR1 is in play, reports from the Hudson tip, Bacardi and Chicken Canyons are red hot. When the bluefin are on RR1, they are also everywhere on the 500-fathom curve, especially in front of the Dip, Middle Grounds, and East and West Atlantis. Lastly, when RR1 is in play, the reports from 20 fathoms in are almost nil.

THE RHINO HORN TO 29-FATHOM SMALL LAKE

From May 15 to June 20 is the most productive time for the area I call the Rhino Horn, located at 15110/43275, as well as the Bacardi Area at 15113/43270. This is not the Bacardi (Durley Chine) Wreck itself, but a nearby area where I have caught several fish. The exact numbers from my logbook are 15113.2/43270.4, 15118.4/43265.7, and 26250/43268.6. I believe the fish travel in a northeast direction, and I set up my trolling pattern and work east-and-west in this area. This sets me up for some sort of intercept with migrating bluefin during the day.

There is also a 29-Fathom Small Lake just to the east of the Bacardi that I like very much. I fish it east-to-west from 26340-26300 to 43275-43260. There is often great concentrations of bait found to the most western edges of this location, and I often park here all day. I have watched more-skilled chunkers than myself from New Jersey catch 30 or more fish during the day while diamond jigging and drifting—but to me, the troll bite is what it's all about.

HUDSON TIP AND THE FIVE FINGERS AREA

Nearby is also the Hudson Canyon tip, located at 15050/43200, 15056.4/43202.7, 150559/43197.6, and 15068/43202.7. This has been a great place for bluefin, and is usually productive the week before the fish show up at the Five Fingers to the north. Bait concentrations are thick here, and I like working north-and-south, on-and-off the bank. It's interesting I have NEVER EVER caught yellowfin here from May through the first week in June, but have found success with yellows at the 41-fathom Fingers during those same times.

The Five Fingers area is a block of real estate on RR1 that over the last 20 years has produced for me between May 20 and June 10, sometimes to as late as June 17 or June 20 (in a cold year). Many, many giants have been caught here in addition to the regular school tuna. They are located at 26265/43250-43330 (Finger 1), 26235/43270-43320 (Finger 2), 26210/43265.8-43338.7 (Finger 3), 26175-26189.4/43270.8-43339.7 (Finger 4), and 26150-26138/43260.7-43323.6 (Finger 5).

As you plot these numbers, you need to use your imagination to see the five actual fingers—15 years ago we drew them on the chart and they have stuck. Make no mistake, many a dream has come true on the Fingers. It's a magical area when the the fish are in resident.

Just east of the Five Fingers is the area I call Thin Lake, located at 15040-14975 to 43214-43250. The eastern range of Thin Lake is where I often lose the fish going into the Five Fingers. I hardly ever find the bluefins way east of here, they always head northeast on RR 1. A friend of mine caught a giant weighing 845 pounds smack on these numbers three years ago on June 2—what a great area to target early in the season. I work this corridor southwest-to-northeast and back.

Here's a shot of some school bluefin feeding on the surface at the 41-Fathom Fingers on Red Route 1.

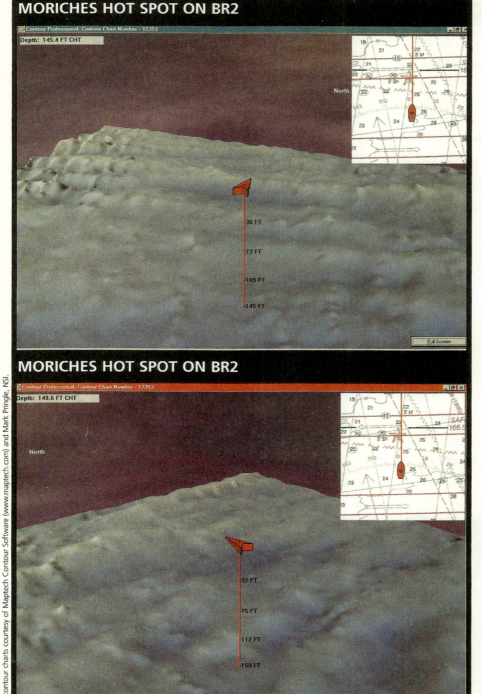

along the 30-fathom curve. If you can find the bluefins home at the Fingers, you are in for a treat.

We also see more black-back gulls and terns here than at any other place. Remember, if you find large concentrations of birds just sitting in the water away from a dragger, don't leave—whatever you do—don't leave! Even if you don't see fish, where there's birds there's bluefin, and you can take that to the bank.

Coming east-to-west, my first leg is to fish from 14850/43450 to 14800/43525. I call this the Riffle and this place holds bait! Often the fish hold here for two weeks at a time. The three 41-fathom Fingers at 14775.9/43525, 14765.3/43520 and 14812.8/43462.7 are consistent winners.

A great way to fish this area is to troll right up the 41-fathom curve, hitting each one of the spots mentioned above. I have found that fishing this entire area from the northeast-to-southwest is more productive than any other headings.

HOT SPOTS EAST OF THE 41-FATHOM FINGERS

About three miles to the east of the 41-Fathom Fingers there are seven spots that have produced. Look at the chart carefully, they are all over impressive bottom contours. The numbers from my logbook are 14775.3/43450, 14725.6/43500, 14720.6/43482.6, 14712.7/43500, 14714/43490, and 14713.4/43482.7. Another great range is the outer 41-Fathom Finger. Straight troll from 14760/43400 to 14725.2/43475.9. Many a Shinnecock boat will have stories to tell you about this area.

We all know each day is a new day, and my logbook may be no better than yours, but "12 captains" confirmed the numbers mentioned above as being great real estate. The question is why—but who cares as long as the reel goes off. There will also be some who argue that these numbers mean nothing and that everyone knows the 41-fathom area is a hot spot. Well, these are my personal numbers and I have caught spring bluefins on them consistently for years. The 41-Fathom Hot Spot to me is extremely significant. I believe it is part of the RR1 bluefin internal compass. Spring bluefin consistently show up if bait is here.

You may be asking, why do the fish always seem to make a turn inshore here? Why has my trolling along the 43550 to the east been unproductive from this spot? Why do we find more bait in this area in early spring? Why do I consistently see bluefin commercial boats here looking for giants early in the season? Why

THE 41-FATHOM FINGERS

Moving from southeast-to-northwest on RR1, 40 fathoms rules. I find this fascinating. I also find it miraculous that at around 43520 and 14600, the bluefins appear to turn inshore. My logbook shows consistently that once the bluefin are in the 41-fathom Finger Area, an incredible hot spot, they turn inshore. I don't know why, but my trolling to the east of here has been fairly unproductive.

The 41-fathom Fingers are pure magic. This area (the large yellow circle on the map) is the finest piece of spring real estate going on RR1. My log shows consistent concentrations of fish between May 15 to June 19, and often to June 25. When RR1 is in play and there is bait present, often the bluefins stay here for two weeks and feed. There's tremendous bottom contour here compared to other spots inshore, several lobster pots, and a tremendous rough edge does the current seem to run northeast-to-southwest here, but 10 miles to the west, appears to run due east? Why is it that in this area the bluefin shift gears from the 41-fathom edge to the 30-fathom edge? Ok, let's follow RR1, continuing to the northeast now in my own personal logbook. I think I know the reason, and the description of the following areas may help explain these phenomena.

THE PEAKS

I believe the area I call the Peaks is another critical, migrating bluefin internal compass-type area on RR1. It's a transition spot from 41 fathoms to 30 fathoms. Though these numbers are my own, I have never caught a bluefin here. I cannot get a bite here. The fish are always on the move, in full migration, and not feeding. I find this fascinating, and would love to hear if anyone has ever hooked up at the Peaks. There are three peaks which mark the travel corridor: 14675/43665, 14665.2/43672.4, and 14650/43675. What a funnel this is on RR1. Why, I have no idea. Many captains call the area to the east of here the Aquarium, and it is a great spot in the fall and summer, but early in the spring it does not pay off for me.

31-FATHOM FINGERS

This next area is what I call the 31-fathom Fingers, and again is pure magic. The bluefin really feed here and I have caught and released over 30 fish here a day. They're here to feed, and it is consistently a great spot from June 2 to June 31. In this area, the bluefin are almost always moving to the northeast, so by trolling a pattern east-to-west, your chances of intercepting your quarry improve. The first block of terrific numbers from my logbook includes 14600/43712.7, 14600/43715.4, 14600/43721.7, 14610/43715.7, 14612/43718.7, 14615/43717.2, and 14618/43719.6. The next block includes 14650/43700, 14655.2/43710.4, 14658/43725, 14657.7/43732.6, 14650/43715.7, 14660.2/43712.4, 14662.6/43715, 14667/43717.8. The final block of productive numbers in the 31-Fathom Fingers area is 14600/43700, 14610/43705.4, and 14608.7/43709.4.

If you see fish and birds in this area, you need not travel any farther. Spend the day, and don't get frustrated if you see fish without actually hooking up. Slowdown, use small jet heads, light leaders, small hooks, watch your flat lines—and pay your dues.

Beyond the 31-Fathom Fingers area along RR1, my knowledge stops. I know the Montauk fleets do well to the east, but I don't.

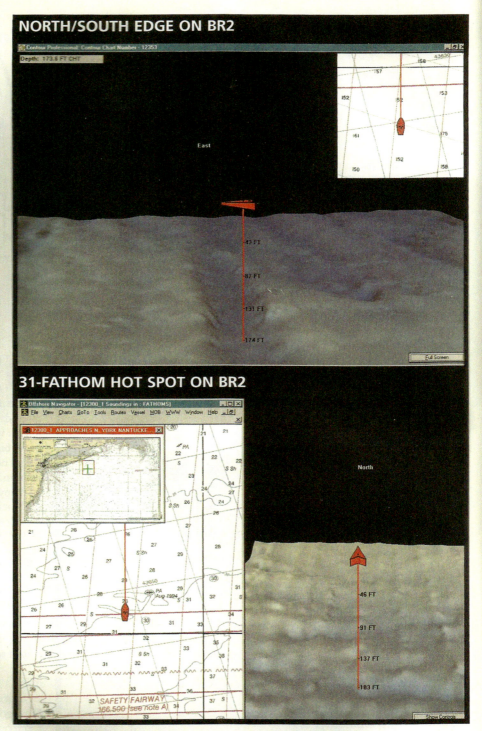

I always lose the fish, and it is a long run from Shinnecock. But I know the 31-Fathom Fingers is the last place I find them, and once the bluefins have left here they are gone, or as least gone from the Shinnecock fishery. By this time the canyons have really lit up and we are fishing for yellowfin and albacore anyway. I know a lot of the Montauk, Block Island and Nantucket crews follow these fish all the way to the BB Buoy. My knowledge is not great here.

How is it that after fishing for bluefins on RR1 for three weeks from the Hudson—often seeing thousands of bluefins on top from May 1 to June 15—that all of a sudden between June 15 and the 30, yellowfin show up at the 31-Fathom Finger. How did they get there? Why do I see so many sharks on top in late June at the 31-Fathom Fingers? Where did they come from? Why does the bait hold so well here? Why do the bluefins take off and go due east from here? Why can't

BR2 AND RR1 OVERLAP AREA

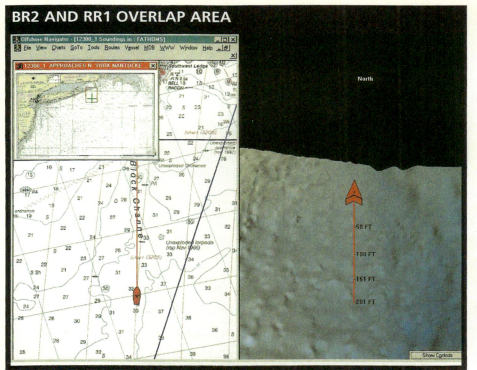

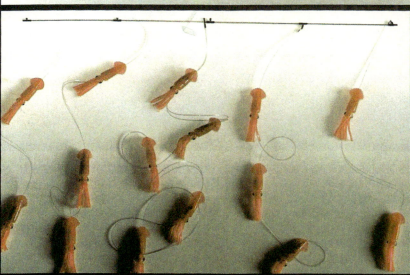

Because migrating bluefin are feeding on small baits, sometimes no bigger than 3 inches, the author pulls only the smallest lures, like these 5-inch jets and 3-inch squid spreader bar. "Low profile" and "low signature" are terms you'll hear Tred use over and over when referring to his trolling spread.

photos: Ray Geminski

I find the fish again once I loose them here? All good questions and no answers.

BLUE ROUTE 2: INSHORE MIGRATION ROUTE

In this the 2001 season, the bluefin followed BR2 and the signs were plain as day. To start, the reports from Virginia, Maryland, Delaware and New Jersey all confirmed the bluefins were in 20 fathoms. The Hudson area was devoid of bluefins for weeks and the lack of fish in the deep was very apparent.

THE MORICHES HOT SPOT TO THE 31-FATHOM HOT SPOT

The first hot spot on BR2 is in front of Moriches, located at 15100/43600, 15075/43600, 15078/43610.7, and 15072/43612.7. Look at the bottom here, it can be a great spot. The next area moving east is a North/South Edge running from 14975/43600 to 14950/43650. The Moriches boats absolutely clobber them here—it's a great spot.

Usually, I miss this bite and my friends from Moriches tell me about their great catches. I'm always a day late and a dollar short in the three-day stretch they're in front of Shinnecock. The fish eat well here, but make no mistake, they're on the move big time.

And now one of my favorite spots on BR2, the 31-Fathom Hot Spot (also called the 31-Fathom Fingers by many). It is a great spot and holds plenty of bait. A block of great numbers is 14875/43640, 14872/43642.7, 14871.4/43630.6, 14860/43612.7, 14862/43616.7, 14861/43618.2, 14850/43625.7, and to the east a touch, 14850/43650 and 14852/43636.4.

This is really a great place to intercept the bluefin, and I troll east-to-west, then go north, then east-to-west again, then north again, etc. Basically, you're trying to work the area in a grid, not simply meandering about. (This place also produces in the fall, but that's a secret!)

RR1 AND BR2 MERGE

Notice RR1 and BR2 are close and merging. Now go to the east on BR2 and whammo! We find common ground on RR1 and BR2, and the best overall spot in the world in late spring for bluefin trolling. This is the 31-Fathom Fingers in general. This overlap area is between these ranges: 14675/43700 to 14675/43750 to 14575/43750 to 14575/43700. This block is common to RR1 and BR2 and is an incredible spot. The problem is, if you want to extend your season, you have two to four weeks before the fish get here. This spot is extremely active between May 20 and June 15.

This area is serious business. When there is bait here, you might call this "Heaven on Earth." I have seen 20

BARTA'S "K.I.S.S." SPREAD

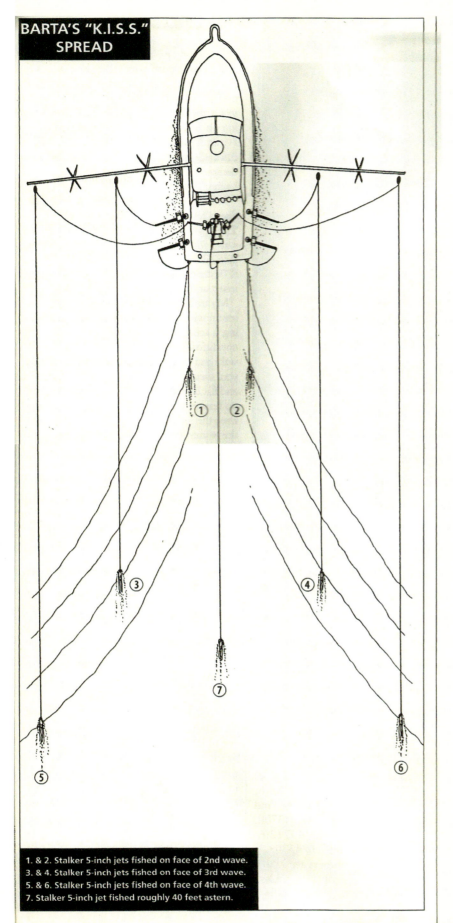

1. & 2. Stalker 5-inch jets fished on face of 2nd wave.
3. & 4. Stalker 5-inch jets fished on face of 3rd wave.
5. & 6. Stalker 5-inch jets fished on face of 4th wave.
7. Stalker 5-inch jet fished roughly 40 feet astern.

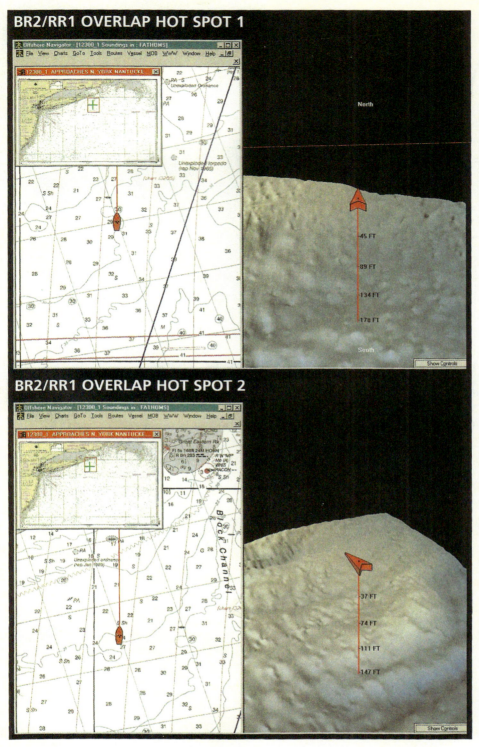

BR2/RR1 OVERLAP HOT SPOT 1

BR2/RR1 OVERLAP HOT SPOT 2

BARTA'S BASIC SPREAD

My basic all-around trolling spread for these spring run bluefin consists simply of seven Stalker jets in purple-and-black, mackerel-and-black, blue silver, or all black. I do not troll the traditional green-and-yellow or zucchini that many use. I know what these fish are feeding on and I know what color the bait is, so I "match the hatch." The color mackerel-and-black is a custom-made skirt that I exclusively designed with Stalker three years ago, and am having good success with it.

For my leaders, I use 50- to 80-pound test fluorocarbon or Momoi up to 130-pound test. The key is to get that damn leader out of the water with just the jet head skimming the surface. Also employ small hooks like 7/0s and 8/0s, the proper chaffing gear, a bell tube, Teflon insert and loop protector.

My trolling speed is 5.8 to 6.4 knots maximum with trim tabs up. When you are working a school don't turn too much. In calm conditions, bluefin don't like to cross the wake and can spook easily. It's important to keep your short and long 'riggers even, and the short and flat lines even, so you can turn hard. I fish no teasers or birds, keep my spread short, and keep the leader and wind-on sections out of the water. It's a low-signature, low-profile spread—remember, you are emulating a school of baitfish. It's that simple. This pattern is devastating on bluefins and is my favorite.

Only if this pattern does not produce will I opt to vary it. The first way I may vary this pattern is to add a Stalker 3-inch squid spreader bar to each long 'rigger and one down the center, for a total of three bars. In this bar pattern, I will also run a split-bill ballyhoo from each short 'rigger, so they run just below the spreader bars.

If that proves also ineffective, I go to a third pattern which consists of the same 5-inch jets on both the short and long 'riggers, two daisy chains made of six 5-inch Stalker jets run on the flat lines, and a Stalker squid spreader bar down the center. Again, I prefer the "Keep It Simple Stupid" approach, and will stick to a spread of all jets if possible.

Lastly, never leave fish to find fish. If you see bluefins on top and they're not feeding, don't give up. Don't change the technique that works for you. I'm very rigid in how I fish; many people think I am too rigid. For better or for worse, these are my three patterns for bluefin and I stick to them. Upon landing a bluefin, immediately bleed, gut and ice down the fish. School bluefin are great on the grill, make perfect sushi, and my wife Stacie likes to can them for the winter.

boats catch 30 to 40 fish each per day on the troll! I have seen things here in spring most people can only dream about—the shame of it is, most boats are still on dry land when the bite is the best.

Let me give you four blocks of numbers where I consistently catch bluefins just west of this spot on the RR1 and BR2 Overlap Area. The first block includes 14700/43700 (the 700 square), 14701.5/43702.6, 14705.8/43705, 14712/43712, and 14716/43713.2. Second spot includes 14750/43725, 14752/43716.7, and 14758/43718.2. The third spot includes 14775/43725, 14778/43728.6, 14779.4/43730, and 14752.6/43720.4. And the fourth spot includes 14800/43700, 14805.7/43702.6, 14802/43712.6, 14809/43716.2, and 14807.6/43708.7. You'd better put these numbers above in a guarded place—a lot of people would like you not to have them.

BARTA'S "SQUID BAR" SPREAD

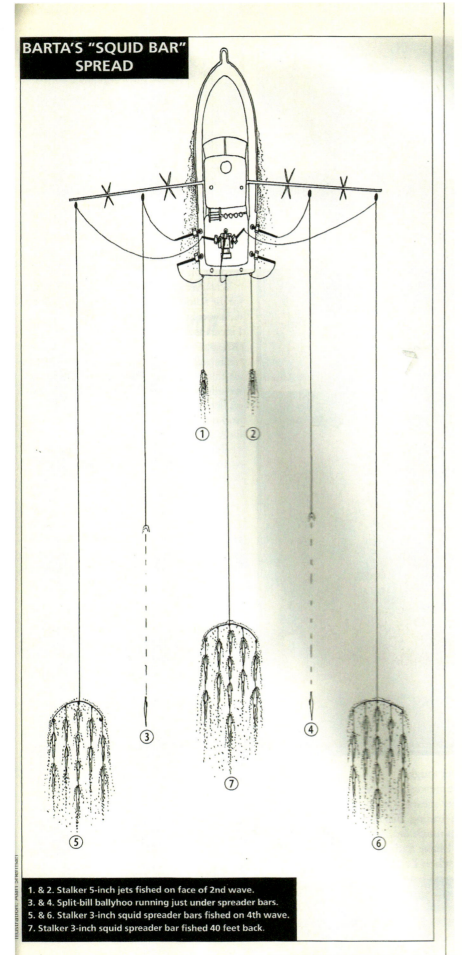

1. & 2. Stalker 5-inch jets fished on face of 2nd wave.
3. & 4. Split-bill ballyhoo running just under spreader bars.
5. & 6. Stalker 3-inch squid spreader bars fished on 4th wave.
7. Stalker 3-inch squid spreader bar fished 40 feet back.

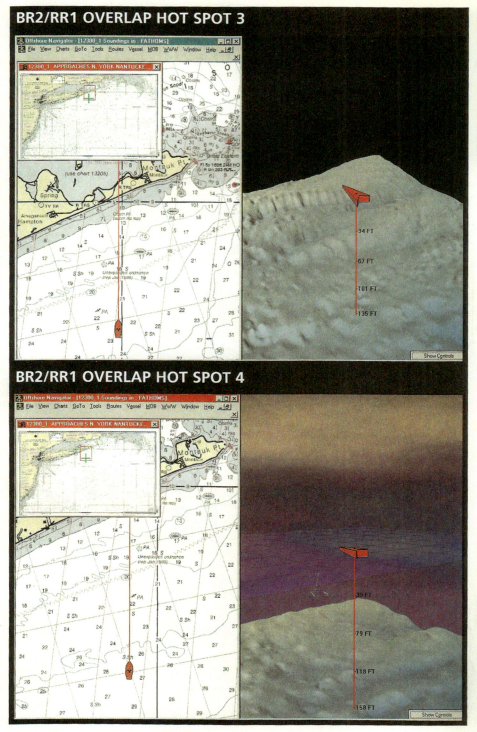

BR2/RR1 OVERLAP HOT SPOT 3

BR2/RR1 OVERLAP HOT SPOT 4

The incredible 3-D images featured in this article are from Maptech's latest creation, Contour Professional Version 4.0. This new edition not only adds new graphics, but also new features such as Contour Dead Ahead and the new Contour Data Collection feature. Now you can create custom Contour Charts from the data you collect. For more information, contact Maptech Inc., 10 Industrial Way, Amesbury, MA, or call 1-888-839-5551. Visit them on the web at www.maptech.com.

are feeding on small bait mostly the size of your thumbnail—some 4- to 6-inch tinker mackerel and squid mostly the size of your hand. There is no better lure than a jet head for tuna feeding on these baits.

Whatever specific trolling spread is out, I aim for the school and when I get in the fish doing 6.2 knots, I do ridiculous things with the boat—I increase boat speed to 9 knots, run over the fish, turn violently left and right, make hard turns, pull the power off, slam in on—just do anything non-standard. Often, or should I say sometimes, I get covered up like this. Obviously, it's not my first choice, but it works. The second non-standard technique is to put small lures out—the entire spread some 50 to 100 yards behind the boat—and troll fast from 8 to 11 knots. I have also seen that work.

RED ROUTE/BLUE ROUTE ROUNDUP

To me bluefin tuna fishing inshore is as good as it gets. It's close to home. My entire family—Stacie, Lauren and Hunter—get to see hundreds of fish on top, whales, and thousands of gulls. The sight will literally take your breath away.

In closing, I have shared 20 years of my personal logbook. If you have the opportunity to get in on this fishery, do it. The net results is, school bluefin will extend your season by almost two months and the action is great. Watch your regulations closely, they seem to change weekly. I hope this article will help other fishermen enjoy this great resource. And keep in mind one fact: The most important thing about this fishery is its proximity to home. Bring your kids, your family and friends and enjoy yourself. Share the information on the radio, leave all the secret channels at home.

I'm about to head off for a 17-day moose, caribou, sheep, goat and grizzly hunt in British Columbia with my recurve bow. They guys at THE JOURNAL just sent me the Maptech 3-D Contour Professional charts of my designated RR1 and BR2 locations. I'm literally blown away at what I see. I showed the charts to the other captains who contributed to this article and they could not

WHEN BLUEFIN WON'T EAT

Bluefin can be incredibly frustrating. As we all know, they either bite your hooks off or are incredibly hard to entice into striking. I have had days where I have trolled ballyhoo, squid, eels, strip baits, jet heads and spreader bars through literally 50 schools of 200 to 500 tuna each on top, without a single boil. And then a fleet of over 50 boats did it all day without a touch. The problem is that they are on the move and not eating. That's when the going is super tough.

The newest technique is to chum and shower spearing as you slow troll. Another is live-baiting. But neither has changed the results much on a bad day. Let me tell you how I have had some limited success on days when I can't beg a bite and schools of bluefin between 40- to 200-pounds are on top migrating to the northeast.

The strike is everything, and these fish in general are leader shy and very cagey. They believe it either. You'd be wise to study them carefully.

After seeing these 3-D charts, I've draw a few new conclusions. First, there is bottom contour just to the east of almost all my hot spots. This is incredibly revealing because it means the current which generally runs east-to-west is hitting the raised contour and creating current breaks and upwellings. This could explain the large concentrations of bait and also why the fish hold at these locations. Maptech does not know it yet, but they are going to have a unit on MAKAIRA very soon—I just hope I'm smart enough to know how to use it.

Till next tide on Red Route 1,
Capt. Tred

ABOUT THE AUTHOR

Capt. Tred Barta needs no introduction, but as time goes on some clarification. While the saying, "Tred is the captain some love to hate," may be getting old, the fact is he is an advocate of family values and perhaps the greatest champion of promoting kids participation in our sport. Tred's Barta Blue Marlin Classic at Walkers Cay, Bahamas, and the Barta Irizarry Blue Marlin Classic in the Dominican Republic so far have raised $409,500 for the IGFA Junior Anglers Program. Tred's tournaments are a sight to behold—90 boats, 400 anglers and a couple hundred guests. His honor system scoring, 30-pound line/single-hook requirements was a format few thought would work—but work it did. Tred also gives over 20 appearances a year for charity, and for no re-numeration. With this latest effort for THE JOURNAL, you're in store for a real treat. The man who has caught more bigeye tuna on rod and reel than anyone else in the world has shared with us his thoughts on offshore safety and fishing with children.

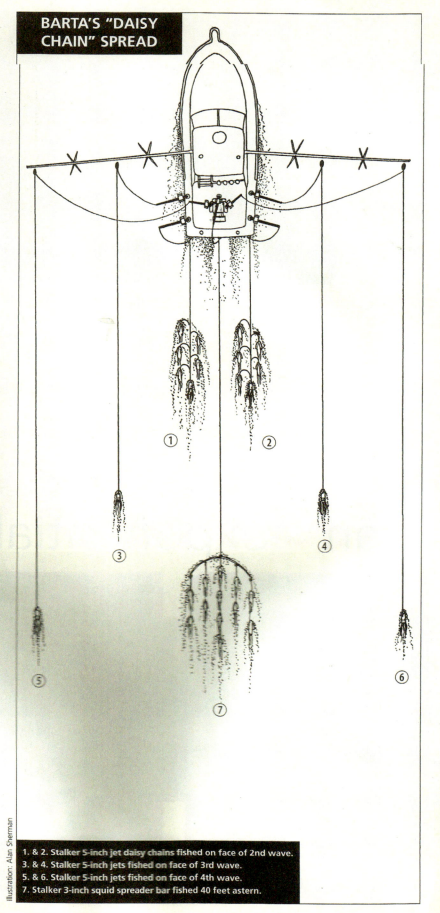

BARTA'S "DAISY CHAIN" SPREAD

1. & 2. Stalker 5-inch jet daisy chains fished on face of 2nd wave.
3. & 4. Stalker 5-inch jets fished on face of 3rd wave.
5. & 6. Stalker 5-inch jets fished on face of 4th wave.
7. Stalker 3-inch squid spreader bar fished 40 feet astern.

Illustration: Alan Sherman